D0523604

BARBARA DE ANGELIS, Ph.D.

ARE YOU THE ONE FOR ME?

Thorsons

An Imprint of HarperCollins*Publishers*

Thorsons
An Imprint of HarperCollins *Publishers*
77–85 Fulham Palace Road,
Hammersmith, London W6 8JB

Published by Thorsons 1993
First published in the USA by
Delacorte Press, Bantam Doubleday Publishing Group, Inc.,
666 Fifth Avenue, New York, NY 10103, 1992
1   3   5   7   9   10   8   6   4   2

© Barbara De Angelis 1992

Barbara De Angelis asserts the moral right to
be identified as the author of this work

A catalogue record for this book
is available from the British Library

ISBN 0 7225 2866 3

Printed and bound by
HarperCollins Manufacturing, Glasgow

All rights reserved. No part of this publication may be
reproduced, stored in a retrieval system, or transmitted,
in any form or by any means, electronic, mechanical,
photocopying, recording or otherwise, without the prior
permission of the publishers.

ARE YOU THE ONE FOR ME?

May this Book
helps you to find
the necesary knowledge
(~~that~~) to recognize the
one to accompeny you
in your precious Journey.

. . . . . .

. . . . .

.   .   Life/Death/e.Je.

From a soul sister
Elisabeth

Also by Barbara De Angelis

SECRETS ABOUT MEN EVERY WOMAN SHOULD KNOW
HOW TO MAKE LOVE ALL THE TIME

I dedicate this book
to my mother, Phyllis Garshman,
and my stepfather, Daniel Garshman,

▼

For loving me unconditionally,
for always being there when I needed you
and for showing me, by your example,
how wonderful love can be
when you're with the right person.

ACKNOWLEDGMENTS

▼▼▼

I want to express my gratitude to the following people:

To my incredible staff at the Los Angeles Personal Growth Center—April Whitney, Linda Boswell, Marla Campbell, Alicia Smith, and Jill Cresap: Thank you for sharing my vision, for working so hard to manifest it, and for trusting me so completely. I feel so fortunate to have each of you in my life.

To my assistants staff for Making Love Work Seminars over the past two years: Maria Talamini, Dennis Cohen, Madelon Cohen, Steve and Wendy Vitalich, David Davison, Suzi Ogulnick, Judy Murphy, Victoria Pruett, Rebecca Gerber Kahane, Stephanie Livingston, Dave Pearson, Mike Handron, Paul Belanger, Fred Balch, Chris McRae, John Heaviside, Kathy Elliott, Steve Hargett, and especially Kevin Roesch. Thank you for your continued love and support; for merging your dreams of healing the planet with mine and making them a reality month after month. What a joy to be traveling together!!

To Harvey Klinger, my literary agent: Thank you for believing in me, for knowing exactly what I need, always getting it for me, and for coming up with the title for this book! You are the best there is!

To David Sams, my business partner and manager: Thank you for always holding the big picture and supporting me in taking the time off from our projects to write this book. I am so grateful for all you've done for me, and mostly for your friendship.

To Mark Fisher, my business manager: Thank you for always watching over me and my business with such a loving eye, and for being true family.

To everyone at Delacorte Press: Especially Carole Baron—Thank you for trusting me so completely with this book; Roger Bilheimer—Thank you for always being there for me; and Jill Lamar—Thank you for your sensitive editing.

To Ruth Cruz: Thank you for always taking such good care of me and my home so I can do things like write this book. I feel blessed to have you in my life.

To the thousands of men and women who have shared their pain and growth with me on the radio, through letters, and through my seminars: Thank you for showing me that I needed to write this book, and for having the courage to heal your heart.

To my best friend and animal companion "Bijou," who sat or slept next to me for every one of the thousands of hours I spent at my computer writing this book, never leaving my side: Thank you, precious puppy, for showing me such total love and devotion, for being a never-ending source of comfort, for knowing just when I'd had enough and taking me for a walk, and for reminding me about what really matters.

And most of all, to my heart's true companion, Jeffrey James: "Thank you" does not begin to express my gratitude for your love, your kindness, your patience, and your loyalty. Without you I could not have written this book, for I wouldn't have had the experience of a healthy relationship to talk about. Thank you for being my teacher, my light, and my anchor. Thank you for loving me not just when I'm beautiful, but when I'm sitting at the computer in my bathrobe and glasses for hours on end. Thank you for helping me heal the frightened little girl inside me by not going away. I love you always.

CONTENTS

▼

UNDERSTANDING
YOUR LOVE CHOICES

▼

▼

AVOIDING WHO'S WRONG

▼

▼

KNOWING WHO'S RIGHT

▼

UNDERSTANDING
▼
YOUR
▼
LOVE
▼
CHOICES

▼▼▼

You are lying in the dark next to the person you love. You can tell by his breathing that he's asleep, and as you gaze at the outlines of his face, you wonder about the future of this relationship. You know he wants to marry you. You love him; you can't imagine living without him, but the thought of marrying him scares you to death. What if you make the commitment and find out later that there's someone you're more compatible with? *How can you be sure he's really the one for you?*

You and your husband are eating pizza and watching a movie on television. This is the first chance you've had to be alone together all week. It's hard to believe that next month will be your tenth wedding anniversary. It's been a good ten years, and although there are no big problems in the marriage, sometimes you wonder if you made the right choice. You love him, but don't feel as "in love" as when you met. You glance over at him sitting on the couch and ask yourself whether you're really fulfilled, or just "comfortable." *Would you be happier with someone else? Is he really your perfect partner?*

You're sitting in your attorney's office, looking down at your divorce papers. Once you sign them, your marriage will be officially over. The pen trembles in your hand, and your eyes fill with tears as dozens of memories flood into your mind: the first time he kissed you; the night he asked you to marry him; the joy you felt on your wedding day; the fun you had fixing up your first home; the closeness you felt when your children were born; the safety you felt in his arms; the hopes and dreams and plans for the future. Never in your wildest dreams did you imagine that it would turn out this way. You were so sure it would work, so confident that he was the right person for you. But now, as your signature severs the marriage forever, you ask yourself, "**Why didn't I see it?** *How could I have known it wouldn't last? Why did I make the wrong choice?*"

1

▼▼▼

LOVE IS
NOT ENOUGH

▼▼▼

Falling in love is a magical and powerful experience. Each kiss, each conversation, each moment in the beginning seems so right, so perfect. But soon attraction and infatuation become a "relationship," and we are brought down to earth with the challenging realities of sharing our life with another human being. And as those first enchanted weeks turn into months, one day we find ourselves asking: *"Is this person right for me?"*

If you've ever been in a serious relationship, you've asked yourself this question—before you made a commitment, before you got married, or, if the relationship didn't work, before you decided to leave for good.

I used to hear this question every day when I had a radio talk show in Los Angeles. I received more phone calls about this problem than any other.

▶ *"I love my boyfriend, but I'm afraid to make a commitment and marry him. What if I meet someone I love more in a few years? How can I tell if we're compatible enough?"*

▶ *"I've been dating a woman for two years, but she has children I don't get along with. Do you think this relationship can work?"*

▶ *"My husband and I argue all the time. He refuses to go to counseling, and we hardly ever have sex anymore. I love him and don't want to hurt the children, but I'm totally miserable. How can I be sure it's really over before I leave?"*

▶ *"I've just come out of a very painful relationship. I want to find a partner to share my life with, but I'm afraid of getting hurt again. How can I tell the next time if I'm with someone who is wrong for me* before *my heart gets broken?"*

I understand the pain and turmoil these people are going through, because I've been through it, too. Since my first serious relationship at seventeen, and, until recently, I fell in love without giving serious consideration to whether the person was right for me, let alone whether they loved me enough. Someone showed up, and if he had something lovable about him, I would start a relationship. I'd convince myself he was *"the one,"* only to find out that we were incompatible and watch the relationship fail. Then I would feel sorry for myself and wonder what I was doing wrong.

After too many heartbreaks, I was forced to face the sad truth: **In spite of my experience, education, and my intense desire to be happy, I continually chose partners who were not right for me. I was falling in love with the wrong people for the wrong reasons.**

I'm happy to say, I've spent the past five years of my life learning how to help myself and others make better love choices, and the results have been truly amazing. When it was time to choose a topic for my third book, I knew right away what it would be. My first two books were about *how* to love; this book is about *whom* to love. It's about knowing when someone is right for you, and avoiding those who are wrong. I hope that what you learn in this book will give you the understanding and support you need to create the passionate and fulfilling relationship you deserve.

HOW COULD I HAVE BEEN SO BLIND?

We all want to be happy in our love life, and we want our relationships to work. So, obviously, none of us deliberately sets out to choose partners who are wrong for us. We truly believe we are making the right decision when we select a mate. But the sad reality is that, more often than not, those choices turn out to be painful mistakes.

▼

Many of us are choosing the wrong partners and wondering why our relationships are not working.

▲

Have you ever thought or said the following about one of your relationships?

▶ "How could I have been so blind? Why didn't I see what he/she was really like?"

▶ "I felt so sure that, this time, it would work. Where did I go wrong?"

▶ "He seemed so wonderful when we first met. I can't figure out why he changed into someone I can't stand."

▶ "All the signs were there from the beginning that she didn't feel the way I did. I guess I just ignored them and convinced myself things would get better."

▶ "We loved each other, but we couldn't agree on anything, and all we did was argue."

▶ "I was so sure he was different from the other men I'd been with. It took me almost two years to find out that I'd picked the same type of guy all over again! How could I have wasted so much time?"

▶ "I remember feeling really in love with her at the time, but the truth is, I never told anyone we were together because I was embarrassed to admit I was even involved with a woman like that."

▶ "Everything about him seemed so perfect; I kept telling myself that I should be happy with him, but there just wasn't any chemistry between us."

There is an old saying, "Hindsight has 20/20 vision." It's always so much easier to look back and see things clearly that we could not see at all then. It's much easier to be wiser about the mistakes we made yesterday than the ones we are in the process of making today. Yet, I've always lived by the philosophy that there are no "mistakes"—only opportunities for growth and learning. And learning from the past gives meaning, and even purpose, to some of the pain and heartache collected along the way.

This book contains everything I have learned about choosing the right partner, from my own experiences and those of the men and women I have counseled and worked with. It's about understanding why you make the love choices you do, and learning how to make more fulfilling ones. It answers the questions, "How could I have been so blind?" and "How can I tell if I'm with the right person?" and hopefully will give you the vision you need to see the truth about your own love life.

IF YOU ARE SINGLE, I hope this book will give you tools and guidelines for making healthy, successful choices in your partner for your next relationship.

IF YOU ARE RECOVERING FROM A BROKEN HEART, I hope this book will help you understand why your relationship choices were not good ones for you, and will give you information that will help you make much wiser and less painful choices next time.

IF YOU ARE UNMARRIED BUT IN A RELATIONSHIP, I hope this book will support you in getting clear about whether your relationship is right for you, so you don't have to waste time and energy on a relationship that won't work.

IF YOU ARE IN A COMMITTED RELATIONSHIP OR MARRIAGE, I hope this book will show you that many of the conflicts you and your partner experience may stem not from lack of love, but lack of compatibility, and that understanding your differences can help you live more peacefully and passionately together.

WHY SOME RELATIONSHIPS DON'T WORK

Relationships don't work for one of two reasons:

1. **You are with the right person but *you are loving wrong*.**
   - ▶ You and your partner have poor communication habits.
   - ▶ You don't know how to create real intimacy.
   - ▶ You don't ask for what you want, and end up feeling resentful.
   - ▶ You neglect the relationship.

or

2. **You are with the *wrong person*.**
   - ▶ Your love or life-style is incompatible with your partner's.
   - ▶ You do not share enough common values and commitments.
   - ▶ Your partner has "fatal flaws" that make having a successful relationship impossible.
   - ▶ You can't give each other enough of what you need.

Several years ago I wrote my first book, *How to Make Love All the Time,* as a manual to help people learn how to love one another in a way that creates healthy, passionate, fulfilling relationships. The book was really about how to stop loving the wrong way and start loving the right way, reason number one above. But that information, as valuable as it has been to millions of my readers around the world, is incomplete without the material I've included in this book, be-cause **if you are loving the wrong person, loving the right way won't make a difference.**

WHOM YOU CHOOSE TO LOVE IS AS IMPORTANT AS HOW YOU CHOOSE TO LOVE.

WHY WE FALL IN LOVE

Ask most people why they fell in love with their partners, past or present, and you'll probably hear answers like this:

► "I met Kathy at the gym where I work out. Something about the way she got so into that aerobics class and gave it so much energy really appealed to me."

► "Donna was a bridesmaid at my cousin's wedding. She looked so beautiful in this pink strapless dress—I knew on the spot I was going to fall in love with her."

► "Jo Anne and I knew each other since we were kids. Everyone always said we'd probably get married when we grew up, and I guess I never even questioned it—it seemed like the right thing to do."

► "Alex and I were assigned to work together on a project in our office. I think it was watching him problem-solve—he is so crea-tive—that attracted me to him."

► "I've always been a sucker for music, so when I heard Fred play the guitar at a friend's house, I knew he was the one for me."

► "This sounds terrible, but I always had this fantasy of a tall, dark-haired man with a mustache. Dennis looked exactly like that, and nothing else really mattered."

► "My ex-husband was so selfish and controlling. After my divorce, I think I was attracted to Stan because he was such a nice guy. He always seemed so sweet and considerate."

These may seem like good reasons to start a relationship, but they are NOT:

▶ All Kathy's boyfriend knows about her is that she has a lot of physical energy.

▶ All Donna's boyfriend knows about her is that she looks good in pink chiffon.

▶ Jo Anne's husband has been so influenced by what his friends and family think that he doesn't even know why he loves her.

▶ Alex's girlfriend is enthralled with his business skills but has no idea what his emotional skills are.

▶ Fred's partner has fallen under a musical spell—she knows nothing about him except for the romantic personality she assumes all guitar players have.

▶ Dennis's girlfriend likes the way he looks—she is attracted to a fantasy, but doesn't know anything about the person underneath.

▶ And all Stan's wife knows is that Stan is definitely different from her ex-husband. But whether he is what she wants and needs is a different story.

None of these people thought they were making the wrong decision. They all sincerely believed that they were making intelligent, sensible choices in their partners. But the frightening truth is that **many of them will discover in a month, or six months, or six years that they are in a relationship with the wrong person.**

▼

MOST PEOPLE PUT MORE TIME AND EFFORT INTO DECIDING WHAT KIND OF CAR OR VIDEO PLAYER TO BUY THAN THEY DO INTO DECIDING WHOM TO HAVE A RELATIONSHIP WITH.

▲

Is it any wonder, then, that our relationships don't turn out the way we want them to, that our hopes and dreams turn into heartache, disappointment, and despair?

TEST YOUR LOVE IQ

Part of the reason why so many people choose to be in a relationship with the wrong person is that they have what I call a low "Love IQ." Your Love IQ is based on how much you know about creating and maintaining a healthy relationship with another person. Therefore, whether your Love IQ is high or low determines how good or how bad your choice in partner will be. If you have a high Love IQ and are "Love Smart," you will probably still make some mistakes in love, but not as many as if you have a low Love IQ. Then you are "Love Stupid."

Here is a quiz to help you determine your Love IQ. It contains ten statements about love. **Grade yourself according to how much each statement describes the way you have felt about love, now or in the past, and how often this belief has affected your life.**

If the belief about how love should feel expressed in the statement has affected you in your past or present relationships:

Very frequently .... **Give yourself 0 points**
Often .... **Give yourself 4 points**
Occasionally .... **Give yourself 8 points**
Rarely or never .... **Give yourself 10 points**

WARNING:

You will be tempted to take this quiz from the perspective of how you think you should feel about love and romance, instead of being honest about how you actually felt in your past. Don't respond to each statement only on the basis of your present attitudes and all you have learned; respond honestly, based on a summary of all of your relationships throughout your life.

Why is this important? For instance, let's take the first statement in the quiz:

"If my partner and I really love one another enough, none of our problems or personality differences will threaten the existence of our relationship."

Perhaps you're in a new relationship, where, for the first time, you're being honest about problems rather than avoiding them. You might feel that this statement doesn't apply to how you feel now at all. You want to answer "Rarely or Never" and give yourself a quick 10 points. But let's say that in your previous relationships, you've ignored conflicts and flaws by telling yourself you loved the person so much that none of his or her hurtful or unloving behavior mattered. From that point of view, this statement applies very much to how you felt. So you should answer "Very Frequently" and give yourself 0 points!

The reason you may be tempted to answer from the point of view of your new understanding of love, rather than how your relationships have really been in the past, could be that you just don't want to appear unenlightened or messed up. As a member of my office put it, "Can't I just answer from the past six months of my life? Do I have to include all those years when I didn't know what I was doing?" My answer is, "If you want to be honest with yourself, and learn from your mistakes, *yes,* you must include your past."

YOUR LOVE IQ QUIZ

1. If my partner and I really love one another enough, none of our problems or personality differences will threaten the existence of our relationship.

2. If I am finally with the right person, I won't ever be really attracted to someone else, because I will be so in love.

3. If it's really true love, I'd know the moment I see the person for the first time.

4. The right relationship will always be interesting and exciting.

5. If it's really true love, I won't feel complete and whole when I'm not with my partner.

6. The sex in a relationship can't be really fabulous unless it is true love.

7. My perfect partner will give me everything I need and will fill in all the empty spaces in my life—I won't really need anyone else.

8. If I'm really in love, I'll feel excited and nervous each time I see my partner; being with him/her will give me goose bumps.

9. If I'm with the right person, we will be so in tune with each other, we'll always know how the other person is feeling.

10. If I'm in the right relationship, it will feel naturally harmonious, and we won't have to work that hard to make it work.

Now total your points:

▶ **80–100 POINTS: CONGRATULATIONS! YOU HAVE A HIGH LOVE IQ.** You are realistic in your understanding of relationships and realize that love is not enough to make a relationship work— it takes communication, compatibility, and hard work. To avoid future problems, work on those areas in which you have a low score.

▶ **60–79 POINTS: YOUR LOVE IQ ISN'T BAD, BUT IT COULD BE BETTER.** You are still letting your romantic ideals and fantasies determine your attitudes about relationships. Pay more attention to how you are feeling and not to how you want the relationship to look. Don't be so afraid of conflict. Remind yourself that true love doesn't mean things have to be "perfect" all the time. The exercises in this book will help you raise your Love IQ.

▶ **40–59 POINTS: WARNING!** *Your Love IQ is dangerously low, but you probably already know this because you have been hurt so much in relationships.* The reason you continue to be disappointed in love is that you don't pay enough attention to whom you are with. You put your partners on a pedestal and are more "in love with love" than with them. If you want to stop suffering and be happier, you will need to make some major changes in the way you choose and behave in relationships. Use the information in the rest of this book to become much smarter about love.

▶ **0–39 POINTS: EMERGENCY!** *Your Love IQ is so low that you are guaranteed to get your heart broken over and over again.* Your love life needs immediate attention. It's time to grow up and leave your fantasy world behind. Your relationships can work, but only if you commit yourself to understanding what you've been doing wrong and learn how to make better choices for yourself. Stop blaming the partners who have let you down and take a good, hard look at how you set up relationships to fail from the beginning. The rest of this book will help you find the answers you need to create healthy relationships.

If you ended up with a very low Love IQ, don't feel too badly. When I first devised this quiz and took it myself, I scored a meager 28 points! Obviously I knew that these ten statements about love were unhealthy attitudes, but I tried to be totally honest with myself about how I have viewed love in my past, and that's how I scored 28 points. By the time you finish reading this book, your Love IQ will be much higher and your confidence in your ability to make successful love choices will be much greater.

UNCOVERING YOUR LOVE MYTHS

▶ Have you ever convinced yourself you were in love when you were really in lust?

▶ Have you ever been involved with a partner who was all wrong for you and not realized it until months or even years later?

▶ Do you ignore the problems in your relationship because you don't want to "rock the boat"?

▶ Have you had a habit of mistaking drama and tension for true love?

▶ Have you ever talked yourself into staying with someone who was mistreating you because your relationship "looks good" on the outside?

▶ Do you ever question a really healthy relationship because you don't feel head over heels in love with your partner all the time?

▶ Do you suspect that you choose partners with whom you are not compatible and ignore the people with whom you could be truly compatible?

If you answered yes to any of these questions, it's because you've been affected by what I call:

THE FIVE DEADLY MYTHS ABOUT LOVE

Love myths are beliefs many of us have about love and romance that actually prevent us from making intelligent love choices. These beliefs or attitudes are false notions about relationships that we develop from:

▶ **watching television and movies**

▶ **reading romantic novels**

▶ **never being taught about love**

Consciously and unconsciously, we base our decisions in relationships on these Love Myths. Let's look at five of the most deadly Love Myths. As you read each one, think not only of your present relationship but about your past relationships as well.

▼

1. **TRUE LOVE CONQUERS ALL.**
2. **WHEN IT'S REALLY TRUE LOVE, YOU WILL KNOW IT THE MOMENT YOU MEET THE OTHER PERSON.**

3. **THERE IS ONLY ONE TRUE LOVE IN THE WORLD WHO IS RIGHT FOR YOU.**
4. **THE PERFECT PARTNER WILL FULFILL YOU COMPLETELY IN EVERY WAY.**
5. **WHEN YOU EXPERIENCE POWERFUL SEXUAL CHEMISTRY WITH SOMEONE, IT MUST BE LOVE.**

LOVE MYTH

1

True Love Conquers All

Deep in our hearts, we all secretly believe this myth about love—that if we really love our partner, we will be able to make the relationship work. **No problem, no conflict, no set of circumstances is insurmountable if we just love enough.**

Exercise: Think back to your past relationships, or to problems in your present relationship, and fill in the blank to this sentence for yourself. Make a list of *at least a dozen responses* that refer to different partners you have had.

► **If I love my partner enough, it won't matter that (problem)**

► **If I love my partner enough, it won't matter that** _____

► **If I love my partner enough, it won't matter that** _____

_____

_____

_____

_____

_____

_____

_____

_____

EXAMPLE: **If I love my partner enough, it won't matter that:**

▶ he drinks
▶ our sex life isn't great
▶ she criticizes me all the time
▶ we fight constantly over how to raise the children
▶ he is a strict Catholic and I am Jewish
▶ I'm not really sexually attracted to her
▶ he doesn't have a job and hasn't worked in two years
▶ she has a terrible temper and blows up all the time
▶ he constantly flirts with other women
▶ I don't get along with her children
▶ he has a hard time telling me how he feels
▶ his family doesn't accept me
▶ I want children and he doesn't
▶ she still hasn't gotten over her ex-boyfriend
▶ he's thirty years older than I am
▶ we live on opposite sides of the country

Here are the consequences of believing in Love Myth #1:

1. You avoid facing your relationship problems, or seeking solutions to those problems, by telling yourself: "If we love each other enough, none of these conflicts or personality differences will matter."

Dennis, thirty-seven, called me on my radio talk show one day and explained that he was Jewish and his fiancée, Alice, thirty-five, was Catholic. They had been dating for two years, and although they talked about their difference in religion, they never really resolved their feelings about it. "I always worried that one day it would be a problem," Dennis confessed, "but we got along so well in so many other ways, and I didn't want to rock the boat. Then Alice and I started to talk about marriage. When I thought about my future, and about having children, I realized that I wanted my kids to be brought up in the Jewish faith, and that there were things about Alice not being Jewish that I also missed but had never told her. I asked her to convert, but she refused. She is a pretty strict Catholic, and says she wants to be married in the Church by a priest, which means she couldn't marry a practicing Jew. I keep feeling like our love should conquer these differences, but they don't seem to go away."

The love Alice and Dennis felt for one another was not enough to overcome their lack of religious compatibility. Although many couples can make interfaith marriages work, Alice and Dennis were each too deeply entrenched in their own religions to compromise. No matter how much they cared about one another, they could not be happy and true to their own beliefs by staying together. But they had put off facing these problems by telling themselves, **"If we really love one another, our differences won't matter."** They kept trying to love and accept each other more, never facing the obvious until the very end.

2. You stay in unloving and unfulfilling relationships even when they are not working by telling yourself, "If I just love him more, he will change."

Kimberly, twenty-eight, and her husband David, thirty, came to me in hopes of saving their marriage. They had been together for six years but couldn't seem to get along without constant arguing. "I love David so much," Kimberly explained with tears in her eyes, "but I am constantly criticizing him. It's driving him crazy, and I hate myself for doing it." I asked Kimberly to list her complaints about her husband. "David is a quiet type of guy. He's pretty introspective, and not much for socializing with a lot of people. I'm totally the opposite—very outgoing and talkative, and I love having fun, being with friends, and living life passionately. I hate to say this, but I feel bored a lot of the time with him. It seems like we don't have anything to talk about, and I feel like I'm always pulling him out of his shell."

"I've told Kim that this is the way I am," David responded tensely. "I want to make her happy, but I feel like she is asking me to be someone I am not. I've always been low-key, and I really don't want to change."

As we talked more, I learned that Kimberly married David because she was looking for stability after having been cheated by a college boyfriend. She was so concerned with making sure he was a nice guy that she never asked herself whether they would be compatible together. *Kimberly and David had so many differences in life-style, temperament, and personality that living together harmoniously was next to impossible. They loved one another very much, but it was not enough to make their relationship work.*

But Kimberly believed Love Myth #1, that true love conquers all, and continued to stay with David, hoping that if she just loved him more, he would change. She never considered the possibility that David wasn't changing because David didn't want to change. She just kept trying to be the perfect wife, believing her love would transform David from the man he was into the man she wanted him to be.

Sadly, belief in this Love Myth can cause you heartache, pain, and even physical harm because it convinces you to stay in relationships that are not healthy. *People with very low self-esteem or a childhood history of neglect or abuse often set themselves up in toxic relationships they find difficult to leave, convincing themselves that if they just loved their partner more, his/her harmful behavior would disappear and be replaced with love and affection.* This is a trap. Your partner's dysfunctional behavior is determined by forces that have nothing to do with how loving you are.

3. You beat yourself up emotionally when a relationship doesn't work, telling yourself, "If I had only loved him/her more, I know I could have saved it."

Eileen, fifty-four, was married to Raoul, sixty, for thirty-one years. Raoul was an alcoholic whose rages and irresponsibility had tortured Eileen and her three children throughout their lives. After pleading with her husband to get some help, and facing his total denial of the problem, Eileen found the courage to leave. Two years after their divorce, she came to me for help with her feelings of depression. When I asked Eileen what she thought was bothering her, she replied, "I guess I feel guilty."

"Guilty about leaving your husband?"

"Not just about leaving him," Eileen said with tears in her eyes, "but guilty for not trying harder to make it work. I feel like I abandoned him. Maybe if I had gone to more Al-Anon meetings myself, I would have understood him better, and he would have stopped drinking. Or maybe if I had been more affectionate, or satisfied him more, he would have given up the alcohol."

The more we talked, the more obvious it was that Eileen was still punishing herself for what she saw as her failure to save her marriage. Eileen's mother had always told her that "a good wife stands by her man through thick and thin," and so Eileen felt that she was an inadequate wife. Eileen's depression was brought on by her belief in Love Myth #1—that if she had just loved Raoul more, their marriage would have worked. The reality of love is very different from the myth. Of course, love is the foundation for a good relationship. But if a relationship is going to survive and grow, it needs a lot more than love.

Here's the reality about Love Myth #1:

▼

LOVE IS NOT ENOUGH TO MAKE A RELATIONSHIP WORK — IT NEEDS COMPATIBILITY AND IT NEEDS COMMITMENT.

▲

The sad truth is, very few relationships end because the two partners do not love each other; they end because they are not compatible partners.

I know this from my own painful experience in several of my past relationships. Like many people with the wrong partner, I attempted to make up for the lack of compatibility by trying extra hard and loving with added intensity. But in the end, we were not compatible enough to live peacefully and happily together. For years I blamed myself, thinking that if I had loved more, the differences wouldn't have mattered. Now I know I was wrong. Differences do matter, sometimes just enough to make a relationship challenging, but often enough to make it unhealthy and unfulfilling. Throughout the rest of the book we'll look in more detail at how to tell if you are compatible with another person.

LOVE MYTH

▾　　▾　　▾　　▾　2　▾　　▾　　▾　　▾

When It's Really True Love, You Will Know It the Moment You Meet the Other Person

When you watch a romantic film, you see it.
When you listen to a romantic song, you hear about it.
When you are single and lonely, you dream about it.

LOVE AT FIRST SIGHT

I think we all secretly believe in "love at first sight," the idea that if it is really true love, you will know it the moment you meet the other person. Oh, there may be other kinds of love, but according to this Love Myth, *true love* will strike you like lightning.

I remember first hearing this myth as a young girl, and I longed to be swept away during a powerfully romantic moment in which I'd look into a man's eyes and know instantly, and without a doubt, that this was my lifelong soulmate! I dreamed about "some enchanted evening," as the famous ballad from the play and movie *South Pacific* described it, when I would "find [my] true love . . .

across a crowded room." Anything less than this kind of intense emotional recognition seemed a pale imitation of what I was sure true love should feel like.

You can call it "love at first sight" or "instant chemistry," but the possible problems are the same if you believe in Love Myth #2:

1. You dwell on the intense connection or chemistry and avoid examining the rest of the relationship.

Skip, thirty-two, is a very successful entrepreneur, who me* Marcia, a twenty-seven-year-old accountant, at a wedding. "My firs. thought when I saw her," he told me, "was, 'God, she is beautiful,' and my second thought was, 'I'm going to marry this woman.' That night was probably the most romantic night of my life. It was a beautiful summer evening, and we danced together on an outdoor patio under the stars. Marcia even caught the bridal bouquet, and everyone kidded us about being next.

"We dated each other for the next ten months, and then she told me she wanted me to make more of a commitment—in other words, to propose to her. I told her I needed more time, that I didn't want to rush things, but she kept pressuring me until one day she gave me an ultimatum: marry her or she'd leave.

"I knew something was wrong, because I just wasn't happy, but whenever I'd question whether I was making a mistake, a little voice in my head would say, 'How could she be wrong for you if you had "that feeling" when you first saw her?' I couldn't answer that question, and I kept remembering how crazy I'd been about Marcia in the beginning. I told myself that my concerns were born from my unwillingness to grow up. So I married her."

"Are you still married?" I asked Skip.

"No," he answered with a sad grimace. "I left Marcia after two years. The truth was, our relationship didn't live up to that first magical evening—Marcia is beautiful, but she is also very angry. She controlled me with her rages, and she drank too much, which made the blowups all too frequent. I put off breaking up with her for much longer than I should have, because I kept doubting my own feelings and thinking about how perfect things were when we met. I didn't want to see the truth; the romantic picture was much nicer."

Skip was a victim of Love Myth #2—he hid behind his intense first impressions of Marcia, and used them to fuel his fantasy of their relationship, rather than facing the reality of how unhappy he really was.

2. You get addicted to flashy beginnings and miss opportunities for real, lasting love.

Alexia was a petite, striking thirty-six-year-old woman who owned a children's clothing store. She came to me to decide what to do about her relationship with Kent. "I'll tell you right away that in the past, my relationships haven't been great," Alexia began. "I seem to have been attracted to these flashy, exciting men who end up leaving me or cheating on me or somehow hurting me. These relationships always seem so powerful when they start, and I feel so wildly and desperately in love, and then—POW!—I get hurt.

"Last year I decided to swear off men entirely, and then I met Kent. He is the cousin of a good friend of mine, and a bunch of us started spending time together on the weekends. I liked Kent from the moment I met him, but never considered dating him because he wasn't 'my type.' We became really good friends, talking for hours on the phone at night, sharing things with one another we'd never told anyone else. It got to the point where we called each other several times a day and spent most of our free evenings together.

"Suddenly one night while we were driving back from seeing a movie, Kent leaned over and kissed me on the lips. At first I was shocked and thought, 'You shouldn't be kissing him—he's your friend!' But then I started getting into the kiss and realized that I liked it. Kent looked at me and confessed that he'd been wanting to kiss me for months and that he thought he was falling in love with me."

"How did you feel about that?" I asked Alexia.

"Totally confused. Excited, frightened, all mixed up. Kent was supposed to be just a friend, not a lover. He's not the kind of guy that I picture myself with."

"And what kind of guy is that?"

Alexia looked a little embarrassed as she replied sarcastically, "Oh, you know, the kind that sweeps me off my feet and then knocks me down again."

"Alexia," I answered, "your relationship with Kent sounds *healthy*. I don't think you've ever known what healthy love is supposed to feel like."

Alexia believed so strongly in the Love Myth of love-at-first-sight that she was invalidating her growing feelings for Kent. She couldn't imagine that love could be real if it didn't hit her over the head in the first five minutes of the relationship. **Like many "love-at-first-**

sight junkies," Alexia was addicted to the instant high of infatuation and therefore couldn't even recognize the real love that had developed in her relationship. She almost sabotaged the first healthy romance in her life.

Being a "love-at-first-sight junkie" is one of the most deadly ways in which we lower our "Love IQ."

"LOVE-AT-FIRST-SIGHT JUNKIES" OFTEN LOOK FOR ALL THE WRONG QUALITIES IN A MATE AND OVERLOOK THE RIGHT QUALITIES.

WHAT IS LOVE AT FIRST SIGHT?

Just what is it that you feel when you meet someone and have that instant feeling of falling in love? If it isn't love at first sight, what is it?

▶ **Lust-At-First-Sight:** You experience raw, sexual chemistry between you and another person, and assign more emotion to the bond than there actually is. *You can't stop thinking about the person, not because you are in love with them, but because you are turned on by them.* Intense physical attraction, especially with someone who fits your mental picture of the "perfect" partner, can easily be mistaken for love, especially if you are looking for an instant high. But the high of lust-at-first-sight is often followed by the low of the disappointment you feel when the relationship doesn't turn out the way you hoped it would. (See Chapter Four for more about "Lust Blindness.")

▶ **Infatuation with their image: Sometimes when you think you are falling in love with someone, you are actually 'in love' with their image:** how they look; their profession; how much money they have; the car they drive; the things they've done in their life. You build a fantasy relationship in your head, telling yourself, "My boyfriend is a doctor," or "I'm dating a woman with the perfect body," and thus you ignore the real person.

In spite of these dangers, is it possible to feel at the moment you meet someone that this is the perfect partner for you, and to be correct? What about those couples married for thirty years who say they knew they were right for one another on their first date? Wasn't that love at first sight? I like to think that they experienced a powerful attraction and emotional connection that grew into a strong and successful relationship. *They recognized something special in one another at "first sight," but the true love developed over time.*

Here's the reality about Love Myth #2:

▼

IT TAKES JUST A MOMENT TO EXPERIENCE INFATUATION, BUT TRUE LOVE TAKES TIME.

▲

Imagine sitting in a cabin on a cold, snowy night. You decide to build a fire to keep yourself warm. You have a choice of using newspapers for the fire, or logs. If you know anything about fire, you know the answer to this puzzle—the newspaper would create a big blaze quickly but would die out just as quickly. The logs would take longer to catch, but would burn slowly and steadily for a very long time.

I've seen so many people, including myself, make the mistake of looking for that instant blaze at the beginning of a relationship rather than looking for a partner with whom they can build a solid and lasting relationship. I'm not saying you can't have both, just as you can use newspaper and logs to build a strong fire. But if you have found yourself choosing inappropriate partners over and over again, perhaps you'd be better off looking for Mr. (or Ms.) Log instead of Ms. or Mr. Flammable!

HOW I ALMOST MISSED OUT ON THE BEST RELATIONSHIP OF MY LIFE

In case you haven't guessed by now, I was a "love-at-first-sight-junkie" myself. The more infatuated I felt with someone, the more credibility I gave my feelings about him and my new relationship. I'll share more about my own mistakes in the following chapters of this book, but first let me tell you about how my search for instant chemistry came close to ruining my chances for true romantic happiness.

About four years ago I was in the process of ending an extremely painful relationship with a man I had loved for a long time. I was fortunate enough to have two best friends, both male, named Kevin and Jeffrey. I originally met Kevin and Jeffrey through my seminar work, and they eventually became facilitators in my organization. Through their support I found the courage to admit to myself that I wasn't getting what I wanted in my relationship, and to face the fact that I needed to leave.

During the many months over which I came to terms with my decision, Jeffrey and I became very close. We talked every day on the phone. We worked on many projects together. We joked around that we were really like brother and sister, since we look alike. I knew women really found Jeffrey attractive, although I told myself he wasn't my "type," and he would often kid me and say if he could find a woman like me, he'd take her. I found myself making excuses to see or talk to him, but I told myself it was just because I was going through such a hard time. I noticed we were finding more reasons to hug or touch one another, but I convinced myself it was because we felt so safe together.

One evening as Kevin, Jeffrey, and I were in a meeting discussing some seminar business, Kevin looked at us and said, "What's going on with the two of you?"

"What do you mean? Nothing's going on," I responded quickly.

"Well, it's just that when you are together, you look like you are in love," he answered.

"Don't be silly," said Jeffrey. "We are just great friends. You can't actually believe that we would be any more than that, can you?"

"All I know is that when I'm around you, it sure feels like more than friends," Kevin said with a smile. "Look, I'm going to leave the room now, so you can both talk about it." And with that, Kevin walked out.

Jeffrey and I sat across from each other on the couch in silence. For a moment we looked into each other's eyes, and then we both started to cry, for Kevin had put something into words that we had both avoided talking about, or even admitting to ourselves: We were indeed falling in love.

Jeffrey reached out and took my hands. "I can't believe this is happening," he said. "We are supposed to be just friends."

"Maybe it is just something temporary," I answered in a frightened voice. "Maybe we just think we feel this way, but it will pass."

And in that moment, I truly wanted to believe that my feelings for Jeffrey would fade, because I couldn't totally accept the fact that I loved *him.* Dozens of questions forced their way into my mind all at once: If I loved him, why hadn't I known about it until tonight? How could I feel so close to someone I hadn't been attracted to initially? Since it hadn't been love at first sight, did that mean the relationship would be passionless?

Like many "Love-At-First-Sight junkies," I didn't trust my feelings for someone unless they hit me over the head. *I looked for all the wrong signals to determine whether I was "in love"—drama, intensity, fear of loss or abandonment, extreme highs and lows—all signs of an unhealthy relationship.* For the first time in my life I had developed an emotional connection with a man based on friendship, trust, openness, safety, consistency, and true caring, and I hadn't even recognized it because

it felt too peaceful to be love.

For several months I struggled with my emotions: One day I'd want to go ahead with the relationship, and the next day I'd decide that I was kidding myself and should break it off. There were many moments in which I questioned whether my feelings for Jeffrey were strong enough, all because the relationship had crept up on me rather than arriving all at once. I put poor Jeffrey through hell with my lack of certainty and came close to losing him for good. It took me almost a year to let go of my Love Myth about the way we should have met and the way I should have felt, and to finally appreciate the depth and the joy of how I did feel. That was four years ago, and looking back, I thank God that Jeffrey was so patient and that I didn't throw away the best thing that ever happened to me. Instead I threw away the Love Myth that had gotten me into one dysfunctional relationship after another.

A first impression of someone is not enough to determine whether he or she will be a healthy and loving partner. You need a second, third, fourth, and fifth impression. You need time to discover someone's character, not just their exterior.

Remember: Falling in love is the easy part, but building a healthy relationship takes hard work.

LOVE MYTH

▼　　▼　　▼　　▼　**3**　▼　　▼　　▼　　▼

There Is Only One True Love in the World Who Is Right for You

There comes a time in every relationship when we ask ourselves this question:

"Is he the one for me?"
or
"Is she the one for me?"

Part of the problem we have answering this question is the phrase **"the one."** It assumes that *for each person in the world, there is one and only one right partner, and we need to find that person or we will never be happy.* No imposters will do, no imitations. We must make sure we have fallen in love with our real soulmate.

So when we are single, we walk through life suspiciously scrutinizing each potential partner, cataloging every flaw as evidence that this is *not* **"the one." The one** would be a better dancer; **the one** wouldn't have two children from a previous marriage; **the one** would be making more money; **the one** wouldn't be ten pounds overweight. But in our attempt to avoid making a mistake and missing out on our one true love, we often deprive ourselves of experiencing truly wonderful relationships.

And when we are in a relationship, especially during rough times, we secretly ask ourselves, "I wonder if _____ is really my perfect mate? I wonder if there is someone else out there somewhere who I would be happier with?"

Here are the consequences of believing Love Myth #3:

1. You compare your partner to your fantasy picture of "the one" and miss out on appreciating their uniqueness.
Tammy was a very attractive, outgoing thirty-four-year-old flight attendant who came to one of my seminars in hopes of figuring out why she couldn't develop a serious relationship with a man. "I don't know what's wrong with me," she began, "but all of my friends are either married or engaged or at least in love, and I can't seem to find anyone who's right for me."

"Do you date a lot?" I asked.

"That's just it—I meet guys all the time who are interested in me, and at first I feel really enthusiastic about them. But within a month or two I get turned off and stop seeing them. Last year I thought I'd finally found someone I could really spend my life with. We went together for eight months. And for the first four or five, everything was perfect. But then little things about him started to bother me, and for the last few months of our relationship we fought all the time until I finally broke it off."

As I talked more with Tammy, I discovered that she thought a relationship was working only when things were "perfect," and to her "perfect" meant no conflict, no differences, and most important, nothing about her partner she didn't like. Tammy had grown up believing in Love Myth #3, that somewhere out there in the world, this "perfect" man was waiting for her, and that he and only he would make her happy. So at the first sign of challenge in her relationships, she bailed out, unconsciously comparing her boyfriends with Mr. Perfect. Naturally, they all flunked the test. And in the process she never had an opportunity to truly appreciate the individual she was with and to fall in love with him.

I worked with Tammy to help her understand the origin of her fantasy picture of men and how it prevented her from having any real relationships. Three months later she wrote me a letter to let me know she was dating her old boyfriend again. "I can't believe how different it feels," she marveled. "He is the same person, but I've stopped expecting him to be perfect, and it's making it so much easier to love him as he is."

2. It prevents you from being open to a new relationship after one has ended.

The second problem with believing Love Myth #3 is that it can inhibit you from starting over again after the relationship you hoped would last a lifetime ends through breakup, divorce, or death. If you really believe in one true love, and you lose that person, you are left facing the rest of your life with a lonely heart, sure that no one could replace your mate.

Several years ago, I met a woman through a mutual friend I'll call Doris. Doris was sixty-one years old at the time and had been widowed for two years after almost forty years of marriage. Her husband had fought a long battle with cancer, and Doris had spent the past few years adjusting to life without him. Now, her family and friends were encouraging her to date again, but she was resistant and reluctant.

"I had the love of my life," she explained to me over lunch. "We had many wonderful years together. Why should I run around trying to find someone who doesn't exist to replace my husband? You only get one true love like that in a lifetime."

I explained to Doris that a new partner would never replace her deceased husband but would offer her an opportunity to experience a totally different relationship. "I don't know," Doris said hesitantly. "I think I'm too old for that kind of thing."

Six months passed, and I received a phone call from Doris. "I think I need some help!" she begged. Doris had met a sixty-four-year-old gentleman named Saul through a charity she was involved with. Saul had been divorced for fifteen years but had never found a partner he wanted to share the rest of his life with, until Doris. "He's crazy about me!" Doris explained. "And the scary part is, I think I'm crazy about him, too. We've been seeing each other for four months. At first I thought of him as an escort or companion to social engagements, but lately I can't stand to be without him. Now he's talking about marriage, and when he brings up the subject, I feel like I can't breathe. I keep thinking about how different this relationship is from my marriage, and feeling like I already have a husband, so what am I doing with him?"

"You're loving him," I answered with a smile, "not in the same exact way you loved your husband, but in a new and different way. That's what is so wonderful about love—you can experience it in so many different expressions."

"You mean it is okay for me to love him?" Doris asked sheepishly.

"It's okay, Doris," I reassured her.

Two months later, Doris and Saul were married. They are gloriously happy together, and from time to time Doris calls to tell me how she is doing. "I can't get over this relationship!" she always says. "I loved my first husband so much, but I love Saul just as much, only in different ways. Who would have thought a grandmother would get a second chance!"

Doris almost missed out on a wonderful life with Saul by believing in Love Myth #3, that there is only one true love.

THERE ARE MANY RIGHT PARTNERS FOR YOU

The love reality for Love Myth #3 is:

▼

IT IS POSSIBLE TO EXPERIENCE TRUE LOVE WITH MORE THAN ONE PERSON—THERE ARE MANY POTENTIAL PARTNERS YOU COULD BE HAPPY WITH.

▲

I can't tell you that there are X number of potential partners for each of us roaming around the earth, but I do know that the possibilities of your experiencing happiness in love are not limited to one person. I know from my own experience that the human heart has a tremendous capacity for loving, and that we limit the amount of love we allow ourselves to enjoy because of the Love Myths we believe. I believe that if you selected just about any two people in the world and stranded them alone on a deserted island for the rest of their lives, they would probably become romantic partners. While this may not be your romantic fantasy, it illustrates the point that the act of loving itself is inherently so enjoyable, that if given the opportunity we find ways to love people we thought we couldn't.

Each true love we have stretches our heart in a different direction, and each relationship serves us in a different way. Does this mean that it really doesn't matter who you are with? Of course not—in fact, it makes the issue of compatibility even more important. *Finding a partner with whom you are compatible, as well as one you love, is the formula for a healthy, lasting relationship.*

LOVE MYTH

▾　　▾　　▾　　▾　　**4**　　▾　　▾　　▾　　▾

The Perfect Partner Will Fulfill You Completely in Every Way

Imagine sitting in a job interview for a position you are interested in.

"Could you tell me about this job?" you ask the person who would be hiring you to work for him.

"Basically, I expect you to fulfill my every need. I expect you to know what I want, even when I don't tell you what I want. I want you to read my mind and know all of my secret expectations and deliver them. I want you to have the answers for me when I am confused, cheer me up when I am down, and make me love myself more when I don't feel confident. You will, of course, entertain me constantly so I never get bored, and enjoy all of my hobbies and interests so you can be the perfect companion."

I'm sure you agree that these expectations are outlandish and that no amount of money could tempt you to put yourself in such a highly pressured and impossible situation. And although this story is slightly exaggerated, the truth is **that many of us walk into relationships unconsciously expecting our partner to fulfill our every need, and when they do not, we become resentful and disillusioned.** I call this "setting someone up," especially because you may be unconscious of what some of those needs are and therefore can't articulate them to the person you love.

Here are the negative consequences of believing in Love Myth #4:

1. You fail to recognize a good relationship because your partner isn't fulfilling the needs you should be filling yourself.

"I think I should divorce my husband," Andrea proclaimed as we sat in my office. She had made an appointment with me to discuss her relationship, which was in major crisis. Andrea was twenty-seven, cute, and very athletic-looking. She had been married to Benjamin for almost two years.

"What's the problem?" I asked.

"I don't know," Andrea answered. "I'm just not happy. I thought marriage would be better than this, would change things for me, but it hasn't seemed to make any difference, and I'm disappointed."

"What did you think marriage would change?"

"I guess I wanted to feel more confidence, more clear about my life and where it is going; instead, I just feel confused."

"Let's talk about the rest of your life. What do you do?" I inquired.

"Well, not anything right now. I had a job six months ago, but I quit because I didn't like it. I don't really know what I want to do. I keep thinking that if I get out of this marriage, I'll feel better."

"Is there a particular complaint you have about Benjamin?"

Andrea thought for a minute and then replied: "No, not exactly. He's really loving and sweet to me. He just doesn't make me happy."

After talking to Andrea for a while, it was obvious to me that the problem in her relationship wasn't her husband, but herself. Andrea had no direction, no goals in her life. She married Benjamin hoping he would fill that empty place inside her, the place where she harbors her low self-esteem. But that was Andrea's job, not Benjamin's. And instead of pursuing a career or getting an education,

Andrea spent her days going to the gym and working out, or watching television.

Andrea was a self-indulgent woman who had never really grown up. But no matter how much Benjamin loved Andrea, he couldn't fill that void inside her. Because she felt empty, she assumed the marriage was not fulfilling her. The truth was, Benjamin was a good husband to Andrea, but Andrea wasn't very good to Andrea. *Her dissatisfaction wasn't with her marriage—it was with herself.*

The fantasy that your true love will "make everything okay" is a deadly one. It can cause you to end a perfectly good relationship because you expect your partner to do for you what you should be doing for yourself.

IF YOU FEEL EMOTIONALLY EMPTY BEFORE YOU START A RELATIONSHIP, YOU WILL FEEL JUST AS EMPTY ONCE YOU ARE IN A RELATIONSHIP.

---

2. You resent your partner for not giving you what you should be finding elsewhere.

Another pitfall of believing that your perfect partner will fulfill all your needs is the pressure you put on him or her to be everything to you. How many times have I heard women complain that they wish their husbands would go shopping with them, or spend a Saturday browsing for antiques, or cared more about how they redecorated the house! It took me years to figure out that there are needs we have as women that men just can't and shouldn't have to fulfill—not basic needs like those for love, affection, friendship, etc., but needs women have to enjoy themselves. Face it, ladies: Most husbands are never going to enjoy coordinating the decorations for your child's birthday party, sorting through fabric samples for the new couch, or spending hours roaming the mall for sales as much as most women do. These are needs better fulfilled by other women.

Men seem to have lower expectations in these areas than women, but men, too, experience their share of disappointment that we aren't fulfilling them in every way. Jeffrey went through this stage a few years into our relationship and began to doubt whether I was right for him. Naturally I was scared to death, but as we talked about it, his concerns focused on one area: sports. He is very athletically talented and loves sports of all kinds. Although I enjoy them, I tend to make other things a priority in my life. The more we discussed this issue, the more Jeffrey realized that his Love Myth told him that the "right woman" would want to go out and throw a baseball around with him, play racquetball every weekend, and do some serious bodybuilding. Jeffrey was depriving himself of doing these things himself because he wanted me to do them, too. "I guess I've been resenting you for depriving me of enjoying my interests," he confessed. We agreed that I would make an effort to share more athletic activities with him but that he would fulfill *himself* by joining a softball team, making workout dates with friends, and taking the time he needed to do what he enjoyed.

Here's the truth about Love Myth #4:

▼

THE RIGHT PARTNER WILL FULFILL MANY OF YOUR NEEDS BUT NOT ALL OF THEM.

▲

We each have our "wish list" of what we want in a perfect partner, but here is the point: There are some needs only your partner should fulfill. But there are others that your family, friends, and acquaintances can fulfill for you.

IT'S IMPORTANT TO DISTINGUISH BETWEEN WHAT YOU WOULD *LIKE* IN A PARTNER AND WHAT YOU REALLY *NEED* IN A PARTNER.

If Jeffrey hadn't challenged Love Myth #4, he might have ended our relationship and gone in search of Miss Junior Athlete of 1992, leaving behind the deep and powerful connection we have.

LOVE MYTH

▼   ▼   ▼   ▼   **5**   ▼   ▼   ▼   ▼

When You Experience Powerful Sexual Chemistry with Someone, It Must Be Love

Have you ever convinced yourself that you really loved someone as an excuse to continue having sex with them?

Have you ever been in a relationship where the only time you got along really well was in bed?

Have you ever pursued someone, telling yourself that you were madly in love, and after consummating the relationship sexually, realized it wasn't love, but lust?

Boy, does this Love Myth get us in trouble! It has its basis in the inherent guilt many of us in our culture feel about acknowledging and enjoying our sexuality. *Since society, our upbringing, and our morality often don't give us "permission" to be sexual for its own sake, we imagine that we have romantic feelings for partners we simply have the hots for!*

I call this the "Lust into Love Formula." Here's how it works:

▼

THE LUST INTO LOVE FORMULA

1. First, you feel powerful sexual chemistry with someone or, in raw terms, *lust*.
2. Next, you act on those urges and have sex with that person.
3. Then you experience some guilt or discomfort having been so sexually intimate with someone you aren't that emotionally connected with.
4. Finally you create a relationship with that person to legitimize your lust.

▲

Obviously I'm *not* saying that every time you form a relationship with someone you are following the Lust into Love Formula. However, if you are a strong believer in Love Myth #5, you may find yourself in this situation more often than you'd like to admit.

Here are the negative consequences of believing in Love Myth #5:

1. You get involved with people you are not compatible with.

Ann is a twenty-six-year-old buyer for a clothing store. Here is her story about how Love Myth #5 got her in real emotional trouble:

"Brian and I met while we were both skiing in Colorado. I guess being away from home combined with the cold and how cute he looked on skis took precedence over my better judgment, and I slept with him on our second date. Maybe it was the altitude, but I'd never had such exciting sex in my life. Brian prided himself on being a great lover, and he was. I was sure I had fallen head over heels.

"Our vacation ended—he went back to Seattle, I returned to San Francisco. We talked on the phone every few days, and I told him how I felt about him. For six months we spent every other weekend together, and, you guessed it, most of the time we were in bed. *The physical passion between us was spectacular, and so I assumed I must love him very much to feel that way.* We even began talking about marriage.

"That summer, we both decided to take two weeks off from our jobs and spend it together at my house. I could hardly wait for Brian to arrive. The first few days were wonderful, as usual. But then things began to fall apart. We started arguing about everything. First it was Brian's smoking—I'd known he smoked, but we were in bed so much that it wasn't that frequent. Now that we had more time together, he seemed to be smoking constantly. And I'd never realized how negative he was. He found something bad to say about my friends, the way I'd decorated my house, even the way I drive. Things got progressively worse until we weren't having sex at all, and I could hardly wait for him to leave.

"The night he went back to Seattle, I lay in bed crying my heart out. I was so confused, and I felt like my dreams were shattered before my eyes. I spent the next few days really thinking about my relationship with Brian, and suddenly everything became clear: *I'd never had a relationship with Brian. All we ever did was make love.* Our meeting was a romantic fling, and the six months afterward were filled either with phone calls that consisted of a lot of flirting and joking, or short visits during which we were in bed the whole time. I'd never seen Brian as a person, just a sexual partner. Once I did, I didn't even *like* him very much!"

Ann had never had really good sex with any of her previous boyfriends. So when she met Brian and the sparks flew, she assumed it must be love. It was also hard for her to admit that she could be that sexually turned on with someone she didn't love or wouldn't marry. She learned the hard way that passion doesn't always come from love. All she and Brian had in common was that they loved to ski and loved sex—enough for a fling, but not enough to make a long-term relationship work.

2. You stay in relationships longer than you should, and have a hard time letting go of partners who are not right for you.

Jamal approached me after a seminar in which I talked about

Love Myths. "You were describing me!" he exclaimed. Jamal is thirty-eight, divorced, and a teacher. Here is his story:

"I got married when I was really young to my high-school girlfriend. I was pretty inexperienced sexually, and she had never been with anyone but me, so it took me a while to realize that we were sexually incompatible. As the years passed, I lost all attraction to her, though I loved her very much. We had three children, and I tried to make it work for them, but finally when I was thirty-one I left and we got a divorce.

"I was on the dating scene for the first time since I was nineteen years old, and I was ready to roll. I promised myself that I'd never end up in some sexless relationship again, and I have to admit I was pretty wild for those first few years. I was so afraid I'd fall in love with someone I wasn't attracted to that I would only date women I felt totally and immediately turned on by.

"That's how I met Sabrina. We were at a jazz coffeehouse, and she was sitting at the bar. The first thing I noticed about her was her body—she looked like my fantasy woman. We started talking, then dancing, and I could hardly keep it together until we went back to her place and got it on. Man, I thought I had died and gone to heaven. She was like a wild pony. It felt the way I always thought it should be with a woman.

"I had promised myself that I wouldn't get involved again until I was completely sure of the relationship, but my resolve was shot to pieces. Sabrina would purr and wrap herself around me until she got her way. I ended up moving into her place within a month, and that's when the trouble began. I found out Sabrina had no money—she'd been supported by an ex-boyfriend, and she had a stack of unpaid bills. I was under her spell, so I agreed to help her out until she got back on her feet.

ESCAPING THE PRISON OF SEXUAL PARADISE

Jamal continued: "Six months passed, and our relationship was like a roller coaster—one minute we'd be fighting and the next we'd be having wild sex. Sabrina was like a spoiled, irresponsible child. She never even looked for a job, and was draining me of all of my energy. I knew I had to get out, but each time I told her I was leaving, she would seduce me and I'd end up staying.

"Finally, one day when Sabrina came home with a thousand dollars' worth of new clothes, I couldn't take it anymore, and I left. I felt free for the first time in months. Unfortunately, that feeling didn't last. Sabrina would call me at my new place and show up dressed in what I call a 'screw me' outfit, and I'd lose my willpower. We'd see each other a few days, then I'd break it off again for a month or two. Then one night she'd call me, tell me she was lonely, and I'd find myself back in bed with her again. I was disgusted with myself.

"I hate to admit this, but I was so hooked into the great sex it took me two years to finally let go of Sabrina."

Jamal's story is dramatic but not that uncommon. He was sure that if sex with Sabrina was that good, she was the right woman for him. It took several years of drama and humiliation to teach Jamal that good sex didn't necessary mean healthy love.

Here's the reality about Love Myth #5:

▼
_____

GOOD SEX HAS NOTHING TO DO WITH TRUE LOVE, BUT MAKING LOVE DOES.
_____
▲

If you have fantastic sex with a partner:

▶ it does not necessarily mean you love them
▶ it does not necessarily mean you are meant to be together
▶ it does not necessarily mean you have a good relationship

It does mean:

▶ you have good sexual chemistry
▶ one or both of you are skilled lovers

It might mean:

▶ you have a strong attraction that can be the basis for a healthy, whole relationship *if you are compatible in other areas outside the bedroom*

THE TRUTH ABOUT LOVE

You have probably been able to relate to one or all of these five Love Myths. Isn't it amazing to realize how they've contributed to some of the mistakes you've made in love?

Here are the five Love Myths again, and the five love realities we came up with:

LOVE MYTH	LOVE REALITY
1 True love conquers all.	Love is not enough to make a relationship work—it needs compatibility and commitment.
2 When it's really true love, you will know it the moment you meet the other person.	It takes just a moment to experience infatuation, but true love takes time.
3 There is only one true love in the world who is right for you.	It is possible to experience true love with more than one person—there are many potential partners you could be happy with.
4 The perfect partner will fulfill you completely in every way.	The right partner will fulfill many of your needs but not all of them.
5 When you experience powerful sexual chemistry with someone, it must be love.	Good sex has nothing to do with true love, but making love does.

CREATING THE LOVE YOU DESERVE

I recently gave a public lecture to a large group of people, and as I was autographing books at the end of the evening, a young woman approached me with tears in her eyes. "I am so inspired by everything you said," she began. "I attended the seminar you and your boyfriend gave last month as well, and I just hope one day I am lucky enough to have a relationship as good as yours."

There was a line of about fifty people waiting to speak with me, and normally I would have thanked this woman and gone on to talk to the next person. But something made me stop and take her hands. "I want you to know something," I said, looking into her eyes. "I do feel very blessed to have such a wonderful man in my life. **But luck had nothing to do with it.** I've made so many unhealthy love choices in my past. I've found men and tried to change them into who I wanted them to be. I've had partners I was totally incompatible with, and told myself it didn't matter. I've loved men for all the wrong reasons. **It's not luck that is making this relationship work—I finally chose the right person,** and together we've worked very hard to create the kind of closeness and harmony we have. And you can have the same thing in your life!"

Perhaps you, too, have felt unlucky in love, and have lost the hope of having the kind of relationship you dream of. Or perhaps you do have someone special in your life but want to feel closer and more loving and aren't quite sure how. I'm happy that you've found this book and have chosen to read it. I know it will help you find the power and wisdom that wait within you to guide your heart toward love that is healthy, joyous, and real.

2
▼▼▼

WHY WE CHOOSE
THE PEOPLE WE LOVE

▼▼▼

► Have you ever wanted a responsible, mature partner, only to end up with an irresponsible, unreliable person who drove you crazy?

► Have you ever told yourself you were ready for a long-term, committed relationship, and were looking for someone who felt the same way, only to end up falling in love with someone who was unavailable or incapable of making a commitment?

► Have you ever vowed never again to get involved with someone who was emotionally shut down and distant, only to find yourself hopelessly infatuated with someone who couldn't love you back the way you deserved to be loved?

► Have you ever wondered why you've ended up with the partners you've had?

We all think we know what we want in a mate. We don't want any unhealthy or negative qualities, just lots of great ones. So we get frustrated and disappointed when we end up in a relationship with someone different from, and usually much less wonderful than, our ideal.

I'm sure you've read the "Personals" in magazines and newspapers, those columns of ads where single people advertise for the kind of mate they would like to meet. If you had to write an Emotional Want Ad describing the kind of partner you were looking for, it would probably sound something like this:

WANTED:

Attractive, sensitive, caring person for permanent relationship. Must be emotionally open, able to talk about feelings, unafraid of intimacy. Successful but not a workaholic, with a great sense of humor. Knows how to make me feel really loved and appreciated. If you are healthy, honest, faithful, and ready for a commitment, I'm the one for you!

The truth is, if you had to match your Emotional Want Ads to the partners you have actually ended up with, they might read more like these:

WANTED:

Self-absorbed, damaged *loser* who has lots of potential and is doing nothing with it. Must be immature, irresponsible, and lazy. Low sex drive a bonus. No skills, background, or success required. If you are looking for someone to make empty promises to and like to blame others for your failures, call me now. Note: Men with jobs need *not* apply.

WANTED:

Are you married? Engaged? Unable to make a commitment? Then I'm the woman for you. I'm looking for an unavailable man for a long, painful, and frustrating relationship. No time or energy required. I'll do all the work. Call anytime, day or night; I'll be waiting. If you like being dishonest, stringing me along, and thinking only about yourself, you're my type of guy.

Obviously none of us would ever write ads like these last two or even agree to accept these kinds of relationships into our lives. And yet, we often end up with partners who fit these descriptions.

This chapter is designed to help you understand why you have chosen the partners you've been with, or the one you are with now.

CHARTING YOUR LOVE CHOICES

The following exercise will give you an overview of the relationships you have been in. I've taught this process for years in my seminars, and it is always an eye-opener for each person who does it. **NOTE: This is one of the most important exercises you will learn in this book. Please read the instructions carefully, and take all the time you need to complete each portion.**

Here's how it works:

STEP 1 On a blank piece of paper, list the names of each partner you have had a significant relationship with, including the one you are with now. *Don't* include someone you dated only a few times. *Do* include anyone to whom you were very emotionally attached. Leave space after each name so you have room to write. If you have had only one partner in your life, just put down that name.

STEP 2 After each person's name, make a list of their *most negative qualities*, those parts of their personality you dislike the most. Don't write a whole sentence—rather, sum up the quality in a word or two. *Example: Marcy's boyfriend could never keep a job during their four years together. So Marcy should write "jobless" on her list.* **Do not** list positive qualities.

STEP 3 Once you have finished, read over all of your lists and circle any words or qualities that seem to repeat themselves from one person to another.

STEP 4 Make a *"summary list"* of those words or qualities you used more than once or that stood out to you.

STEP 5 Take some time to think about your summary list and your individual lists. Ask yourself the following questions:
   ► Are there some patterns in my relationships of which I need to be aware?
   ► Is there a trend I can see in my relationships over time? Getting healthier? Getting worse? Getting better and then a relapse?
   ► Were some partners easier to list negative qualities about than others?
   ► Is my present partner significantly different from previous partners? Better? Worse? The same?

Example #1. Ann's Love Choices Chart

EDDIE
Dishonest
Manipulative
Space case (lives in dream
   world)
Impractical
Controlling
Self-absorbed
Explosive temper
Sexually dysfunctional
Moody
Uses me for money
Can't keep a job

DAVID
Low sex drive
Moody
Deceptive
Explosive temper
Stubborn
Can't talk about feelings
Unfaithful
Impractical
Self-absorbed

JERRY
Space case
Moody
Self-absorbed
Unromantic
Explosive temper
Impractical
Professionally passive

SEAN (ex-husband)
Angry
Unfaithful
Critical
Moody
Jobless
Deceptive
Controlling
Low sex drive
Emotionally distant
Self-absorbed
Rebellious
Hates talking about feelings
Uses me for money

ADAM (husband)
Not romantic enough
Low sex drive
Hard time talking about
   feelings
Temper
Rebellious
Serious

Ann, thirty-nine, has listed five important men in her life. She is married to one now (Adam), another previously (Sean), and the other three men were long-time partners. When Ann looked over her list, several things were obvious:

1. Her list of negative qualities about Sean was the *longest*, accu-

rately reflecting that this had been the most painful relationship in her life.

2. Her list about her present husband, Adam, was the *shortest*, accurately reflecting that this is the healthiest and most satisfying relationship in her life.

3. There was an enormous contrast between her relationship with Sean and her present husband, Adam, indicating some real growth on her part.

In Step 3 of the exercise, Ann circled similar qualities that seemed to repeat themselves on the lists and then made a summary list.

STEP 4: ANN'S SUMMARY LIST OF SIMILAR OR COMMON QUALITIES

Angry
Dishonest
Moody
Irresponsible and unreliable
Sexually dysfunctional
Self-absorbed
Jobless
Hates talking about feelings
Controlling

"This is embarrassing," Ann complained as she read her summary list. "I never realized these men had these traits in common. I always told myself how 'different' each new one was from the last. I guess they looked different on the outside, but they were very similar. At least I've improved over the years, and married a loving, reliable man."

Ann's Love Choices Chart helped her understand exactly why her relationships didn't work. Once it was on paper, it was easy for her to see what kind of men she had been attracting and why she had been so unhappy.

Example #2. Mitchell's Love Choices Chart

Mitchell is a thirty-six-year-old attorney who wanted to figure out why he couldn't find the right woman to marry. "I'm looking for a powerful, independent woman who won't smother me in a relationship," he explained, "But somehow I end up with the opposite."

VALERIE
Emotionally unstable
Insecure
Drama queen
Clinging
Irrational
Obsessive (looks)
Victim
Whiny
Manipulative
Childish
Helpless
Sexually damaged

LINDA
Manipulative
Drama queen
Temper
Controlling
Always tense
Whiny
Emotionally unavailable
Sexually repressed
Frightened
Too attached to parents

SHERYL
Domineering
Critical
Selfish
Addicted/food
Drama queen
Complainer
Negative
Nervous
High-strung
Closed-minded
Victim
Draining

STEP 4: MITCHELL'S SUMMARY LIST OF SIMILAR OR COMMON QUALITIES
Drama queen
Controlling
Obsessive
Victim
Emotionally unstable
Immature
Sexually damaged

When Mitchell looked at his summary list, he was amazed. "I found these women so compelling," he admitted, "but for all the wrong reasons. I'm obviously attracting weak, little-girl types with a victim mentality and a real addiction to drama. You can imagine how turbulent these relationships are. The women fall apart and go from one crisis to the next, and I try to rescue them and fix everything."

Mitchell learned several things from his Love Choices Chart:

► He not only attracts women who are addicted to drama, but he himself is obviously addicted to drama, since he puts up with this kind of behavior.
► He gets to feel superior to his partners by choosing women who are a mess, and helping them get their lives together.
► Even though he says he wants a strong, independent woman, he finds women who are dependent and not self-sufficient, and once again he gets to feel needed and important.

CREATING YOUR EMOTIONAL WANT AD

Now that you've made your Love Choices Chart and worked on your summary list, it's time for you to face the truth about the kinds of partners you've chosen in your life.

▼

TO FIND OUT WHAT KIND OF PERSON YOU'VE BEEN SEEKING, LOOK AT THE KIND OF PARTNERS YOU'VE ENDED UP WITH.

▲

► **You don't end up with your mates by accident.**
► **You don't attract someone because you have bad luck.**
► **You don't find the same type of person over and over again by coincidence.**

You get what you ask for!

I believe that we get back what we put out, that our unconscious mind has certain "agendas" or needs, and based on these needs, we choose particular partners in our lives. Ann could insist to herself and her friends that she truly wanted a loving, open, stable, responsible man, but in truth, and as shown by her summary list, she attracted men who were angry, unreliable, self-absorbed, jobless, and sexually dysfunctional. Mitchell claimed he longed to find a strong, independent woman, and yet he continually attracted immature, overly dramatic women who needed rescuing.

One of the most effective ways to sum up the kind of person you've been unknowingly seeking, whether in your past or today, is to create your own Emotional Want Ad. You've actually already found the ingredients for your want ad in your Love Choices summary list.

Here's what to do:

Write a want ad using the characteristics you have on your summary list. Make the ad as direct and as humorous as you can. It's okay to make fun of yourself and your past choices. *In fact, the more dramatic and outrageous your ad is, the more it can help you to break free from the negative emotional patterns that have been hurting your love life.*

Here is Ann's Love Choices summary list once more:
    Angry
    Dishonest
    Moody
    Irresponsible and unreliable
    Sexually dysfunctional
    Self-absorbed
    Jobless
    Hates talking about feelings
    Controlling

Now here is how Ann's Emotional Want Ad might sound:

WANTED:

Angry, unemployed control freak for long, demeaning relationship. **Must be moody, manipulative, and an expert at making me tiptoe around in fear, because that's what I like. The more you keep me guessing, the happier I'll be. Men with ambition or a clean credit record need not apply. If you are looking for someone to love you no matter how unavailable and obnoxious you become, then I'm the girl for you. Chronic lateness and lying are real pluses. Don't worry if you can't get it up—I'll pretend you're normal and won't ever complain. Call whenever *you* want to—after all, you're the boss.**

Here is Mitchell's Love Choices summary list once more:
    Drama queen
    Controlling
    Obsessive
    Victim
    Emotionally unstable
    Immature
    Sexually damaged

Here's how Mitchell's Emotional Want Ad might sound:

WANTED:

Do you hate yourself? Do you hate the world? Do you like to blame everyone else for what's gone wrong in your life? I'm looking for an immature, sexually damaged woman who will whine and complain twenty-four hours a day. Eating disorders, drug addiction, or other obsessions are definite pluses. You must be good at jumping out of moving cars, hanging up on me on the phone, and throwing temper tantrums in expensive restaurants. Hate being touched? Then you are perfect for me! If you call your parents less than once a day, don't bother applying, because I'm not looking for a grown-up. Call me in the middle of the night, or better yet, at work during an important meeting. Don't worry about interrupting— nothing is as important as you and your latest crisis.

Writing your Emotional Want Ad can be very confrontational, because it forces you to look at the message you've been giving out about the kind of partner you are willing to accept. *But it is a powerful way to break your own negative programming by taking what has been unconscious and making it conscious.*

DON'T SKIP THIS EXERCISE, EVEN IF IT IS UNCOMFORTABLE. WORK ON YOUR WANT AD UNTIL IT IS SO STRONG THAT IT MAKES YOU LAUGH.

Here are a couple more samples written by some of the participants at my seminars:

Cynthia was married for thirty-two years before she divorced her husband. She wrote this want ad based on her list formulated from their relationship:

WANTED:

Moody assbole who doesn't know how to talk. Sign language O.K. I'm looking for a man to glue himself to the couch, watch sports day and night, and belch. The more boring you are, the more I like you. No need to shave or shower frequently. I like to be disgusted. Denial a must. Don't ever admit that we have any problems. Erections not necessary.

Carl, thirty-six, keeps attracting women who don't think he is good enough for them. Here is his want ad:

WANTED:

I know you are out there. You: gorgeous, superficial, obsessed with money, cars, and being seen by the right people. Me: not good enough for you. Together we'll be perfect. You'll constantly put me down, and I'll love it. I need a woman who will make me feel inadequate. Humiliation in public a big plus, especially around your friends. If you spend hours getting dressed and putting on makeup and haven't read a book in years, you are just what I am looking for. Please call—I need you to make me feel worthless.

Francine, forty-three, has a history of attracting charming but cruel men. Here is her want ad:

WANTED:

Hey There! Do you like hurting the one you love? Are you interested in a long, drawn-out, painful relationship fraught with multiple breakups and reconciliations? I'm looking for someone to make me miserable. I'm not picky; addictions welcome. Call any time day or night. My good night's sleep is nothing compared to the pure pleasure of hearing from you. Your thoughtless impulse to call after an evening of drinking and whoring will be viewed as the ultimate in attentiveness and a compliment to my desirability as a woman. Hurry. There are many men even more troubled than yourself applying at this very moment.

Over the years I've helped thousands of people understand more about their relationships through making Love Choices Charts and Emotional Want Ads. Remember: **We're not looking at the positive qualities in your partners, but the pattern of negative or undesirable qualities.**

▼

LOCATING THE PERSISTENT, NEGATIVE PATTERNS IN YOUR RELATIONSHIPS IS THE FIRST STEP TOWARD ELIMINATING THOSE PATTERNS.

▲

UNDERSTANDING YOUR EMOTIONAL PROGRAMMING

Have you ever wondered:

▶ why you've stayed in relationships with people you knew weren't good for you?

▶ why you've attracted the same kind of person over and over again?

▶ why the very characteristics you dislike in a person are the ones your partner possesses?

As the saying goes, **"If I'm so smart, how did I end up in such a dumb relationshp?"**

The answer lies in understanding why you've chosen the partners you have in your life.

WHEN YOU UNDERSTAND WHY YOU'VE MADE THE LOVE CHOICES YOU HAVE, YOU WILL THEN BE FREE TO MAKE NEW AND BETTER LOVE CHOICES.

The rest of this chapter is dedicated to helping you gain insight into your relationship choices, past and present. As you read, remind yourself of your summary list of negative characteristics and your Emotional Want Ad. This will keep you focused on the particular issues you'd like to know more about.

As I said earlier, it is not by accident, nor by virtue of your bad luck that you've ended up with the partners you have. Rather, it is due to your *emotional programming.* **Your emotional programming is simply a set of decisions and beliefs you made about yourself, others, and the world in general when you were growing up.** Each day that you are alive, you collect experiences, and each experience helps you form decisions about yourself, about people, and about life. In the same way you would program a computer with basic information, so you program your mind with these beliefs. For the rest of your life this "program" affects how you think and behave.

In other words, your **life experiences** cause you to make certain **decisions** about yourself and others. The combination of all of these decisions is your **emotional programming,** which in turn causes you to make certain **love choices** as an adult.

Life Experiences → Decisions →
Emotional Programming → Love Choices

Here's something else to be aware of: The majority of this emotional programming occurs when you are still very young. Psychologists estimate that:

▶ **Between birth and five years of age—you receive 50 percent of your emotional programming.**

▶ **Between five and eight years of age—you receive 30 percent of your emotional programming.**

That means, by the age of eight, you are 80 percent programmed, psychologically.

In other words, 80 percent of your decisions about yourself and others have already been made.

▶ **Between the ages of eight and eighteen—you receive 15 percent more of your emotional programming.**

So by the time you are eighteen years old, you're 95 percent done! That leaves 5 percent left for the rest of your life. This may not seem like much, but it's that 5 percent that I work with when I help people make changes in their lives. And the good news is that you can use that 5 percent to understand and change the other 95 percent.

Perhaps now you can better understand why, even though the 5 percent of your mind that is conscious says, "I want a wonderful partner who loves me and treats me well," the 95 percent of your mind that is *unconscious* is responsible for making your poor love choices.

Once you understand why you've been doing what you've been doing, you will be free to change your behavior permanently.

▼

YOUR UNCONSCIOUS EMOTIONAL PROGRAMMING IS RESPONSIBLE FOR MUCH OF THE PAIN YOU EXPERIENCE IN YOUR LOVE LIFE.

▲

DISCOVERING YOUR DECISIONS ABOUT LOVE

Your next step is to understand your own emotional programming, as if you were reading a computer manual for your brain. Here's an exercise that will help you:

Exercise: Making Your Emotional Programming Map

STEP 1 Make a list of the most painful realities or experiences you can recall from childhood, up until you left home. Include things such as ongoing situations (a parent's alcoholism, for instance), or particular events (being punished or ridiculed by a parent).

Sample situations

My parents were divorced.

Mom and Dad always fought.

I was always compared to my "perfect" sister.

I was overweight and always teased.

Dad was never home and cheated on Mom.

We had eight kids in the family and not enough time or money to go around.

Mom was a rageaholic and very moody.

Dad never showed affection or praised me.

Mom died of cancer when I was ten.

I had a stepfather who hated me.

We had a strict religious upbringing and lived in constant fear of sin.

Dad molested me.

Sample events

Younger brother was born and I was ignored.

My parents put my dog to sleep without telling me.

Dad promised to come to my birthday party and never showed up.

I saw Dad beat up my brother.

I found Mom drunk and unconscious.

I thought Mom left me behind in a store.

My parents didn't believe me when I told them my brother had molested me.

My father let go of me in the ocean and I almost drowned.

My best friend dropped me and told everyone she hated me when I was eleven.

STEP 2 Think carefully about each item on your list, and ask yourself, "*What descisions did I make about myself, others, or life because of this experience?*" Then write down your decisions next to the appropriate memory. Take your time doing this, and if you get stuck on one, go on to another and come back to the first one later.

Don't be surprised if many of the decisions you made when you were young are similar.

Examples:

SITUATION OR EVENT	DECISION
My parents were divorced.	I'm not lovable enough.
Dad molested me.	I'm bad and dirty and men who love me control me.
Mom and Dad always fought.	I have to be good so I don't make people mad—it's not okay for me to be angry.
I was overweight and always .... teased.	I'm not okay the way I am so I have to try extra hard to get people to like me.
Dad was never home and .... cheated on Mom.	Men can't be trusted, and women are doormats.
Mom was a rageaholic and very moody.	It's not safe to express myself—I can't make people upset.
Dad never showed affection or .. praised me.	I'm not lovable—I have to work hard to get people to love me.
Mom died of cancer when ...... I was ten.	I have to take care of everyone.
I had a stepfather who hated .... me.	People who love me (Mom) abandon me.
We had a strict religious .... upbringing and lived in constant fear of sin.	It's not okay to have fun or be sexual.
Dad promised to come to my ... birthday party and never showed up.	Men are irresponsible and I can't count on them.
I saw Dad beat up my brother. ..	I have to be good so I don't get hurt/I can't protect the people I love.
My parents didn't believe me ... when I told them my brother had molested me.	My feelings don't count so I should just keep them to myself.

STEP 3 After thinking about the decisions you made due to a particular experience or circumstance, *write down how this emotional programming has affected your love choices and the kinds*

of partners you choose. This is the hardest portion of this exercise, but the most important. You may want to think about this over a period of days, and talk with close friends or your partner to help clarify your ideas. Keep adding to your list as new revelations surface.

We've been talking about Ann throughout this chapter, and earlier we saw her summary list and her Emotional Want Ad: *"WANTED: Angry, unemployed control freak for demeaning relationship."* Now look at her emotional programming table.

Ann's Emotional Programming Table

SITUATION OR EVENT	DECISION	LOVE CHOICE
Dad made promises he didn't keep. Let me down constantly, didn't show up when he was supposed to.	People I love will disappoint me. Men can't be trusted.	Men whom I put on a pedestal and then they disappoint me. Men who are irresponsible.
Never told Mom and Dad were having problems. Wasn't told they were getting divorced until right before.	People I love will lie to me, so I can't trust them.	Men who are dishonest with themselves and with me.
Never saw Dad loving and affectionate toward Mom. Dad cheated on Mom with other women.	Men aren't turned on by their own wives. Women are starved for love.	Men with low sex drive who don't show me they want me. Men who are attracted to other women.
Sick with high fevers as young child. Dad doesn't come home. Mom left alone with me.	I can't count on men to be there for me. I have to take care of myself.	Men with no jobs whom I have to support. Men who are impractical and don't take care of me.

| Neither Mom nor Dad will talk about divorce or how sad they are feeling afterward. Act like everything is fine. | It's not safe for me to share my feelings. People I love don't want to talk about feelings. | Men who have a difficult time discussing feelings and hate my being emotional. Men who refuse to look at our problems. |

Ann's comments: "I never realized how much these childhood events affected me. All along I've known I was choosing the wrong men, but I couldn't figure out why. Reading down that column of decisions I made as a little girl was frightening, but I could feel in my heart that part of me really still believes those things. *I attracted men who made me feel the same way I felt with my father—angry, discounted, betrayed.* The worst part is, I didn't even recognize the pattern because I was so used to having those feelings in childhood."

Now that Ann understands more about why she has attracted the wrong partners, she can begin making changes to attract the right partner.

▼

ONCE YOU BECOME AWARE OF YOUR UNCONSCIOUS DECISIONS ABOUT LOVE, YOU CAN MAKE NEW, HEALTHY DECISIONS.

▲

Later we'll talk more about how to "reprogram" your mind so you can break free from the unhealthy habits of the past.

Here are some more samples of the kinds of love choices you might have made based on childhood events and the decisions about love that followed:

SITUATION OR EVENT	DECISION	LOVE CHOICE
Mom was a rageaholic and very moody.	It's not safe to express myself. I can't make people upset.	Moody partners with bad tempers. Partners who hate when I get upset or emotional and won't talk about feelings.

Dad molested me.	I'm bad and dirty, and men who love me control me.	Partners who are sexually obsessed and very domineering.
I was overweight and always teased.	I'm not okay the way I am, so I have to try extra hard to get people to like me.	Partners who are unavailable or like me as friends, whom I pursue and feel rejected by.
Dad was never home and cheated on Mom.	Men can't be trusted, and women are doormats.	Partners who aren't there for me emotionally, who are workaholics or who are still in love with their ex.
Dad never showed affection or praised me.	I'm not lovable—I have to work hard to get people to love me.	Unemotional partners who don't make me feel special.
My parents were divorced.	People who love me abandon me.	Partners I test by behaving badly and who end up leaving me.
I saw Dad mistreat Mom.	I have to be good so I don't get hurt. I can't protect the people I love.	Partners who have problems I try to fix.

WHY YOU CHOOSE THE PEOPLE YOU LOVE

There are many ways in which your emotional programming can have an effect on whom you choose to love. Here are some of the reasons you might end up with a particular partner.

THE "GOING HOME" SYNDROME

As human beings, we gravitate toward the familiar. We like to sleep on the same side of the bed each night, to park in the same space at work, to go back to our favorite vacation spot. *Returning to the familiar* is a basic instinct that gives our lives a sense of continuity and safety in a chaotic and changing universe. Unfortunately, this instinct can work against us.

WE OFTEN SEEK OUT EMOTIONAL SITUATIONS THAT ARE SIMILAR TO THOSE WE EXPERIENCED IN CHILDHOOD, REGARDLESS OF WHETHER THOSE EXPERIENCES WERE POSITIVE OR NEGATIVE.

I call this pattern *"going home."* Here's how it works:

When you were a young child, your home was the main source of love and safety in your life. Even if there was violence or chaos in your household, it was still "home"—it was where you were fed and had a place to sleep and received some sort of attention. So you associate **love** with **home.** You also associate **home** with other characteristics, based on your experiences at home. For instance, if your parents fought a lot, you might have an equation in your mind that says **home = chaos.** If you weren't shown much love or affection, your equation might be **home = loneliness.** If one of your parents was abusive, it might be **home = fear.**

Remember your basic math from school, where you learned:

$$\text{If } A = B, \text{ and } B = C, \text{ then } A = C$$

Let's use this same principle to illustrate "going home":

▶ If love = home, and home = chaos, then **love = chaos.**

▶ If love = home, and home = loneliness, then **love = loneliness.**

▶ If love = home, and home = fear, then **love = fear.**

YOUR MIND WILL EQUATE WHATEVER ASSOCIATIONS YOU HAVE ABOUT "HOME" WITH WHAT LOVE IS SUPPOSED TO FEEL LIKE.

So if home felt like chaos, you might seek unstable partners who will help you create dramatic, chaotic relationships. If home felt like loneliness, you might seek a partner who doesn't give you enough love, affection, or attention, so that you end up feeling lonely. If home felt like fear, you might attract someone who always criticizes you, threatens to leave, or makes you jealous, so that you always feel fearful. You unconsciously choose what is familiar—**you are going home.**

Obviously, we all have positive associations with home as well, which we also seek to reproduce in our adult life. I've found, however, that *it is the more painful associations that can cause the most trouble, because they are usually unconscious.* In other words, if you came from a home where your parents showed you a lot of affection but criticized one another, you might consciously seek a partner who was very loving, but unconsciously attract someone who was critical.

HOW ANN WAS "GOING HOME" IN HER RELATIONSHIPS

We've been following Ann throughout this chapter. Ann is a thirty-nine-year-old woman with a history of attracting irresponsible, emotionally distant men. Ann is now happily married to Adam, but still finds herself afraid to trust completely because of her past experiences. Reading Ann's emotional programming list, you can see how she went "home" in most of her relationships with men. When I asked Ann to write down her negative associations with home, here is what she came up with:

HOME = **Disappointment**
Denial
Lack of communication about feelings
Betrayal
Inadequacy
Dishonesty
Abandonment

Substitute the word **love** for **home,** and you see Ann's unconscious associations regarding **love:**

LOVE = **Disappointment**
Denial
Lack of communication about feelings
Betrayal
Inadequacy
Dishonesty
Abandonment

Ann was amazed at how similar her negative description of her childhood was to her negative description of her adult relationships. All of her love affairs included the same emotions she felt as a little girl. **Ann had left home physically, but she hadn't left home emotionally.** She continued to re-create the same emotional circumstances, because, as unpleasant as they might have been, they were what she was used to. The good news was that in her marriage to Adam, Ann felt very few of those old, familiar feelings. Unlike Ann's previous partners, Adam was responsible, successful, and emotionally open. "It looks like I'm finally leaving home!" she remarked. "Adam is helping me change many of the negative decisions I'd made about love. Even though there are times when Adam reminds me of my father, we can talk about my reactions together, which allows me to heal."

I asked Ann to redefine her concepts of **home** and **love** by turning each negative quality into its opposite and adding others.

Ann's new list:

HOME & LOVE = **Trust**
Honesty
Communication about feelings
Fidelity
Reliability
Consistency
Safety
Support

WHY MITCHELL CHOSE WOMEN WHO WERE EMOTIONAL BASKET CASES

Remember Mitchell, the thirty-six-year-old attorney who kept attracting women who smothered him and depended on him to fix their lives? Here is his list about **home** and **love**:

HOME & LOVE = **Drama**
Lack of stability
Responsibility
Mom's pain
Crisis
No childhood

Mitchell's mother was an alcoholic who couldn't function as an adult half of the time. When she wasn't passed out, she was on an emotional roller coaster. Mitchell's dad was a quiet, passive man whose method of dealing with his wife's disease was denial. As the oldest child in the family, Mitchell ended up taking on much of the responsibility that should have been his mother's—cooking, cleaning, caring for his younger sisters and brother. In this way, he really had no childhood.

Mitchell's biggest burden, however, was the emotional one he took on in trying to fix his mother. "I loved my mom so much," Mitchell shared, "but nothing I could do would get her to stop drinking. I felt like I was her only hope. No wonder I don't realize how screwed up these women are when I meet them," he exclaimed. "Emotionally unstable, dramatic women seem 'normal' to me. It feels familiar—just like home. It's what I experienced every day of my life."

Does becoming aware of his emotional programming completely eradicate it for Mitchell? Of course not. But now that he is conscious of his "weakness" for rescuing messed-up women, he can be much more vigilant about making sure to choose self-sufficient, healthy partners.

Now it's your turn to look at your emotional programming about **home** and **love**.

Exercise: Defining "Love" and "Home":

STEP 1 Make a list of the negative associations you have with the word "home" from childhood. Try to use a word or phrase, as in the examples above, rather than a long description.

STEP 2 Substitute the word "love" for "home" to understand more about your unconscious programming regarding love.

STEP 3 Compare your "love =" list to your summary list of negative qualities in partners. Notice the similarities, and determine if you've been "going home" by loving the partners you have chosen.

COMPLETING UNFINISHED EMOTIONAL BUSINESS FROM CHILDHOOD

The second way in which your emotional programming affects whom you choose to love is by unconsciously motivating you to complete unfinished emotional business from childhood. Here's how it works. Every child has two basic instincts, or agendas:

▶ They want to feel happy and loved, especially by their parents.

▶ They want to see their parents happy and loved.

If you go through your childhood and these agendas, or desires, aren't met, it is as if you have unfinished psychological business that is left hanging. You somehow feel incomplete, as if something is not right. *Your mind "remembers" that these desires are important to you, and will create circumstances in your adult life to "help" you accomplish these unconscious goals.*

YOUR UNCONSCIOUS MIND WILL SEEK TO COMPLETE ITS UNFINISHED EMOTIONAL BUSINESS FROM CHILDHOOD BY GETTING YOU TO "CHOOSE" PEOPLE WHO WILL HELP YOU RE-CREATE YOUR CHILDHOOD DRAMAS.

Here are some of the ways in which you may be completing unfinished childhood business:

▶ **If you didn't get the love/attention you wanted from a parent, you might** attract a partner who, like your parent, doesn't give you the love you want and makes you work hard to try and get it.

▶ **Or, if you are really angry at that parent, you might** attract a partner who, unlike your parent, *does* give you the love you want, and you reject him, hurt him, or make him work hard to get your love (i.e., retaliation).

ARE YOU FALLING IN LOVE WITH YOUR MOM OR DAD?

Michelle, twenty-nine, is a perfect example of a woman who was unconsciously using the men in her life to complete some emotional business from her childhood. Michelle came to me complaining that she always attracted very critical, controlling men who made her feel she wasn't good enough for them. She found partners who'd tell her she wasn't skinny enough, smart enough, or motivated enough. She'd had three long-term relationships in which each of her boyfriends tried to change her into someone else. Michelle even went so far as to have plastic surgery to increase her bust size because her last boyfriend told her her boobs were too small!

I gave Michelle an assignment—to write out a complaint list about each of her parents, and then to compare the list to her complaint list about her boyfriends. Here is what she came up with:

DAD	MOM
unavailable	critical
passive	demanding
nonexpressive	sarcastic
serious	moody
cold	perfectionist
workaholic	angry

"I can't believe this," Michelle told me. *"I've been falling in love with my mother."* Michelle's mom was a highly critical, caustic woman. Nothing Michelle ever did as a child met her mother's standards. She was always fussing over her daughter and comparing her to other children, both in appearance and behavior. Michelle's dad was a real absentee father, but when he was around, he didn't disapprove or approve—he was just there. Michelle received a lot of attention from her mom, but it was negative attention. Even as an adult, when Michelle calls home with news of a job promotion, or a trip she's planning, her mother still questions Michelle's judgment and makes her feel inadequate.

By attracting men who constantly put her down, Michelle is re-creating a relationship with her mother in which she tries hard to be smart enough, pretty enough, and good enough. It's as if a part of her mind thinks, "Maybe this time I'll get him to think I'm beautiful," or "I know he will love me if I can just be more of what he wants me to be." The little girl inside her has never released her need for Mommy's approval, so she makes poor love choices.

If you suspect that you may be "falling in love with a parent," complete the exercise I gave Michelle: Make a complaint list about your parents, and compare it to your summary list earlier in this chapter. The similarities can be frightening, but you will definitely gain some insight.

ARE YOU PUNISHING MOM OR DAD?

If you didn't feel loved as a child, and you have a lot of suppressed anger about it, you might act out a second option—*finding a partner like your parent and unconsciously setting out to hurt him.* Louisa, forty-one, has been married to Fredric, forty-three, for four years. This was Louisa's third marriage, and they came to me on the verge of divorce. "I feel like I'm seeing the past flash before my eyes," Louisa admitted with a frightened look on her face. "In each of my marriages, I've ended up feeling completely turned off to my husband. The last two times, I've cheated on them, and our breakups were ugly. I love Fredric, and when we got married, I vowed I would never make the same mistakes again, but for the past six months I can't seem to do anything but criticize him."

The key to understanding Louisa's pattern lay in her relationship with her father. Louisa's parents were divorced when she was five. Her father moved to another city, wrote or called infrequently, and visited even less. All through her childhood, Louisa lived for a scrap of love and attention from her dad, and never expressed anything but adoration for him. But the rage she was feeling inside began to manifest itself when she hit puberty and started dating. Louisa became a heartbreaker: She'd find some guy who was crazy about her, get involved with him only long enough to be sure he really loved her; then she'd cheat on him, break up suddenly, or treat him shamelessly. **Louisa was "punishing" her father for abandoning her by abandoning all the men in her life.** It was as if she were saying, "See how bad it feels to be rejected? Now you know what I went through!"

------------------------------▼------------------------------

IF YOU ARE STILL ANGRY AT ONE OF YOUR PARENTS FOR HURTING YOU, YOU MIGHT ATTRACT PARTNERS WHOM YOU HURT.

------------------------------▲------------------------------

ARE YOU TRYING TO RESCUE MOM OR DAD?

Here's another way in which we often unconsciously finish childhood business:

If your parent wasn't happy and loved, you might:

▶ attract a partner just like your parent to love, regardless of whether he is good for you or not, to "prove" to Mom or Dad that you do love them, even if their spouse didn't

▶ attract a partner like your parent and try to fix or rescue him, to try to make that parent happy

► attract a relationship that isn't any better than your parents' marriage, in order not to be any happier than Mommy and Daddy

CASE #1: *How Tammy Tried to Rescue Her Father*

"I am so sick of falling in love with alcoholics!" Tammy complained to me. "Why do I keep finding these guys with addictions and staying with them?" Tammy was a bright, thirty-two-year-old advertising executive with lousy taste in men. No matter how hard she tried, she attracted one addictive man after another. Even though *she* didn't drink, smoke, or do drugs, she somehow managed to fall in love with men who did. Her current boyfriend, Todd, was typical—a charming, successful business owner with a big ego and a big drinking problem.

Tammy's pattern wasn't hard to figure out. She'd grown up on a farm, the youngest of three girls, Daddy's favorite. Tammy's father was a hardworking, affectionate man and an alcoholic. Though no one in Tammy's family ever used that word, everyone knew that living with Dad meant accepting his "crazy times." Tammy spent her childhood watching her mother try to cover up for her husband's problem, and watching her dad suffer financial loss and eventually severe physical disease—all brought on by his drinking. Tammy felt helpless—she loved her daddy so much, but didn't know how to encourage him to stop hurting himself. As a little girl, she used to hide his liquor bottles under the hay in the barn, hoping he wouldn't find them, but he always did.

Soon after Tammy moved away from her home state to a large city, her father was diagnosed with liver cancer and died. Tammy was devastated. Inside, she felt as if somehow she should have been able to prevent his tragic end. At about this time she began falling in love with alcoholics, all of whom she desperately tried to heal. Todd was her latest "case." "I know you are going to tell me to leave him," she told me, "but he really needs me. He had the worst childhood, and I really believe if I'm just there for him, he will finally stop."

To Tammy, leaving Todd would be like abandoning her father and her mission to save him. Tammy was trapped in a self-destructive cycle. *Like all people who have an unconscious emotional program to save Mom or Dad, or to make them happy, she was a prisoner of her past, and her love choices weren't based on who was good for her but who she could help.*

CASE #2: *How Jeremy Married His Mother*

When I first met Jeremy, a forty-five-year-old plumbing contrac-tor, he seemed like a really nice guy. Married for twenty-four years to Becky, Jeremy was in turmoil because he didn't feel in love with his wife but couldn't bring himself to leave. "I've known Becky since college," he told me, "and she's the sweetest person in the world. She's a wonderful mother to our four kids, and a devoted wife. If I'm honest with myself, I have to admit that I've been unhappy with our relationship for most of our marriage. It's not that she does anything wrong, because she's perfect, but I'm not attracted to her as a lover, and except for the children, we have very little in common."

As I worked with Jeremy to understand how his childhood may have affected his relationship with Becky, he began to see why he had been willing to sacrifice his own happiness in order to keep his wife happy for so long. Jeremy's father had deserted his wife and children by running off with his secretary. Jeremy's mother was devastated, and felt totally inadequate as a woman. She never dated or married again. Jeremy was eleven at the time, and the only boy in the family. Though he didn't understand all the details of the scandal, he was sensitive enough to know that his mother felt insecure and rejected. At that point in his life, Jeremy made several unconscious decisions: *to prove to his mother that she was good enough by trying to fill her emptiness with his love, and to prove to his father that he had been wrong to leave by never leaving a woman himself.*

When Jeremy met Becky in college, he felt instantly drawn to her: She was insecure, vulnerable, and afraid of men, just like Mom. From the first, he felt a profound sense of responsibility to protect Becky and make her feel loved. This feeling grew until he asked her to marry him. Only after years of thinking about what made Becky happy did Jeremy finally begin to admit to himself that he wasn't happy. But his emotional programming didn't allow him even to consider doing anything that would hurt Becky, so he stayed in the relationship, feeling more and more trapped with each passing year. To Jeremy, the idea of leaving Becky was unthinkable: It would make him just like his father, and he would be saying to his mother, "Dad was right to leave you because you didn't fulfill his needs, just as Becky doesn't fulfill mine."

I pointed out to Jeremy that it wasn't his love for Becky that was keeping him a prisoner, but his anger at his father and his protection of his mother. His unfinished childhood business had held him hostage for almost thirty years. Jeremy hadn't ever fully

been in a relationship with his wife, because he was still emotion-
ally bound to his mother.

**Give yourself permission to have a wonderful, loving
person in your life.**

I believe that we all have some unfinished emotional business
from childhood, but if you aren't happy with your relationship
choices and suspect you may still be held hostage by your childhood
feelings, spend some time thinking about all you've read and look
for some connections between your past and your present.

FEAR OF INTIMACY

► **Do you attract people who can't make a commitment?**

► **Do you feel frightened or smothered when someone expresses strong feelings of love toward you?**

► **Do you find yourself pushing people away, even when
they're giving you what you want?**

If you answered yes to any of these questions, you may be
affected by the third way in which your emotional programming can
determine your love choices: It gives you a fear of intimacy.

▼

**IT'S NOT INTIMACY WE FEAR,
IT'S THE *CONSEQUENCES* OF INTIMACY.**

▲

Here's how it works: Let's say that, as a child, someone with
whom you were intimate, such as a parent, sibling, or relative, hurt
you in some way. Maybe you loved your mother and she died when
you were a child. Your mind makes an association between intimacy
and that painful experience.

Intimacy = Loss or Intimacy = Shame or Intimacy = Pain

In other words, you associate intimacy with a negative consequence.

Years pass. You consciously tell yourself you want a loving,
intimate relationship with a partner, but your emotional programming associates intimacy with something undesirable. *So your unconscious mind makes choices in partners who will "protect" you*

from intimacy because they are either unavailable or uncomfort-
able with intimacy themselves. "Why can't I attract someone who
will give me the love I want?" you complain. The answer: Because
you don't want to be loved that way. You don't trust it. It caused you
pain in the past, and you are afraid it will again.

Suzanne is a thirty-eight-year-old graphic artist who attended a
women's seminar I gave. "My biological clock is running out,"
Suzanne told us. "All I want is to find a husband, settle down, and
have a family. I've been looking for the right man for years, but I
keep finding the wrong ones—married men, men who don't want
kids, men who are afraid to feel. Why aren't there any good men out
there?"

I listened to Suzanne complain about her love life, and had a
feeling there was something else to it. A few hours later, after an
emotional exercise, I found out what it was. "I've never realized this
before," she began with a shaky voice and tears in her eyes, "but I
don't think I ever forgave my father for leaving me and my mother.
My parents got divorced when I was three years old, and my father
moved to another state. I only saw him a few times after that. I
remember my mom telling me that we were better off without him,
and I think I convinced myself that she was right. I've tried for years
to block him out of my mind, to tell myself his leaving didn't affect
me, but I know it must have. Ever since I walked into this workshop,
I haven't been able to stop thinking about it, and I'm tired of
pretending that it was okay. I'm tired of feeling so numb."

Suzanne continued to attract unavailable or unsuitable men into
her life because she was petrified of intimacy. *To Suzanne, intimacy
meant loss, fear, mistrust, pain, and disappointment. Consciously
she wanted a man in her life, but unconsciously she was emotionally programmed to avoid intimacy at all costs.* Before she could
have a healthy relationship with a man, Suzanne would have to purge
herself of the pain she had avoided feeling for so long, and create a
new, positive picture of intimacy.

Exercise: *Write down any negative words you have
associated with intimacy. Think about why you may have
made those decisions about what intimacy means, and ask
yourself if those decisions have been affecting your choices
in partners.*

LOW SELF-ESTEEM

There's a popular concept in many metaphysical philosophies that says:

YOU GET WHAT YOU THINK YOU DESERVE.

Not only do I believe this, but I have seen it manifest itself in my own life and the lives of thousands of people I have worked with. For many of us, the problem is that we don't think we deserve a lot when it comes to love. This is the fourth way your emotional programming can affect your love life: It unconsciously tells you that you don't deserve the love you consciously think you want.

I could write a whole book on self-esteem, but here's the important point:

----------------------------▼----------------------------

IF YOU WERE TOLD OR CONCLUDED THAT YOU WERE NOT LOVABLE AS A CHILD, YOU MAY HAVE A DIFFICULT TIME ATTRACTING LOVE.

----------------------------▲----------------------------

As children we believe what our parents tell us, because we love them and because they are the only authorities we know. So if your parents told you you weren't good enough, or smart enough, or likable enough, part of you believed them. Even if they didn't actually use these words, but treated you in an unloving way, you probably still concluded that you were unlovable. **When you grow up, you either attract people into your life who can't love you, or mistreat you, or you have a difficult time finding partners at all.**

The big problem with low self-esteem is that you may not even realize you aren't being treated well in your relationships. *People with self-esteem problems typically either make excuses for why their partner isn't loving them enough or blame themselves for their partner's behavior.*

CASE #1

Craig, twenty-seven, is dating a woman who constantly breaks dates, shows up late or not at all, and doesn't call to explain. It's obvious to his friends that she doesn't really care about Craig, but he doesn't see it that way. "Patrice is just really busy," he insists. "She is dedicated to her career, and sometimes things come up at the last minute she needs to do." Craig grew up with a father who told him he would never amount to anything, and a silent mother who was afraid to interfere. Craig is used to being ignored and treated like he is unimportant, so Patrice's behavior doesn't seem strange to him.

DO YOU FEEL TOO GUILTY TO BE LOVABLE?

Sometimes it isn't our parents' influence that destroyed our self-esteem, but repressed feelings of guilt or shame we've been carrying with us since childhood.

▼

IF YOU'VE DONE SOMETHING YOU HAVEN'T FORGIVEN YOURSELF FOR, OR FEEL IN SOME WAY RESPONSIBLE FOR SOMEONE ELSE'S PAIN, YOUR EMOTIONAL PRO-GRAMMING MIGHT HAVE CONCLUDED THAT YOU DON'T DESERVE TO BE LOVED.

▲

CASE #2

Joanie was a vivacious thirty-two-year-old nurse who couldn't seem to meet men, let alone start a relationship. I was surprised to hear Joanie describe her lonely life, since she was so outgoing and attractive. "I don't know what it is about me," she complained, "but no matter what I do, I can't find someone to love. All of my friends are either married or have boyfriends. What's wrong with me?"

As we worked to uncover her emotional programming, we came up against something from Joanie's childhood that she had never connected with her vacant love life. Joanie had a younger sister named Stephanie who was born severely handicapped. As a young girl, Joanie remembered helping carry her little sister every-where, because she couldn't walk, and helping to feed her, because she couldn't coordinate her limbs. Stephanie was confined to a wheelchair at age five, and eventually was put into a home for children with special needs.

"I remember lying in bed as a child next to Stephanie," Joanie reminisced, "and looking at her beautiful face. I couldn't understand why God did this to my little sister. She was my only sibling—my parents didn't have any children after that—and I felt like she was taken from me. Everyone used to tell me how lucky I was to be healthy, but that only made me feel more . . . well, I guess 'guilty' is the right word. I felt guilty to be so normal when poor Steph was so damaged."

Joanie broke down and cried tears of grief and love for her little sister. We talked about the decisions she had made as a child—*that she didn't deserve to be happy if Stephanie wasn't happy; that she didn't deserve to have a husband and a normal love life, since Stephanie would never be able to have one.* Joanie hadn't been aware of what a powerful affect her guilt had on her as an adult. Somehow her feelings translated into behavior that kept men away from her. She was emotionally programmed *not* to fall in love. Now that she was aware of the source of her pattern, Joanie could begin to heal her feelings of guilt and give herself permission to be twice as happy—one dose for herself, and one dose for Stephanie.

USING YOUR PAST TO CREATE A LOVING FUTURE

I'm sure you have been able to relate to some if not many parts of this chapter. Don't be surprised if your personal experience is a *combination* of several things: Maybe you concluded that you've been "going home" by choosing partners who don't make you feel special, because that's what your childhood was like, *and* have been falling in love with men or women just like Mom or Dad in order to rescue them. You may even have to read this chapter over several times before you can digest all of the information it contains. Here are some suggestions that will help:

▶ **Make sure to do all of the exercises I've included.** They really work. Don't avoid the ones that are scary—they are probably the ones you need to do most.

▶ **Write down all of the realizations and insights you have about yourself and your love choices.** Putting your thoughts into words will help make them more tangible and will start the process of helping you change your emotional programming.

▶ **If you are in a relationship, share your insights with your partner, and ask him or her to read the book and do the same.** If you are *not* in a relationship, do this with a close friend. THE MORE YOU TALK ABOUT YOUR NEW REALIZATIONS, THE LESS YOU WILL TEND TO FORGET THEM.

This chapter is titled "Why We Choose the People We love." We've talked about emotional programming, completing childhood business, trying to rescue Mom or Dad, and other unhealthy motivators for choosing a mate.

But what about healthy reasons for falling in love? Don't they exist? *Is it possible to choose a partner because we simply love them?* The answer, of course, is YES. That magical feeling of connection called "love" can draw us to someone. **What's important to remember, however, is that even in the best of relationships, many unhealthy patterns may manifest themselves.** For instance, you could be in a very happy relationship but notice that you have a tendency to try to fix your partner, or rebel against your mate's demands for intimacy. These behaviors probably have their source in that emotional programming we discussed.

So if you are in a good relationship, and have discovered that some of the reasons you are together have to do with your emotional programming, don't panic and think you need to break up or get divorced. Every relationship has some elements of healing in it, and there is nothing better than having a partner with whom you feel safe. You can work together to heal the wounded parts in each of you.

And if you are in a relationship you suspect is not healthy, read Chapter Eleven in this book to help you determine whether to stay in a relationship.

I know this can be a painful, though enlightening, chapter to read, and I'm proud of you for having had the courage to finish it! There is a wonderful quote by George Santayana:

> *"Those who cannot remember the past are*
> *condemned to repeat it."*

None of us can ever fully escape from the influence of our past. I truly believe, however, that by remembering, we can turn the pain of our poor choices into wonderful lessons that help us create the healthy and loving relationships we desire.

3
▼▼▼

FALLING IN LOVE
FOR ALL
THE WRONG REASONS

▼▼▼

A person doesn't need a reason to fall in love.
The experience itself is reason enough.
BARBARA DE ANGELIS, AGE 17
JOURNAL ENTRY

▼▼▼

When I was seventeen and hope-
lessly romantic, I lived in a philosophical world of idealism and
fantasy. The year was 1968. My favorite book was *The Little Prince*
by Antoine de Saint-Exupéry, my favorite song "The Impossible
Dream" from the Broadway musical *Man of La Mancha*. I used to
listen to that song ten times a day because it helped me believe
anything was possible; I believed in people; I believed in the hope of
world peace. And most of all, I believed in love. To me, falling in love
had to be the highest human experience there was. As you can see
from the above quote, I didn't really care about whether a relationship was good or bad, whether the person was right for me or not. I
was fascinated with the mere idea of being in love.

Many years and many lessons later, I have learned that what
should be the joy of falling in love can quickly turn into sorrow if

you are falling in love for the wrong reasons. Can there be wrong reasons for falling in love? In spite of what I thought at seventeen, the answer is yes.

GETTING INVOLVED WITH SOMEONE FOR THE WRONG REASONS IS ONE OF THE WAYS IN WHICH WE CREATE UNHEALTHY AND UNFULFILLING RELATIONSHIPS.

There are many reasons why people decide to have relationships other than being in love. This chapter talks about seven wrong reasons to have a relationship. As you read each one, ask yourself if you've made one or more of these mistakes in your past, or if you're making them in your life even now. *The more of these patterns you recognize, the more you'll understand why some of your past relationships caused you so much pain and disappointment, and the more you'll be able to avoid recreating these patterns in your future relationships.*

SEVEN WRONG REASONS TO BE IN A RELATIONSHIP:

1. **Pressure (age, family, friends, etc.)**
2. **Loneliness and desperation**
3. **Sexual hunger**
4. **Distraction from your own life**
5. **To avoid growing up**
6. **Guilt**
7. **To fill up your emotional or spiritual emptiness**

WRONG REASON

▼   ▼   ▼   ▼   **1**   ▼   ▼   ▼   ▼

Pressure

▶ Are most of your friends part of a couple, but you are still single?

▶ Are you unmarried and over thirty?

▶ Are you the last person in your family to "settle down"?

► Are you recently divorced?

If you answered yes to any of these questions, you probably already know about pressure. Pressure is the influence that your friends, family, society, and your own programming place upon you that gives the message, **"You should be in a relationship, and if you're not, something is wrong with you."** When we feel pressured by those outside influences or our own internal ones, we may choose to get involved in relationships we normally would not choose.

Here are some of the different kinds of pressure people commonly experience:

Age Pressure

► A woman meets a thirty-seven-year-old man who has never been married, and calls up her friend to share her excitement. Her friend's first reaction is "He's thirty-seven and unmarried. What's wrong with him?"

► You attend the wedding of your first cousin. During the reception, you hear the same thing from each of your relatives: "So you're almost thirty. Why aren't you married?"

This is age pressure—the attitude that if you are over a certain age and not seriously involved with someone, you aren't "normal." Of course, just what that age is varies from person to person. Whether you're conscious of it or not, you probably have an age by which you think you should be married, or in a permanent relationship. That number might have come from things your family talked about when you were growing up, or what ages your older brothers and sisters were when they got married, or just an image of at what age a person is really grown up.

To understand the origins of age pressure, we need to go back thousands of years in history. The economic and physical survival of a family was based on how many children there were. Sons could help with hunting, farming, and protecting the family against enemies. Daughters could help with chores and be valuable assets if desired by other males for mates. The sooner a young man or woman married and started his or her own family, the better. It strengthened the family group, or clan, by adding to their number and, in families who owned property, guaranteed that there would be inheritors to keep what the ancestors accumulated. And remember, life expectancy was less than half of what ours is now in the twentieth century. So a girl of fourteen might have had only another twenty or, at most, thirty years left to live. By the time she was in her twenties, she was middle-aged! Therefore it was natural for her family to want her married in her early teens, so she could start having children right away.

Although we've come a long way from those ancient times, we are still influenced by some of the thinking our forebears lived by. So when your Aunt Mabel pulls you aside at Thanksgiving dinner and says, "Sweetheart, I know it's not my business, but why don't you find a nice guy and settle down?" she is voicing a sentiment that has its roots in historical realities.

Whether the pressure comes from your family, your friends, or from your own sense of urgency, the result is the same: **You may compromise your standards for an acceptable partner just to have a relationship with someone.**

ROSEANN'S HIGH-SCHOOL REUNION TRAUMA

RoseAnn had just turned twenty-eight when she received an invitation to her ten-year high-school reunion. "That's when the impact of being single really hit me," she explained. "I'd been wanting to find someone special for a long time, but I was so busy starting my own business that I guess I didn't stop to think about how I was feeling. When I opened up that invitation and thought of seeing all of my old friends, I got so depressed. I had these fantasies of showing up at the hotel, greeted by all of my girlfriends and their husbands carrying piles of baby pictures, and me the only unmarried one there."

"That's when I met Sandy. A friend introduced us, and I didn't really think he was my type, but decided to give him a chance. Before I knew what happened, we were in a relationship. Looking back, I can see that from the beginning, there were big problems. I kept finding things wrong with Sandy, and wanting to improve him. I didn't like his taste in lots of things—clothes, food, movies. Even the way he kissed bugged me. But I found myself tolerating all of this stuff and telling everyone how happy I was.

"Five months after the reunion, I woke up and admitted to myself that I didn't want to be in this relationship with Sandy. I wanted to be in a relationship, period, and the combination of turning twenty-eight and facing the reunion put tremendous pressure on me to find someone so I didn't look like I was alone. Breaking up with him was painful, because there was double pressure—all my friends and family had already been asking, When's the wedding?, and now I had to disappoint them as well as Sandy."

RoseAnn is a perfect example of someone who got involved with a partner to lessen the pressure, not because she was really in love.

Pressure from Family and Friends

Some people are very susceptible to the opinions of their family and friends and allow themselves to be pressured to get into or stay in relationships that aren't making them happy. If you don't have a strong sense of yourself, or if you are very enmeshed with your family members, you could end up having a relationship because everyone else thinks you should, not because you truly want to be with that person.

HOW LENNY LET HIMSELF BE PRESSURED INTO MARRIAGE

Lenny sat with his head in his hands. "I've let everyone down," he said with a moan. "What am I going to do?" Lenny, forty-four, and his wife, Krista, forty-three, had known each other since grade school. Their families belonged to the same church and were good friends, so when Lenny and Krista began dating in junior high, their parents were delighted. "I can't remember a time when it wasn't just assumed that Krista and I would get married one day. Everyone talked about it like it had already happened—Mom would make comments like, When you and Krista get older, Grandma's china will be passed down to you, or Dad would say to Krista's father, You know, Samuel, I always did feel like you were family, and hopefully one day, you will be. And Krista had been trying out my last name with hers for years.

"When I graduated from high school, I went into the Navy, again because my dad thought it would be good experience for me. Everyone seemed to think that when I got out, I'd ask Krista to marry me, and I did. If I look back now, I don't remember deciding to do it. It was just the thing I was supposed to do. You can imagine how happy they all were. That's when I started going numb. It's not that I didn't love Krista; I did, in a certain way. But I wasn't ready to marry her, or anyone.

"It's been almost twenty years, three kids, and four affairs later, and I just can't handle it anymore. I'm so lost, I'm hurting my wife and children, and letting everyone I love down."

I watched Lenny weep like a frightened little boy, and felt so much empathy for this man who had been under pressure for so long to live up to everyone else's expectations of how his life was supposed to be. **The truth was that Lenny had been *letting himself down* for years by not listening to his own heart, by making decisions others thought were best, not because he thought they were.** In doing what his friends and family thought he should, Lenny had robbed himself of a chance to experience true love and happiness.

When you make a decision to be with someone because of the pressure you feel (from yourself or others) rather than because the person seems right for you, you are giving your power away and ensuring an unhappy end to your love story. If you have been in this position often, or are in it now, ask yourself what *you* want and need, and give that first priority over what anyone else thinks.

WRONG REASON

▼　　▼　　▼　　▼ **2** ▼　　▼　　▼　　▼

Loneliness and Desperation

▶ You're lying in bed at night, alone. It's been a long time since you've been in love, let alone made love. Your body feels empty, your heart hurts. Your mind thinks back to your ex, and the one before him, and remembers the happy times when you had someone to hold you and make you feel special. And then you hear yourself say, "Maybe I should just call him up and tell him I miss him. It can't hurt, can it? Maybe it wasn't so bad after all."

▶ It's Friday afternoon, and once again you have nothing exciting planned for the weekend. You are tired of being single. You're beginning to dread Saturday nights, renting a video and sitting home without anyone to share it with. Then you remember the guy you met at the car wash who asked you out for Saturday night. You told him you would get back to him today when you found out if you were free. Of course you're free. But do you want to go out with him? He seemed kind of boring. You decide to call him. After all, it's better than a date with the video store.

▶ You're out on a date with a woman you've seen a couple of times.

You know she likes you, but she isn't really that appealing. You finish dinner, and she invites you over to her apartment. On the way there in the car, she puts her hand on your thigh. She obviously likes you. You aren't really attracted to her, but it's been over five months since you've been with a woman, and you miss the closeness. So what if you decide to sleep with her. It doesn't mean you have to marry her, does it?

We can all relate to these stories, because we have all experienced loneliness, periods in our lives when we felt so emotionally empty that we were desperate for someone, anyone to love. But unfortunately, what starts out as a lonely act of reaching out to another human being can end in a very complicated and hurtful relationship.

Take the woman in the first story above. She'll call up her ex-boyfriend and tell him she is lonely. He'll decide to come over and "cheer her up," and they'll end up in bed. Suddenly they're involved again—except he neglected to tell her he's seeing someone else. She'll go through months of "back and forth" with him until they finally break up, this time for good. All of that pain from one desperate night of loneliness.

The woman in the second story will end up going out with the guy she's not really interested in. Six months later, when they're still involved, she'll meet someone she really cares for. Now she has to hurt the first man, whom she was really only using, and tell him she doesn't want to see him anymore because she has met a man she loves more.

The man in the third story may think he is in for a simple one-night stand, but this girl may have other things in mind. By always being there for him, making it easy for him to be in the relationship, she may indeed end up getting him to marry her. One day he'll wake up and finally admit he isn't in love with his wife, break her heart, upset their families, and feel like a heel.

These three people didn't just end up in these unfortunate circumstances because of bad luck; they got involved with people for the wrong reasons, and doomed their relationships to unhappy endings.

WHEN YOU ARE FEELING LONELY OR DESPERATE, YOU ARE MUCH MORE LIKELY TO MAKE POOR LOVE CHOICES AND END UP IN UNFULFILLING RELATION-SHIPS.

HOW RHONDA'S LONELINESS ALMOST KILLED HER

The story of Rhonda is a sad example of the pain we can create for ourselves and others when we choose love out of desperation. Rhonda, thirty-five, had been overweight as a child. While her friends were dating in junior high school, Rhonda stayed home and absorbed herself in her schoolwork. Because of her tremendous scholastic achievements, Rhonda won a scholarship to a private university in the Northeast. She arrived at college never having been on a date in her life.

In her first year of school, Rhonda lost fifty pounds (she says it was getting away from her mother's cooking). She could hardly believe what she saw when she looked in the mirror: She actually looked attractive. And when young men began to ask her out, Rhonda knew her transformation was real. She went out on one or two dates before she met Karl.

Karl was a senior in college and from a very wealthy family. He was athletic, good-looking, and very domineering. When he asked Rhonda out, she was sure he'd made a mistake. She never expected anyone that handsome to be interested in her. In fact, Rhonda had no idea what to expect in a relationship. She'd never been in one. So as the months passed, and they began dating exclusively, Rhonda was so overjoyed she didn't pay much attention to some of Karl's characteristics that were, to say the least, a bit strange. For instance, Karl liked to gamble—not just small amounts of money, but also large ones. He also liked his sex rough and dirty, and needed to push Rhonda around to get really turned on. And when he wasn't with Rhonda, he frequented porno film theaters and strip bars.

Rhonda was a smart girl—in the back of her mind, she knew something wasn't right. But she didn't want to lose Karl. After all, he was the only man who had ever really wanted her. So she ignored the problems and worked hard to please him. And when Karl suggested they get married, Rhonda was sure her dreams were finally coming true.

When Rhonda came to me fifteen years later, she was on the verge of a nervous breakdown. Her dream of a happy marriage had quickly become a nightmare. Karl was a compulsive gambler and a sexaholic with a violent temper. His behavior had progressively deteriorated until he'd gambled away most of his family inheritance, and like many men who link sex and anger together, his need for violent sex increased until he would beat Rhonda before he slept with her. The fat little girl who lived inside Rhonda was so afraid of losing Karl that she put up with this treatment until the night before she called me, when, for the first time, Rhonda fought back against Karl's abuse and he raped her. Fearing for her life, she fled with her two small children to a friend's house.

Rhonda's healing was not just in leaving Karl, but in forgiving herself for staying with him for so long. She needed to work hard to understand that her desperation to be loved had driven her to tolerate such inhumane treatment by her husband.

Rhonda's case is extreme, but the pattern is not. If you suspect that you've allowed your emotional vulnerability to influence your choice of partners, and you have ended up in unhappy relationships, you should be excited to know that happy relationships are just a decision away. The solution for you is to **BE MUCH PICKIER. DON'T LOWER YOUR STANDARDS JUST BECAUSE YOU'RE FEELING TIMES ARE TOUGH. YOU'RE NOT A STORE TRYING TO GET RID OF OLD MERCHANDISE THAT PUTS IT ON SALE—YOU ARE A VALUABLE, LOVABLE HUMAN BEING WHO DESERVES TO HAVE THE KIND OF RELATIONSHIP YOU WANT, NOT JUST THE KIND YOU THINK YOU CAN GET.**

WRONG REASON

▼　　▼　　▼　　▼　　3　　▼　　▼　　▼　　▼

Sexual Hunger

► Have you ever been so horny that you talked yourself into believing you cared much more for someone than you actually did?

► Have you ever overlooked things in a partner you didn't like so you could prolong your relationship and keep having sex?

You know what I'm talking about—it's been a while since you've had sex, and you get involved with someone you normally wouldn't be with, because you feel "the hunger." Eventually you face the fact that the relationship is not what you want, and have to admit to yourself that you were probably just horny. How embarrassing! How humiliating! But how common.

I've heard countless stories of people who ended up in relationships simply because they wanted the intimacy of physical touching and the release of sex so badly that they took whomever they could get. When you are feeling this kind of sexual pressure, you become good at having a relationship with just about anyone, and at making tremendous compromises to convince yourself you are doing the right thing.

Here's an important point: I'm *not* talking about falling in love with someone because you have intense sexual chemistry. I call that "Lust Blindness," and we'll talk about it in Chapter Four. With sexual hunger you may not even feel attracted to the person you get involved with. You just want to be with *someone*.

HOW LONNIE'S SEXUAL HUNGER LEFT HER STARVING FOR LOVE

"I'm disgusted with men," Lonnie complained to me. She'd called my radio talk show to ask my advice on a pattern in her life. "I'm twenty-four years old and I've had eight relationships in five years," she began. "I have really bad luck. I meet these men and have a brief affair with them, but when we stop seeing one another, they go out, find a woman, and get married. I'm not kidding, Dr. Barbara, all eight of them got married after being with me. I can't figure out what I'm doing wrong."

My first question to Lonnie was, "Where do you meet these guys?" When she answered "in bars," I saw part of the problem. My second question was, "How long do you know them before you sleep together?" When she answered "one night to a week," I saw more of the problem. Then I asked her what she'd been taught about sex growing up. "My mom told me that all men want women for is our bodies," Lonnie said. Now I saw the whole problem.

"There is no such thing as bad luck, Lonnie," I told her. **"But there is such a thing as bad choices, and you keep making them."** You have such a strong need to be loved by a man, and you think that means a man who wants you sexually, you'll take anyone who'll sleep with you, which is just about any man. You don't love them, or even like them—you like *the attention* they are giving you. They fill up that empty place inside your soul. Then, when they leave to find a complete relationship, you feel angry and rejected. You set the whole thing up as a way to hurt yourself."

Lonnie was getting involved for all the wrong reasons, and her self-esteem was paying the price.

THE HIGH PRICE NICHOLAS PAID FOR BEING HORNY

"I'm in big trouble, Dr. Barbara," Nicholas said with a pained expression on his face. Nicholas was a nice-looking thirty-five-year-old dentist attending a lecture series of mine. "I met this woman, Jackie, three months ago. She was an ex-girlfriend of a friend of mine, and I wasn't really that attracted to her. But it had been over a year since I'd slept with a woman. A year! I felt like something was wrong with me. I felt like people could just look at me and say, 'Hey, that guy looks like he hasn't gotten laid in a long time.' I just hadn't met anyone I really liked, and the months went by. So when Jackie came along, I thought, what the hell, I don't really like her, but at least I'll break the cycle.

"We went out once or twice and ended up sleeping together. The big joke was, the sex wasn't even that good. I knew it was going nowhere, but I figured since I didn't know when I'd have sex again, I might as well stock up now. I know it sounds awful, but it gets worse. Six weeks passed, and I'm geting disgusted with myself, so one day I decided to tell Jackie that night that we really shouldn't see each other anymore. That afternoon I got an emergency call at my office in the middle of fitting a patient for dentures—it was Jackie, and she had to talk to me immediately. When I picked up the phone I heard her say, 'Nicholas, I'm pregnant.' I was so shocked, I dropped the man's teeth right on the floor.

"That night I went over to Jackie's house and we talked about everything. Dr. Barbara, she wants to keep the baby. I told her I didn't love her, that I didn't even like her, that it was wrong of me to sleep with her and lead her on, and she told me that she didn't care how I felt. She loved me and wanted my child. I can't believe this is happening to me."

Nicholas didn't plan on paying such a high price for his sexual hunger. Jackie had his child, and Nicholas pays child support and sees his daughter fairly frequently. He has a lot of anger at Jackie, and even more anger at himself, especially for not insisting on using birth control. And although he claims he wants to find a woman to love, he hasn't found anyone yet.

WHAT'S YOUR SEXUAL HUNGER LIMIT?

Do you have a Sexual Hunger Limit (SHL), a period of time beyond which you feel "something is wrong" because you haven't been sexually active? If you're single, ask yourself what your limit is—a few months or a year or more. You might have to look back through your calendar or datebook to figure it out, but it's well worth the effort. Remember, I'm not talking about what makes you physically uncomfortable, but what time period makes you psychologically uncomfortable. It's good to know your **Sexual Hunger Limit.** *You might want to put it on your calendar as the time approaches, so you can be careful to avoid getting involved with someone for the wrong reason!*

WRONG REASON

▼   ▼   ▼   ▼   4   ▼   ▼   ▼   ▼

Distraction from Your Own Life

Have you ever thought about how distracting it is to be in love? You think about how the other person is feeling, what they need, what makes them happy, how your behavior affects theirs, just to name a few examples. **It's no wonder, then, that we often get into relationships *not* because we have found the right person but as an excuse to avoid our own life.**

▼

Are You Using Relationships To Avoid Dealing with Your Own Life?

Read each of the following statements and ask yourself if it applies to you now, or if it has applied to you in the past:

► I have a history of unfulfilling relationships.
► I don't go for long periods of time without being in a relationship.
► The relationships I get involved in are very time-consuming.
► There are many areas of my own life that are not operating the way I'd like them to.
► There are projects or dreams I've had for a while that I haven't followed through with.
► When I'm in a relationship, I devote less time to my own interests and friends.

► I tend to become romantically involved with my partners rather quickly.

► As a rule, I don't enjoy spending time alone, and would rather be with other people.

► When I am working on a task or project, I tend to become easily distracted by phone calls, unimportant errands, other people's needs, etc.

► I find it easier to motivate others to solve their problems than to motivate myself to solve my own.

▲

If you relate to several of these statements, you may be using relationships to avoid taking care of your own life. What you have been thinking is your obsession with love could very well be your addiction to not facing yourself and your problems. After all, if you are busy loving someone else and working full time to make them happy and meet their needs, you won't have much time left to meet your own needs or realize your own dreams.

Some people have relationships because they are bored with the lack of passion and purpose in their lives, and rather than looking within to find out why they feel that way, they get involved in a love affair and make that their purpose. These relationships never work *because you aren't in love with the person—you're in love with the distraction.* And when the relationship ends, you're left with yourself once more.

WHY MARY BETH NEEDED TO GO ON A "RELATIONSHIP FAST"

Mary Beth stood up in one of my seminars and announced that she was suffering from "relationship burnout," a syndrome I wrote about in *How to Make Love All the Time.* "I am so sick of going from one man to another," she complained. "I feel like moving to the mountains and becoming a nun. I get in these stupid relationships and stay until I can't take it anymore, and then I leave. For a few weeks I am so happy to be on my own. I clean up my apartment; I do the things I've been wanting to do but didn't have time to when I was seeing my latest guy. But all of a sudden I start to feel restless, and before I know it I'm at a party or a bar and getting fixated on some new man."

I asked Mary Beth what she did professionally, and noticed that she instantly became uncomfortable. "Well, right now I'm doing hair in a salon downtown, but that's just until I start my own business."

Mary Beth had a dream of being an interior decorator. But as I questioned her, it became clear that she had never done anything about it. She kept telling herself she should go back to school and get a degree, or look for a job with someone in interior design. Yet she never did. Each time she would be single again, she'd get excited about her goals for a few days or weeks. Then she'd come up against her fear of failure. And suddenly she was on the prowl for a partner again. *She used each new relationship to keep her from facing her procrastination.*

I pointed out to Mary Beth that she was using the men in her life as distractions in the same way that some men use women for sex. She agreed to go on a *"Relationship Fast"* for six months—no dates, no bar-hopping, nothing. During that time she would start to develop a relationship with herself and embrace her dreams again. Once she focused on getting her life in order, she wouldn't need to hide behind her love affairs, and she could take her time looking for a partner with whom she could have a healthy, long-term relationship.

If you suspect you've been using relationships to avoid dealing with yourself, try going on a *"Relationship Fast."* It may be difficult at first, but it will force you to face all the issues in your life that you've been avoiding.

WRONG REASON

▼   ▼   ▼   ▼   **5**   ▼   ▼   ▼   ▼

To Avoid Growing Up

Some people get into relationships not because they are ready to share the fullness of their own life with someone *but because they want to be taken care of*. These men and women are trying to avoid growing up, so they find partners who will play "Mommy" and "Daddy" roles for them. These relationships are not about learning and growing together—they are about *dependence*. You may be in this kind of relationship when:

► There is a big age difference between you and your partner.

▶ There is a big difference in the financial and professional success of you and your partner.

▶ There is a big contrast in the life experience level of you and your partner.

▶ One partner is always looking to the other for help and advice.

In these relationships you convince yourself you are in love when, in reality, you have simply found a replacement for Mom or Dad.

Katrina, a twenty-five-year-old actress, is a classic example of a woman who had a habit of falling in love for all the wrong reasons, and her favorite reason was to avoid growing up. She came to me for help when her two-year relationship with Simon, a thirty-four-year-old attorney, was in major trouble. Simon had become disenchanted with their romance and was thinking of leaving, and Katrina was in an emotional panic. "Simon is my whole life," she cried. "I can't function without him. I'll do anything to get him to stay."

I listened to Katrina describe her relationship with Simon, and realized that although she loved the way Simon had been taking care of her, she didn't really love *him*. When she talked about their time together, she would detail what he bought her, where he took her on vacation, how he gave her career advice, and how good he was at helping her with her problems. I don't even think Katrina knew Simon that well. He was just "Daddy," who'd be there for her no matter what. Katrina's own father had left when she was four, and she'd seen him only twice since. She was hungry for strong, male caretaking energy, and that's what she'd found in Simon. Her two prior boyfriends were also older and more mature. Katrina fooled herself in thinking, "I guess I just like older men."

When I met with Simon, I found myself talking to a sensitive man overwhelmed with guilt. "I love Katrina," he told me, "but I don't think we're right for each other, and I don't think Katrina is ready to have a relationship with anyone right now. When we first got together, I felt very protective of her, and probably took care of her more than I should have. In the past six months I realized that those roles had to change, but the more I try to let go and encourage her to stand on her own two feet, the more she accuses me of abandoning her. At this point I feel like leaving for good. I'm not sure she even wants to grow up."

Simon's assessment of Katrina was accurate: **She didn't want to grow up, and she used her relationships with men as a way**

to avoid it, finding partners who would play a caretaking role with her. Katrina was falling in love to fulfill needs left over from childhood and to avoid taking responsibility for her own life.

As I'll discuss later, all really good relationships have an element of healing within their dynamics, and there are times when the woman plays Mommy for her partner and he plays Daddy for her. *However, when you live out these roles the majority of the time, you are using the relationship to remain in a childlike, or irresponsible, state.*

WRONG REASON

▼   ▼   ▼   ▼ 6 ▼   ▼   ▼   ▼

Guilt

► Have you ever ended up in a relationship *because you didn't want to hurt the other person's feelings by rejecting him?*

► Have you ever stayed in a relationship much longer than you should have *because you were afraid to hurt your partner by leaving?*

► Have you ever been with someone you knew cared more about you than you did about them, *but you felt too guilty to break it off?*

If you answered yes to any of these questions, you understand the sixth wrong reason to fall in love: guilt. Guilt might seem like a strange motivation for getting into or staying in a relationship, but it happens all the time. You tell yourself it's love, but it's really sympathy, or in extreme cases, pity. **You remain in romantic situations not because you want to stay, but because you are afraid of what might happen if you left.** You are a prisoner of guilt.

Is Your Love Life Run by Guilt?

Read the following statements, and notice how many apply to you, either now or in the past.

► You have a difficult time saying no to people, especially those you care about.

► You came from a dysfunctional family in which your feelings didn't count (e.g., alcoholic, critical, or controlling parents).

► You grew up feeling responsible for making others happy (a parent with problems who needed rescuing, a single parent who leaned heavily on you for affection, etc.).

► You have a hard time knowing what your needs are, and an even harder time asking those you love for what you need.

► You pride yourself on being a sensitive and giving person and would feel very hurt if someone labeled you "selfish."

► You dread hurting other's feelings, and go out of your way to make sure nothing you say or do offends those you care for.

► You have a much easier time spending time and money on someone other than yourself.

► You have a difficult time hearing someone you care for talk about their problems without feeling compelled to help them find a solution.

► You find yourself backing down from expressing an opinion or a feeling you have if you notice that it upsets the person to whom it is directed.

► You feel uncomfortable being happier, wealthier, or more successful than those with whom you are close.

▲

If you can relate to only a few of these statements, you're probably affected by the same amount of guilt as most people. If more than four of these statements apply to you, you may have a tendency to allow guilt to influence your love choices. If you can relate to almost all of them, you are definitely falling in love for the wrong reasons!

HOW DANIEL'S GUILT GOT HIM INTO A ROMANTIC NIGHTMARE

I can't think of a better example of falling in love for the wrong reasons than Daniel. He was handsome, in his early thirties, and a successful television director, but Daniel's love life was a mess.

Daniel was the only son of a very dramatic mother and an invisible father. Daniel's mother was extremely demanding of his time, attention, and love. If she didn't receive it, she would pout, cry, and even become physically ill. Daniel's father had obviously been treated the same when he first married his wife, and wisely spent as much time as he could working. "My mother was an expert at making me feel guilty," Daniel recounted. "In high school she would conveniently become sick on weekends when she knew I had a date. She'd lie on the couch with smelling salts in one hand and a cold washcloth in the other, saying, 'Don't worry about me, honey, go out and enjoy yourself. If things get really bad, I'll just call an ambulance'."

When Daniel went away to college, he thought he'd left his unhealthy relationship with his mother behind. As we saw in Chapter Two, however, our emotional programming stays with us even after we are physically separated from our parents. So when Daniel told me about his relationship with Elsa, I wasn't surprised.

Elsa was a very pretty, feminine-looking twenty-six-year-old photographer's assistant whom Daniel met at a party. "The first thing that struck me about Elsa was how fragile she looked—like a china doll," he remembered. "We struck up a conversation, and she told me she had just ended a terribly abusive relationship. Her eyes filled with tears as she described what she'd been through, and I felt so sorry for her."

Daniel and Elsa began dating. He knew Elsa's self-esteem was low, so he would call her several times a day to reassure her how special she was. Soon Elsa began to look to Daniel as her savior.

TRAPPED BY GUILT

At first, Daniel felt good about the relationship. But after a few months he began to feel restless. "I was feeling emotionally stifled by Elsa's intense neediness," he explained, "but when I'd mention to her that I needed some space, she would totally freak out—sob, scream, beg me not to abandon her. It would shake me up so much that I'd promise her whatever she wanted, and for a while, things would calm down. Then I'd feel uncomfortable again, and the cycle continued.

"Don't even ask me how we ended up engaged," Daniel continued. "It had something to do with Elsa's birthday and my inability to break her heart. **I felt trapped—if I did what would make me**

happy—leave—it would kill her. If I went through with the marriage, it would destroy me. I walked around for weeks in a depression, and that's when I met Josie. She was content, independent, and strong, and I was desperate to be with a woman who didn't make me feel obligated and so damn guilty. Four days later, we ended up sleeping together.

"Dr. Barbara," Daniel said with a moan, "Elsa and I are supposed to get married next month. I know I can't go through with it, but I feel so terrible about the way I've hurt her—I can't bear to think about what will happen if I tell her the truth."

My heart hurt for Daniel as I saw the genuine anguish in his eyes. Here was a man who had started out with what he thought were good intentions—to help a woman who had been badly hurt—and he was going to end up hurting her even more. **How did Daniel get into this painful situation? He allowed himself to be motivated by *guilt* rather than by *real love*.**

If you've been a prisoner of guilt in the past, or are in a relationship now only because you feel guilty about leaving, think about this:

▼

WHEN YOU DECIDE TO BE WITH SOMEONE OUT OF GUILT AND NOT LOVE, YOU ARE RIPPING THEM AND YOURSELF OFF.

▲

WRONG REASON

▼ ▼ ▼ ▼ 7 ▼ ▼ ▼ ▼

To Fill Up Your Emotional or Spiritual Emptiness

I believe that each of us is here, in this lifetime, struggling to understand our relationship with the whole, and longing to feel part of, and not separate from, the universe we inhabit. This is our *spiritual hunger*, the urge to connect in some way with a Higher Power or meaning. And we are also here as children in grown-up bodies, yearning to feel loved, accepted, and whole. This is our *human hunger*, the urge to connect with those around us.

The wonderful thing about love is that it can fill you with a sense of joy and belonging unlike anything else in the world, and in this way satisfy those hungers. *Love gives meaning to your existence and heightened purpose to everything you do. Yet these same gifts can be dangerous when they are used to try to fill an emotional or spiritual void you carry into a relationship, a void you should be learning to fill yourself.*

A truly healthy relationship will give both people a heightened appreciation of the magic and mystery of the universe and will open the doors for their spiritual growth. It will also help each person heal the wounds of childhood, and gain a stronger sense of themselves through feeling so loved and accepted by their partner. But **when you enter a relationship with a tremendous amount of emotional and spiritual emptiness, you risk creating pain for yourself and your partner.**

There are two problems that arise when you are emotionally or spiritually empty:

1. **You get involved in relationships to fill yourself up, rather than because you have found someone who is right for you.**

   If you walk around with a big emotional or spiritual void, you are constantly feeling empty. That emptiness can be experienced as discomfort or tension in its mild stages, becoming pain, depression, and hopelessness in its more acute stages. Just as a starving animal will eat anything to get rid of its hunger pangs, so you may seek any kind of relationship to get rid of the pain of your aloneness. *Whether the relationship is healthy or unhealthy, loving or abusive, fulfilling or draining will be unimportant to you, at least in the beginning. Just the thought "I am in a relationship" will temporarily take the edge off of your "appetite."* Lying in bed with someone, anyone, will feel wonderful for a while, because you won't have to feel yourself. Spending time with someone, anyone, will feel satisfying because you won't have to be alone with yourself.

   You can see how vulnerable a person in this situation would be to getting involved in the wrong relationships with the wrong partners for the wrong reasons. Only after the high of being with someone has worn off are you left to face the person you've chosen to love. And how painful to discover that you are not filled up after all and, even worse, that being in this person's presence makes you feel even emptier and more alone than you did before.

You might find yourself going from relationship to relationship, never satisfied, always wondering when you will find the "perfect partner." **Your liberation will come when you realize that you need to feed your own heart and soul first before you are ready to have a healthy relationship.** Just as diet experts will tell you never to go shopping on an empty stomach because you'll pick all the junky, unhealthy foods, my advice is not to shop for a partner until you have filled yourself up, at least enough so you aren't "starving for love."

2. You get involved in relationships that *could* be right for you, but look to them to fill you up in ways you should be filling yourself.

How often do I hear someone complain that their partner doesn't make them feel whole and complete and that the relationship isn't worth staying in! So often this is a person who is lacking wholeness and completion in himself or herself, and is expecting their lover to fill the emotional and spiritual voids they've been carrying around long before the couple even met.

If you have deep places of emptiness within you, no partner, regardless of how much they love you, will be able to fill that emptiness.

You can ruin a perfectly good relationship by looking to your mate as your emotional and spiritual savior. Only you can fill those empty places; only you can save yourself. It *is* reasonable to expect your mate not to add to your emptiness, and to love you in a way that supports you in your healing process and teaches you how to love yourself again. *But in the end, you must be your own hero.*

Are You Emotionally and Spiritually Empty?

Here is a quiz to help you determine if you are suffering from emotional or spiritual emptiness. Think about each statement carefully. **If it describes how you feel:**

Very frequently . . . . **Give yourself 0 point**
Often . . . . **Give yourself 4 points**

Occasionally .... **Give yourself 8 points**
Rarely or never .... **Give yourself 10 points**

1. I have a difficult time being alone and doing "nothing." I need to have the radio or TV on, have someone with me, or keep myself busy.
2. I have no strong sense of purpose in my life and feel I don't really know what I'm doing here.
3. I'm not sure what my basic values and beliefs are, and I feel confused about what is right and what is wrong.
4. I don't do loving things just for myself, like making a fancy meal, going on a trip, dressing up, or otherwise pampering myself. I do these things when I have a partner, but not alone.
5. I don't feel comfortable thinking or talking about my feelings regarding the meaning of life, death, religion, God, my childhood, etc.
6. I like things to be predictable and under control. When I am faced with sudden change, I feel a sense of panic.
7. I compare myself and my life unfavorably with the success and happiness of others. There are many people with whom I would like to trade places.
8. I feel best when my time is scheduled and my activties are planned. I prefer structure to spontaneity.
9. I have a difficult time acknowledging good things about myself, giving myself credit for a job well done, receiving compliments or gifts, or trusting that others really love me.
10. Even when I am being loved, or good things are happening to me, I have a difficult time really feeling it and letting it in.

Now total up your points:

▶ **80–100 points: You have a healthy spiritual and emotional relationship with yourself.** Your appreciation of your inner world is as deep as your enjoyment of your outer world. *You have a strong sense of who you are and your purpose in life, and should be able to bring a lot of fullness and love into a relationship.* Take some time to think about those statements that received lower scores, and work on those areas of yourself.

▶ **60–79 points: Your spiritual and emotional relationship with yourself isn't bad, but it could be much better.** You've made great progress in some areas, but in others you still need some work to feel the peace and happiness you deserve. *Stop being so* *hard on yourself—you are "enough" just the way you are.* Work on trusting more and controlling less. You are ready to have a healthy relationship, just be careful not to sabotage it by expecting your partner to love you more than you love yourself.

▶ **40–59 points: Warning! You are living with a great deal of emotional and spiritual emptiness, and it's keeping you from having a healthy relationship.** You've been focusing too much on your external world. Now it's time for you to turn inward to find out who you really are. You can't keep running away from yourself. *The reason your love life has been so painful is that you don't even have a good relationship with yourself.* If you're single, go on a "Relationship Fast" for at least three to six months— no dating, no flirting, no sex. Instead, spend time getting to know yourself. Read, take classes, go to seminars, meditate, spend time outdoors in nature, keep a journal. If you're in a relationship and want to continue it, do these same things and create a little more space between you and your partner. *No one is going to make you happy until you are happy with yourself.*

▶ **0–39 points: Emergency! You are in an emotional and spiritual state of starvation.** Your life needs immediate attention. Stop expecting someone to come along and rescue you. Only you can rescue yourself. Wake up and remind yourself that you are on this planet for a reason—to learn and grow, *not* to avoid yourself. Stop blaming others for causing you so much pain. Stand up and fight back against your hopelessness. *You need time to discover who you are and how to love yourself before you even think of having a good relationship with a partner.* Find a support system, and follow the guidelines for the category above. You deserve to feel better than this.

Understanding and Healing Your Emptiness

In Chapter Two I talked about the decisions you make in childhood about yourself and about life based on what you experienced in your family. **The less you were loved and the more pain you were exposed to, the more emotional and spiritual emptiness you inherit.** If you received a low score on the quiz, or know you have made poor love choices because of your emptiness, make a commitment to begin deepening your relationship with yourself.

Things you can do:

► **Keep a journal.** This will help you get in touch with your inner self and become familiar with your thoughts and feelings. It will also give you an opportunity to access your own inner wisdom.

► **Learn to meditate.** I've been practicing meditation for over twenty-three years. I began Transcendental Meditation at eighteen, when I realized I had a lot of emptiness inside me. Along with helping reduce stress so you can enjoy life more, meditation can open up subtler forms of awareness and give you a spiritual anchor. There are many forms of meditation to choose from. Find one that feels right for you. It will add a powerful sense of peace to your life.

► **Spend time outdoors in nature.** It is impossible to walk through a forest, sit and watch the ocean, or stand on the top of a mountain and not be affected by the serenity and simple grace that nature reveals to us. In our fast-paced everyday lives, we are bombarded with electronic stimuli, and it is easy to lose touch with the beauty and balance of our home called Earth. Spending time outdoors is an easy way for you to restore yourself spiritually, whether it's just taking a walk, sitting in a park, or planning a day trip to the mountains, a lake, or the ocean. Don't forget to leave those boom boxes at home and keep talking to a minimum so you can enjoy the silence of nature and allow it to fill your soul with tranquillity.

► **Read books that make you think.** We often only choose to read a book when we think we will get specific advice from it. Reading can be a form of meditation, and books that make you think about life's meaning are especially helpful in beginning the process of restoring you to spiritual wholeness. Here are some of my favorites:

Chop Wood, Carry Water: A Guide to Finding Spiritual Fulfillment in Everyday Life by Rick Fields, with Peggy Taylor, Rex Weyler, and Rick Ingrasci. Published by Jeremy P. Tarcher, Inc.

Choose to Live Peacefully by Susan Smith Jones, Ph.D. Published by Celestial Arts.

Emmanuel's Book compiled by Pat Rodegast and Judith Stanton. Published by Bantam Books.

The Autobiography of a Yogi by Parmahansa Yogananda. Published by Self-Realization Fellowship.

As Above, So Below: Paths to Spiritual Renewal in Daily Life by Ronald S. Miller and the editors of *New Age Journal.*

Any books by Alan Cohen.

Falling in Love for the Right Reasons

Now that you know some of the wrong reasons for getting involved in a relationship, you're probably thinking, "What are the right reasons to fall in love?" I feel there are two conditions that should exist in your life before you are ready to participate in a healthy relationship (or be more committed to the one you are already in):

1. You feel full of love and want to share it.

When you feel full of good things in your own life, you come into a relationship truly ready to share, because you have something to share. Like a person whose arms are overflowing with gifts, you can't wait to offer some of your abundance to others. Your relationship becomes focused on what you can give rather than what you can get. This is not the same as the person who gives in order to get. Rather, you give simply because you are so full. *When you are truly in touch with your own goodness you will find it naturally overflows, just as a full river overflows onto the riverbank.*

▼

IT IS FULLNESS THAT MAKES A RELATIONSHIP WORK, NOT EMPTINESS.

▲
---

2. You are willing to learn more about yourself by looking in the mirror of your beloved.

A relationship is not a possession, it is a process. You don't acquire a relationship, you enter into one, and it affects you twenty-four hours a day. I always tell people, "A relationship is the best seminar in town," and I believe this with all my heart. When you are in love, you are faced with a mirror that reflects everything about you back for you to see. You confront your fears, your weaknesses, your selfishness, your insensitivity, your limitations, your emotional programming, and your pride. You get to look at all those parts of yourself that you dislike. *Relationships can be your greatest source of pain, or your greatest teacher.*

If you are not prepared for the intensity of the powerful learning experience love provides, you will resist your relationship and resent your partner. You will become angry at the mirror for the reflection it is showing you. The more open you are to surrendering to your relationship as a gift and a guide, the more you will grow and the easier it will be to make it work. You are ready to have a truly fulfilling relationship when you can say, *"I commit myself to learning everything I can from this person and this experience, even if it makes me uncomfortable."*

If you've read this chapter and realized that you have fallen in love for the wrong reasons in one or more of your realtionships, don't despair! A wonderful quote by metaphysical philosophers P. D. Ouspensky and G. I. Gurdjieff reminds us:

"When one realizes one is asleep, at that moment one is already half awake."

Each realization you have about mistakes you've made in the past opens the door for you to make more enlightened choices in the future. Instead of being *hopelessly* romantic, you can be *hopefully* romantic.

4

▼▼▼

THE SIX BIGGEST MISTAKES WE MAKE IN THE BEGINNING OF A RELATIONSHIP

▼▼▼

When the most important things in our life happen, we quite often do not know, at the moment, what is going on.
C. S. LEWIS

▼▼▼

In the movie *Defending Your Life,* Albert Brooks plays a man who dies in a car accident and suddenly finds himself in Judgment City, a cosmic pit stop between Earth and the Hereafter. In Judgment City, the departed must convince a judge that he learned enough about love and happiness in his previous lifetime not to be sent back to Earth, and thereby is free to move on to a higher plane of existence. During each soul's "appointment" with the judge, he is made to review his life by watching a film of it projected onto a huge screen. Because Albert's character is no longer living that life, but observing it objectively, he can see many things about himself and his choices that were mistakes. Situations he failed to take notice of, warning signs he didn't pay attention to, feelings he ignored, chances he passed up—all of these become painfully clear to Albert sitting in his viewing room in the afterlife.

I remember watching this film and thinking that it would be wonderful if, from time to time, we could all stop, sit back, and "watch" the movie of our own life to gain a perspective that's difficult to obtain while we are busy living it! This would be especially helpful in our relationships, where *it's easy for us to see what the problems were once the love affair has ended, but not so easy to figure out what's wrong while we're still involved.*

In working with thousands of men and women over the years and in analyzing my own love life, I've learned that **so much of the hurt, heartache, and disappointment we experience in love could be avoided if we just *paid more attention* at the beginning of the relationship.** I've watched all the movies of my past love affairs, and have helped my friends and clients watch theirs, and I've concluded that there are six big mistakes many of us make when we first get involved with a partner. This chapter will introduce you to each of these mistakes and will then help you go back and evaluate your own past so you can learn from it.

▼

THE SIX BIGGEST MISTAKES WE MAKE IN THE BEGIN-NING OF A RELATIONSHIP:

1. **We don't ask enough questions.**
2. **We ignore warning signs of potential problems.**
3. **We make premature compromises.**
4. **We give in to Lust Blindness.**
5. **We give in to material seduction.**
6. **We put commitment before compatibility.**

▲

MISTAKE

▼   ▼   ▼   ▼   **1**   ▼   ▼   ▼   ▼

We Don't Ask Enough Questions

Imagine, for a moment, that you have decided to buy a new car. You drive up and down Main Street, where all the car dealerships are located, searching for a car that's right for you. Suddenly you spot it—a cute, sporty little model on the lot up ahead. You park and walk over to the car you are "attracted" to. "I love the way it looks!" you think. You open the door and sit in the car for a moment. "I love how it smells, and the way the seat feels against my body—this is the car for me."

As you get out of the car, a salesperson approaches you. "Can I help you?" he asks.

"I want this car," you exclaim.

"Do you have any questions about it?"

"No," you respond emphatically, "I just want this car."

"Well, would you like to know how it compares to other models, or what kind of warranty it comes with, or the kind of gas mileage it gets?"

"No, talking about all those things would ruin the excitement I'm feeling now."

"What about the price? Don't you want to know that?" the salesperson asks you in a bewildered voice.

"Oh, don't be so logical. The price doesn't matter to me—all that matters is that I love this car, I need this car, and I know it's meant for me."

This is obviously an absurd fantasy. No one in their right mind would make an important purchase such as buying an automobile without asking questions to be sure they were making the right choice. For that matter, you probably wouldn't buy a refrigerator, stereo, VCR, or even a new iron without grilling the salesperson until you felt absolutely sure you weren't making a mistake. **Yet many of us ask less questions before we start a relationship than we do before we buy a pair of shoes!** In doing this, we miss the opportunity to discover things about our potential lover that could be crucial to the success or failure of our relationship.

Why We Don't Ask Questions Before We Fall in Love

Here are some of the reasons why we don't ask questions in the beginning of a relationship:

► **It's not romantic:** Falling in love is romantic. *Interviewing someone is not.* So we allow ourselves to be seduced by going out to dinner, dancing, flirting, complimenting, and all the behaviors that usually manifest themselves when we first meet a potential partner and get *swept away,* so to speak. That's how the movies we saw and the books we read said it was supposed to be. You shouldn't need to ask your date lots of questions about himself. You'd look at your partner and just know he was the one.

But as we discussed in Chapter One, these love myths can get you into lots of trouble. **Asking your partner questions to find out more about them may not seem romantic, but it's the only intelligent way to really get to know someone.**

Brandy, thirty-one, told me a sad story about how she broke off her engagement to Warren, thirty-six, when she found out he had a history of physically abusing women in his life. She'd been seeing Warren for almost a year, and during that time he lost his temper quite often, but he never actually hit her until three weeks after they became engaged. Only after she left did Warren confess that he'd had a problem with violence before. I asked Brandy how much she'd known about Warren's past relationships when she got involved with him: "I'm ashamed to admit that I didn't really know anything about his past," Brandy confessed. "It's not that I didn't think about it—I did. But each time I meant to bring it up, we'd be out having fun, or about to make love, and it just seemed like it would ruin the mood. Now that I look back, I realize I never pressed him to talk about the things he avoided discussing."

I hear these same excuses when people try to explain why they don't discuss birth control or sexual protection with prospective partners.

My answer to this is: **If you want to talk about what's really not romantic, unwanted pregnancy is not romantic; herpes is not romantic; and AIDS is certainly not romantic.** Aside from finding out if you're with the right person or not, *asking a potential partner questions about himself has, in the 1990s, unfortunately become a matter of life and death.*

▶ **You don't want to know the answers.** Another reason we don't ask questions is simply that we don't want to know the answers, because we may not like what we hear. We don't want to hear anything bad. *If you are desperate to get into a relationship, or to make one work, you will avoid discussing anything that might sabotage your "fantasy" that you are with the right partner.*

▼

WE'RE TOO BUSY LOOKING FOR REASONS WHY WE *SHOULD* LOVE SOMEONE TO TAKE THE TIME TO LOOK FOR REASONS WHY WE *SHOULDN'T.*

▲

You finally find a partner after a long period of loneliness, or you finally meet someone who is ready to make a commitment, or you're tired of dating and just want to settle down, so you avoid asking the questions you know might "ruin" this great new relationship. As the saying goes, *"Don't destroy my fantasy by forcing me to face reality."*

► **You don't want your partner to ask you questions about yourself.** The third reason you might avoid asking your partner questions is to prevent them from asking questions of you. This will be especially true if:

► You aren't happy with yourself or your life.
► You are ashamed of or haven't come to terms with your past.
► You feel guilty about things you are presently doing.
► You don't have a good self-image.

When you aren't comfortable with who you are or who you have been, you will unconsciously protect yourself by not probing too deeply into your partner's life, as if to say, "I'll leave you alone, and you leave me alone. Okay?" It's obvious that two people playing this game are going to have a very unhealthy and dysfunctional relationship.

Erica, twenty-seven, spent years becoming a master of emotional hide-and-seek. She'd get into intense relationships with men she didn't know that much about. "I know why I don't get into heavy discussions with these guys," she told me. "It's because I don't want them asking me a lot of questions about me and my past." Erica was an incest victim. She'd been molested by her father from the time she was twelve until she was sixteen, when she finally escaped by running away. But Erica never really left her past behind. Like many incest victims, she tried to erase the memories because dealing with them was too terrifying. She chose men who didn't want to get too intimate with her, so she didn't have to get too intimate with them. Her worst fear was that if she found a man who was willing to share the truth about himself, she would have to reveal her terrible secret, and he'd judge her and reject her for having been part of something she felt was dirty and shameful.

Ignorance Is Not Bliss

In spite of the three reasons just discussed, the truth remains that in love, and in fact all of life,

WHAT YOU DON'T KNOW *WILL* HURT YOU.

The more information you have about someone, the better you'll be able to judge whether or not this person will make a good mate. The less information you have about someone, the more likely you will end up angry, disappointed, or heartbroken.

Here are some of the areas you should ask your partner questions about:

▶ family background and quality of family relationships
▶ past love relationships and reasons for breakups
▶ lessons learned from life experiences
▶ ethics, values, and morals
▶ attitudes about love, commitment, communication
▶ spiritual or religious philosophy
▶ personal and professional goals

MISTAKE

▼   ▼   ▼   ▼   **2**   ▼   ▼   ▼   ▼

We Ignore Warning Signs of Potential Problems

▶ Do you ever feel stupid for not having paid enough attention to something a partner said or did that was a sign of worse things to come?

▶ Do you think or yourself as a positive person who looks for the good in people and situations?

▶ Do you look back on some of your relationships and see things now you didn't see then?

If you answered yes to any of these questions, then you've probably made mistake number two: *You notice something about your partner that should signal you to be cautious, but you choose, consciously or unconsciously, to ignore it.* You may do this by:

Minimizing its importance. "He really doesn't drink that much, mostly on weekends, and besides, it's just beer."

Making excuses for the other person. "I know she seems

overly jealous and possessive, but her ex-husband cheated on her and made her really insecure. She doesn't mean to act this way."

Rationalizing. "It would be stupid for him to get a job now, just when he's about to sell his script. This way, he has time to polish the final version and visit agents and producers."

Denying it. "What do you mean, you think he doesn't treat me well? He's wonderful to me. No one's ever loved me the way he does. You're just jealous that I'm happy and you're not."

Ironically, the more positive and loving a person you are, the more prone you may be to ignoring the warning signs in your relationships. If you have the habit of looking for the good and seeing the potential in people, you might overlook disturbing characteristics or behaviors in your partner, only to find later that you should have paid attention.

This tendency is probably one of the most dangerous mistakes we make in our love life. *We don't see what we don't want to see; thus we set ourselves up for eventual feelings of disappointment, betrayal, and anger.* "You weren't like this when I met you." "If I'd known you had this problem, I would have never gotten involved with you in the first place." "You've changed—you used to be different." These are the things we end up saying when we inevitably face the truth about our partner. And although there are cases in which a person is deliberately deceived by a partner, **most of the time we are deceiving ourselves!**

HOW MARGUERITE SET HERSELF UP TO BE BETRAYED

Marguerite is a thirty-four-year-old graphic artist who came to me to try to heal a broken heart. She'd just ended a two-year relationship with Kenneth, forty-one, because she found out he was sleeping with his ex-girlfriend. "I'm so depressed, I can't function," she told me, sobbing. "I was so sure everything was fine between us. I really believed that he was the one for me and that we would make it work. I can't believe this is happening to me."

Whenever anyone tells me they are shocked about the negative outcome of a relationship, I assume they must have ignored some warning signs along the way.

RELATIONSHIPS DON'T JUST FALL APART OVERNIGHT. IT TAKES MONTHS AND YEARS OF DETERIORATION BEFORE THE LOVE IS FINALLY DESTROYED.

When a person discovers he has cancer, it feels like the disease came upon him suddenly, but the tragic reality is that the cancer has been growing inside his body for a long time. In the same way, you may notice the effects of the deterioration of a love relationship all of a sudden, but in reality the problems have been developing all along. Although modern science may not yet know how to detect diseases such as cancer in their initial stages of growth, you *can* detect potential problems in your relationships as early as the first few weeks.

MARGUERITE'S MOVIE

To help Marguerite gain some insight into her relationship, I suggested that she participate in an exercise I'll teach you later in this chapter. I asked her to close her eyes and to imagine she was sitting in an empty movie theater. In front of her was a huge blank screen. Suddenly the screen lights up and a movie comes on. It is a love story—the movie of her relationship with Kenneth. "I want you to imagine that the movie starts from the very first moment you met Kenneth," I said. "Picture your first encounter, your first date, the conversation you had. Remember it in detail. And **as you are watching your movie, I want you to look for any warning signs, any clues you did not see or did not pay attention to at the time, that are disturbing. When you find one, freeze the scene in the movie, keep your eyes closed, and describe it to me.**"

Marguerite sat quietly for a few moments and then spoke. "Okay, I'm at the party where I met Kenneth. We are talking about ourselves, and when I ask him if he is with anyone, he answers, *"I came with someone, but our relationship is pretty much over."* I remember feeling relieved hearing that because I was so attracted to him. Now, as I watch the movie, I realize what a strange answer that was: If his relationship was over, what was he doing taking her to a party?

"Good," I responded. "Now let the movie start again."

"Oh, I can't believe what I just saw!" Marguerite exclaimed. "I'm at Kenneth's apartment. We've been dating for almost a month, and this is the first night we slept together. He goes in the kitchen to get us a drink, and I'm taking a tour of his place. *On his desk I notice a picture of him and a really pretty woman with their arms around each other on the beach in a tropical setting.* I wonder if it's his past girlfriend, but I'm afraid to ask about it and ruin the evening, so I ignore it. Later I find out that it is she, and over the next year we had many fights about his keeping her pictures out. I didn't even stop to ask myself why he would have his ex's picture on his desk when he's bringing me home.

"Next I see Kenneth and me sitting in a restaurant having a conversation about Julie, his ex. He's explaining to me that she is like family to him, and even though they aren't together, he is all she has, and he's helping her financially until she can get back on her feet again. I can hear him saying, *"I'm just a loyal kind of guy, Marguerite. It's hard for me to close the door on someone who's been part of my life for four years."* I remember feeling a tight nervous sensation in my stomach, but what he was telling me sounded very loving, so I didn't confront him. I feel sick just looking back at this.

"Now it's a few weeks later. Kenneth calls me up to tell me he can't see me on Saturday night because it's Julie's birthday. It seems she called him crying and said she had no one else to be with and started getting nostalgic about this place they went to on her birthday for four years, so he is going to be a 'friend' and take her out to eat. He reassures me that it will only be for an hour or two, and he'll call me when he gets home. I see myself sitting at home waiting for the phone to ring. It's ten o'clock, eleven, midnight. Finally, at one-thirty, the phone rings. *It's Kenneth, apologizing profusely and explaining that after dinner, Julie fell apart and they went back to her place to talk. 'I couldn't leave her when she was like that, honey,'* he told me. I can see myself feeling furious, and yet loving him so much."

At this point, Marguerite began to cry. "It's so obvious, isn't it?" she said in a trembling voice. "I can see it all there in this movie. I **ignored every sign Kenneth gave me that he hadn't really let go of Julie.** I guess I wanted to believe that he had, and maybe he wanted to believe that, too. Toward the end of our relationship, we finally began to fight openly about it. She was calling him a lot, he hadn't stopped giving her money, and I thought that was wrong. He told me I didn't understand, that my jealousy was just because I was insecure."

"Now that you've seen the whole movie, when you watch the end, where Kenneth sleeps with Julie, is it still a shock?" I asked.

Marguerite looked at me with tears in her eyes. "No," she answered resolutely. "It still hurts, but it isn't a shock. I should have seen it coming. I just wasn't paying attention."

I was proud of Marguerite for not remaining a victim and for taking her power back by recognizing how *she* had made the choice to ignore information that would have forewarned her that Kenneth wasn't emotionally available. It didn't eliminate her pain, but it did give her confidence that next time, by paying more attention, she would be able to make a healthier love choice.

WHAT SOME WARNING SIGNS MEAN

Here are some examples of warning signs and possible problems they might develop into.

WARNING SIGNS	EVENTUAL PROBLEM
Avoids discussing his past, dodges direct questions, or makes light of it	*Could be hiding something serious;* won't want to work on relationship
Won't reveal details of family background; doesn't see or speak to family much.	*Difficult time being intimate;* hidden anger and rage at family members that will be projected onto you.
Still in frequent contact with one or more ex's; talks with them on phone a lot; doesn't include you in the friendship or introduce you.	*Won't be able to make a commitment to you;* may get back with ex. May never make you number one.
Very enmeshed with family members. Seems to talk to them too much. Doesn't stand up to them. Let's them tell him or her what to do. No boundaries.	*Won't be able to include you in family.* You will always feel like an outsider. Won't side with you if they attack.
Use of alcohol or drugs. Can't have sex or fun without them. Can't be around people without "partying."	*Could be alcoholic or drug addict.* Will deny it. Expect mood swings, emotional distance.
Extremely attentive and intense person. Showers you with love, constant affection, gifts. Seems to think about you twenty-four hours a day.	*Could be highly possessive and jealous.* Will live their life through you. Won't give you space. You will feel smothered.

Frequent flirting, staring at others. Needs lots of attention from people. Attracts sexual interest like flies.	*Watch out for possible cheater.* Will never make you feel secure. You'll feel like it's your problem.
Angry at past lovers. Feels like a victim. Blames ex's for problems in relationships.	*You're next!* Won't take responsibility for their part in things. Will end up angry at you.
Credit problems, debts, unpaid parking tickets, shaky finances, "temporary bad times."	*Get out your checkbook!* You'll hear lots of excuses but see very little action. You'll play Mommy or Daddy.
Likes to be in charge in and out of the bedroom. Always seems to be strong and to know what he wants. Never shows fear or vulnerability.	*Control freak!* It starts out feeling like you're being taken care of and ends up like you're living with a dictator.

These are just a few samples of warning signs and their possible consequences. In Chapter Six I'll talk about Fatal Flaws and in Chapter Seven we'll look at Compatibility Time Bombs so you can get a much better idea of the kinds of problems to watch out for in relationships.

Watching the Movie of Your Love Life

Now it's time for you to look at some of the warning signs you've received and ignored in past or present relationships, and to gain some understanding of how you could have predicted the problems you'd have with that partner if you had paid more attention in the beginning. You'll need some paper, a pen, and a quiet place where you won't be disturbed.

▼
Watching Your Love Movies

STEP 1 Write down the name of a partner and the dates of your relationship at the top of a page.

STEP 2 Write down the heading "Warning Signs" under the name.

STEP 3 Read these instructions. Then close your eyes and imagine that you are sitting alone in a movie theater. It is dark, and as you look up at the screen, the film suddenly begins. The title flashes on the screen and says (*Your Name*)'s *Relationship with* (*Your Partner's Name*)—*A Love Story* Example: *Barbara's Relationship with Jeffrey—A Love Story.* The first scene is the very first encounter you had. Visualize your whole relationship with that person unfolding. See yourselves talking, spending time together, having sex, etc., in chronological order, as if you were watching a movie of your relationship.

As you watch each scene of the movie, starting from the very first moment you met, watch for any behaviors, comments, discussions or experiences that don't feel right to you. *You can tell which these are by how tense your body becomes when you think about or visualize them in your mind. These are warning signs. As you notice each one, gently open your eyes and write it down under Warning Signs. Then close your eyes again and continue watching the movie where you left off. Do this until the movie is over—that is until the relationship ends or you are in the present.*

STEP 4 When you are done watching the movie, open your eyes, look over the warning signs you wrote down, and based on the problems that developed in your relationship with that partner, write a few sentences describing the outcome of that relationship.

STEP 5 Repeat this same exercise for every person you've been involved with.

▲

JUNE'S LOVE MOVIES

Here's an example of the love movie exercise by a woman named June, who took my seminar.

Name
  David, 1974—77

Warning Signs

- ▶ Acted very mysterious about himself on first few dates.
- ▶ Told me he wasn't interested in settling down.
- ▶ Didn't call me when he left town on business.
- ▶ Answered questions about his attitudes toward love and relationships by quoting philosophers.
- ▶ Wouldn't talk much about his past lovers.
- ▶ Told me to not get too emotionally attached to him whenever I'd say I loved him.
- ▶ Always acted like my superior or teacher.
- ▶ Didn't like when people thought we were a couple.

Conclusion

I was madly in love with David, but it's obvious watching my movie that he wasn't in love with me. *David was petrified of commitment and had a difficult time with intimacy.* He was actually pretty honest about it—I just didn't get the hint, and kept hoping he would love me more in time. Maybe it was the fact that he was unobtainable that I found so attractive. David kept me hanging for several years in an off-again, on-again relationship (it was always on from my side) until he moved to another city and I found out he and my best friend were having an affair. I shouldn't have been surprised, but I was.

Name

Peter, 1979–80

Warning Signs

- ▶ Had four drinks on our first date and got smashed.
- ▶ Seemed passionate but impersonal in bed from the start.
- ▶ Bragged about how bad he'd been in high school and how he almost flunked out (I thought he was "colorful").
- ▶ Drove really fast, ignoring speed limits, and talked about how he could get traffic tickets fixed.
- ▶ Couldn't actually tell me what his job was, but said he had lots of deals in the works that involved finance.
- ▶ His apartment was a pig.
- ▶ Tried to impress my friends when he first met them and told jokes all night.
- ▶ Described all his ex-girlfriends as weak and helpless victims.

Conclusion

I must have been blind not to see from the first night that Peter was a rebel who had never grown up. I saw his behavior as exciting, obviously lying to myself. *I had enough warning signs in the first two weeks to know he would never be a stable, responsible partner, but I ignored them.* The year we were together was turbulent and dramatic. He was like a tornado smashing through the serenity in my life with his bravado and bad attitude toward everything "conventional." The longer we were together, the more it became apparent that he was a "weekend alcoholic," didn't have any real career direction, and desperately needed to be the center of attention at all times. Looking back, I don't even think Peter knew who I really was—he was too busy cleaning up the constant messes in his own life, with my help, of course! I finally left, and he accused me of not being able to "handle his high energy." Give me a break.

Name
Gerald, 1986–present (my husband)

Warning Signs
- ▶ Told me when we first met he had a bad relationship with his mother.
- ▶ Got angry at me for telling our friends we were seeing each other before we had a chance to discuss it together.
- ▶ Had immature, unenlightened friends.
- ▶ Very hard on himself and had difficult time acknowledging his accomplishments.
- ▶ Tendency to get annoyed with people and situations easily.

Conclusion
It was interesting to watch my movie with Gerald since we are married, happily, in my opinion. First of all, it was different from the others in that I wasn't chasing Gerald or trying to get him to love me. Thank God. I finally learned from the past and broke that pattern.

I could see right away that the problems we do have in our relationship could all be spotted in seed form in the beginning. Gerald's mother was never really a good mother to him, so he gets reactive when I try to mother him at all. And because he is so hard on himself, he is hard on other people as well. I'd say impatience and intolerance are his most difficult qualities. He really needs to be included in what's going on—I found that out when we had our first fight about announcing our relationship, and I've remembered that since, and always made sure to communicate with him before I rush ahead. **I think the difference between this movie and the others, aside from the fact that it's still going on, is that *Gerald is just as aware of his warning signs, or potential problem areas, as I am*. We still work through them, along with mine,** of course, but I feel like we are working as a team, and not against each other.

June learned a lot from her love movie exercise. She was able to see clearly that the outcomes of her earlier relationships weren't accidents—she didn't pay attention to the warning signs. And she can trace the trouble spots in her relationship with her husband back to the beginning.

What to Do with the Warning Signs You Discover

The point of this section is *not* to make you so paranoid the moment you see a flaw in a potential partner that you run the other way. As we saw in Chapter Two, all of us bring emotional baggage into a relationship. You won't meet anyone who, if you're really paying attention, doesn't give off some warning signs. The key questions you need to ask yourself are:

▶ Is this warning me about *something reasonable that I am willing to deal with* (partner too serious, not spontaneous enough, needs to trust love more), or is this warning me about *something unreasonable that I am not willing to deal with* (partner has no integrity, cheats, can't feel, makes you feel unloved, has addictions, emotionally screwed up, etc.)?

▶ If I decide I am willing to deal with this, *is my partner also aware of this problem or pattern and willing to work on it as well?*

I believe that with enough love and determination, a couple can overcome many obstacles. But it's almost impossible to make a relationship work when one person knows there is problem and the other is in denial.

MISTAKE

▼   ▼   ▼   ▼   **3**   ▼   ▼   ▼   ▼

We Make Premature Compromises

The third common mistake we make in the beginning of our relationships I call **premature compromise**—*changing or editing* *your own values, behaviors, and habits in hopes that you and your new partner will appear to get along more harmoniously.*

I'm not suggesting that you walk into a relationship thinking, "I'll do anything to get him to like me, even if it means compromising my own values." The process is a lot more subtle than this. It's an adjustment you make in what is important to you as you get to know someone. *When you discover that beliefs you've had, or interests that were important to you, or friends you care for are not acceptable to your partner, you may tend to make these less important in order to create the illusion that the two of you are much more compatible than you actually are.*

THE DANGER IN PREMATURE COMPROMISE IS THAT YOU LOSE YOUR SENSE OF SELF EARLY IN THE RELATIONSHIP AND CREATE A FALSE SENSE OF HARMONY BETWEEN YOU AND YOUR MATE.

Let's look at some common ways in which we make premature compromises:

Compromising Your Beliefs and Values

When you first meet someone, you share your beliefs and values with them and try to discover more about theirs so you can decide how well suited you are for one another. But once you come across a conflict in those values, you have two choices:

---

1. **You can stand by your beliefs and risk tension between you and your partner,**

or

2. **You can compromise your beliefs to "keep the peace."**

You might compromise your beliefs or values by:

▶ allowing yourself to be pressured into having sex with someone before you are ready or feel it is appropriate

▶ not speaking up about something your partner is doing in his life that you feel is wrong

▶ not disclosing your beliefs on a controversial issue (abortion, politics, homosexuality, the environment, religion), or softening or denying those beliefs.

▶ participating in activities you would normally avoid (gossiping, drinking, taking drugs, watching pornographic movies, etc.)

▶ not expressing an opinion if it strongly disagrees with your partner's

▶ going off your diet and eating junk food you'd ordinarily avoid

JUDY TELLS HOW SHE COMPROMISED HER BELIEFS

"I met Daryl through a coworker and was immediately attracted to him. I was twenty-seven, and had dated a lot of men, but no one I really wanted to get serious with. But Daryl seemed like he had a lot going for him, and I found myself interested in pursuing the relationship.

"I guess I was so eager to impress him that I went into our first date thinking more about trying to be who he wanted me to be than the person I really was.

"Looking back at that night, I see the beginning of a pattern. We went out to dinner, and he ordered wine. I don't drink—at least I didn't before Daryl, but I decided to have some wine. A few glasses later, I was getting pretty tipsy. But it didn't stop there. We went to a bar to meet some of his friends and dance, and drank some more. A little voice kept saying, 'Judy, this is totally unlike you. This is everything you disapprove of.' But Daryl was being so sweet to me and I felt so appreciated that I didn't pay attention. By the end of the evening, I was totally bombed. I can't say I didn't have fun, because I did, but not the way I want to have fun.

"Daryl and I dated for five months, and the story didn't change. He'd call me up and say, Let's party, babe, and I'd come running. His whole crowd drank too much and played too much, and I became just like them. I used to go to church at least a few times a month, but I gave that up. I mean, I couldn't really show up with a hangover. Sometimes I'd try to talk to Daryl about my spiritual beliefs, or suggest we calm things down a bit and just stay home together. But he'd always laugh and call me his "little Sunday school teacher," and I'd drop it.

"I broke up with him last year. It was one of the hardest things I've ever done, because I did love him, and he said he loved me. **But** it wasn't me he really loved, it was the woman I turned into when I was with him. The real me went into hibernation when I met him, and I didn't get her back again until I left. It was a painful lesson."

Compromising Your Interests and Activities

Sometimes to make a relationship work:

▼

1. **You will give up your own interests or activities, especially if you suspect they aren't important to your new partner or that they might interfere with your future together,**

or

2. **You will become very involved in interests or activities you really don't care about at the expense of your own, in order to bond with your partner.**

▲

Some ways by which you might do this are:

▶ Stop reading as many books because your partner would rather watch TV in the evenings.

▶ Give up a sport such as cycling, tennis, or weight training because your partner doesn't want to participate.

▶ Stop attending personal growth seminars, classes, Twelve Step meetings, or support groups because your partner isn't interested in or doesn't support these activities.

STEVE TELLS HOW HE COMPROMISED HIS INTERESTS

"When I first met Valerie, she was dating someone else, and I remember telling a friend of ours to let me know if they ever broke up. Six months later I was really surprised when he called. 'Valerie is available,' he announced, and I called her that night. Our relationship started out hot and heavy, and from the first week, I was really anxious to make it work. Saturday morning arrived, and I told her I was going to meet a friend for racquetball, as I did each weekend. "Oh, you can play racquetball anytime," she practically cooed. "What am I going to do all day until you come over?" It took me about ten seconds to decide to skip racquetball and spend the afternoon with her.

"I think I played racquetball twice the whole year we dated. And that wasn't the only interest I gave up. **I stopped watching football because she thought it was "gross." I stopped running every morning before work because she'd coax me to stay in bed with her. I stopped doing anything Valerie didn't like doing.** I never thought that I was sacrificing—I guess I was just trying to avoid arguments. When I finally began reintroducing those things I'd given up into my life, Valerie went crazy. 'You never used to be like this!' she'd scream. 'You've become so selfish!' It took me all that time to figure out that Valerie needed much more attention than I could give her. **I would have seen this in the first few weeks of our relationship if only I hadn't compromised who I was so much.**"

Compromising Your Friends and Family

Other ways in which you may compromise too much in relationships is:

▼

1. **You stop spending time with the friends, family, and people you love if your partner is not comfortable with them**

or

2. **You start spending time with people you don't care for in order to please your partner.**

▲

Judy talked about this in the earlier example. She not only compromised her beliefs and values by drinking and partying with Daryl, but she also compromised her friends by spending less time with them and more time with Daryl's friends, whom she disliked and had little in common with. "The truth is," Judy commented, "if I had stayed in closer contact with my own friends, I probably wouldn't have gotten so far off-track, and the relationship would have ended a lot sooner and with much less pain."

Why We Make Premature Compromises

There are two reasons why you may compromise prematurely in the beginning of your relationships:

1. You must compromise to create some kind of compatibility. Your partner is so different from you in important ways that unless you start editing away parts of yourself, the relationship will be very short-lived. Perhaps your partner even expects you to compromise, and, like Daryl, ridicules or rejects you if you don't.

2. You compromise because you are desperate to be loved and accepted by your new partner and to make the relationship work. Your partner may have no desire for you to give up who you are and what you believe in, but you may walk into the relationship frightened of discovering that this is not the right person for you. So you try to make it look like you are perfect for one another by becoming a "clone" of your mate.

All good relationships contain some degree of compromise. You can't live your life exactly as you did when you were single once you make a commitment to a mate. But:

WHEN YOU MAKE COMPROMISES OUT OF A DESIRE TO AVOID CONFLICT, YOU ARE COMPROMISING FOR THE WRONG REASONS.

What's the solution? *Enter into a relationship knowing what your values, interests, and loyalties are, and be committed first to yourself and second to your partner.*

MISTAKE

▼   ▼   ▼   ▼   4   ▼   ▼   ▼   ▼

We Give In to Lust Blindness

As a seminar leader, I'm always attempting to create new ways of helping people learn through *experience* rather than *information*.

If I have a principle I want to teach, I try to find the most creative way possible to illustrate that principle with an exercise. One of my favorites is designed to show people how prone they are to making Mistake #4. Lust Blindness: Here's how it works when I do this exercise with single people:

Each course participant puts on a blindfold. Then, with the help of my staff, they pair up with a member of the opposite sex. Their instructions are to spend five to ten minutes together getting to know one another as if they were shopping for a prospective partner. I tell them to be as flirtatious or bold as they want to. They can hold hands or be affectionate if they wish. After the time elapses, they make notes to themselves about their reactions, and we place them together with another partner. By the time we are finished, they've had six or seven "minirelationships."

Next, I ask them to rate their partners based on how attracted they felt to each one, placing them in order (number one, number two, etc.), and to write down why they felt that way about each person.

Then the fun begins. We introduce each person to all of their partners. **You can imagine the shock on people's faces when they realize that, with their blindfold on, they felt attracted to *totally different people* than they normally would without a blindfold.** A young, athletic guy whose taste in women is blonde, buxom, and beautiful finds his number one choice was a women who is a little plump and on the plain side and with whom he had one of the most stimulating and erotic conversations of his life. A career woman who has made a habit of getting involved with the most successful guys she can find discovers that her number one choice is a schoolteacher whose voice and sensitivity she fell in love with. I love watching people stand around getting their minds blown and their boundaries broken as they begin to understand how much visual chemistry, or Lust Blindness, has limited their ability to choose partners with whom they are compatible.

I'm not suggesting that you put a bag over your head the next time you go to a party or a bar (although it is an interesting idea— *"Barbara's Bag Bar!"*). As we'll discuss in Chapter Ten, sexual chemistry and attraction is one important element of compatibility. But this exercise always reminds me of how affected we are by Lust Blindness.

How to Cure Lust Blindness

In Chapter One I talked a lot about the "Lust into Love Formula" and how it seduces you into believing you are compatible with people when you really just have the hots for them! **You are in love with the passion, not necessarily the person.** But I wanted to remind you about Lust Blindness again since we are discussing mistakes we make at the beginning of relationships, and to encourage you, if you are single, to **try to wear a psychic blindfold when you meet people so you can see who they really are beyond the physical.**

WHEN YOU LEARN TO FEEL PEOPLE WITH YOUR HEART AND NOT JUST SEE THEM WITH YOUR EYES, YOU WILL ATTRACT MUCH MORE COMPATIBLE PARTNERS INTO YOUR LIFE.

If you have a history of Lust Blindness, I suggest that you **postpone having sex with a new partner until you can't stand it any longer.**

Each of you has your own moral beliefs, and you must follow your own conscience when it comes to sexual activity. I can only share my personal views and what I've found works for people I've helped. If you do plan to be sexually active before marriage, try waiting for as long as you can with a new partner, and I'm not talking about a week, either!

Get to know everything you can about this person, using the information I'll give you in the rest of this book, before you sleep with him or her.

Here are my guidelines for deciding when it's right to become sexual with someone:

When Is It Time To Become Sexually Intimate?

► You should be *intellectually and emotionally intimate* before you are sexually intimate.

► You should spend at least *twice as much time* talking and learning about one another as you do necking or fooling around.

► You should *like* the person. I have a saying:
DON'T SLEEP WITH SOMEONE YOU DON'T WANT TO
BECOME LIKE.

► You should *respect* the person and his or her values.

► You should have gone through some difficult times together (one of you was sick, family crisis, job stress) and
seen how your partner operates under stress and how he
or she treats you when you are under stress.

► You should have *discussed birth control, sexually transmitted diseases such as herpes and AIDS,* and know as
much as possible about your partner's sexual history. If
you haven't been tested for the AIDS virus, I suggest you
do so, and ask your partner to do the same. Why take
chances?

► You should have agreed on *what form of birth control
you are going to use,* and if it's different from a condom,
that you will *use a condom in order to practice safe sex.*

► If you are a woman, you should ask yourself:
WOULD I WANT TO HAVE THIS MAN'S CHILDREN?
WOULD I WANT A SON JUST LIKE THIS MAN?

These questions serve two purposes: First, they remind
you that pregnancy is always a possibility and will ensure
that you are careful about birth control; and second, they
will help you be sure that you are ready to become sexually
intimate with this man. Whether you actually want children
or not, *if you don't like this man enough to want children
that carry his genes, characteristics, and personality, then
what are you doing sleeping with this guy?*

► If you are a man, you should ask yourself:
WOULD I WANT THIS WOMAN TO BE THE MOTHER OF
MY CHILDREN? WOULD I WANT A DAUGHTER JUST LIKE
THIS WOMAN?

I showed this list to a friend of mine as I was writing this book,
and her response was, "My gosh, Barbara, you've taken all the fun
out of sex. Who could possibly pass this kind of test?" My answer to
her and to you is:

▶ What's fun about getting your heart broken because it turns out the person you slept with is seeing someone else?

▶ What's fun about lying in bed at night next to someone you just made love with and feeling alone?

▶ What's fun about having been sexually vulnerable with someone only to find out that he lost interest after he got you in bed?

▶ What's fun about an unwanted pregnancy?

▶ What's fun about finding out your partner gave you herpes?

▶ What's fun about testing positive for the HIV virus?

Making love can be one of the most beautiful and healing experiences in the world, but I've seen it cause tremendous pain, humiliation, and heartache for people when they enter into it blindly.

MISTAKE

▼ ▼ ▼ ▼ 5 ▼ ▼ ▼ ▼

We Give In to Material Seduction

I stood before a group of women during one of my seminars and told them I was about to describe two men, and I wanted them to judge how eligible they felt these guys were. "If you're single," I explained, "judge them on the basis of whether you'd be interested in going out with them; if you're married, judge them on the basis of whether you'd advise your girlfriend or your daughter to go out with them."

"Okay," I began, "let me describe the first man. He's very warm, caring, and open, and interested in having a serious, committed relationship. He has a dynamic personality and loves being around people. He is emotionally healthy and capable of being totally intimate with the person he loves. He is happy with his life and has an adventurous spirit with a great sense of humor. He loves to talk about his feelings and is committed to personal growth."

I looked around the room and noticed that all of the women were nodding their heads and giggling. "All right, how many of you would be interested in this guy?" I asked. All the women cheered and whistled, letting me know Candidate #1 was a hit.

"Okay, next, Mystery Guy #2. He's a very controlling person and likes to have everything his way. He can have a terrible temper and is known for being highly critical. As for sex, well, he's pretty inhibited, but that doesn't matter much, since he's afraid of commitment and has a difficult time being intimate in relationships. Besides, he's a workaholic, so that doesn't leave much time for love."

The women were crinkling up their noses and making strange faces as they listened to my description of Candidate #2. "Well, ladies, how many of you would be interested in this guy?" I asked, and the response of boos and hisses gave me my answer.

"Well, ladies, I'm glad you've made your decisions. But there is something I neglected to tell you about each candidate. **The first man, the one you all wanted to be with, is a trash collector. And the second man, the one you all booed, is a multimillion-aire with homes and yachts around the world and who hangs around with royal figures and celebrities."**

The women looked at me with shock and embarrassment on their faces. I'd fooled each one of them into facing their own attitudes about material wealth and prestige. As wonderful as Mystery Man #1 sounded at first, these ladies had a hard time with the thought of going out with a trash collector. And as bizarre as Mystery Man #2 sounded at first, it would be difficult to turn down a date with a multimillionaire.

How We Become Materially Seduced

In our society, where such an emphasis is placed on outer rather than inner wealth and accomplishment, we often fall prey to material seduction in choosing our partners. We do this by allowing ourselves to be influenced by a person's:

▶ money
▶ life-style
▶ appearance
▶ power
▶ career
▶ reputation

As much as we would like to believe that our values are so lofty that these things wouldn't have an effect on us, it is difficult to be completely immune to them.

It makes me sad that, as women, we have been so disempowered throughout history that we look for sex with famous or rich men, or for a husband with an important job and standing in the community, or a boyfriend with a nice car and a condo to make us feel worthwhile *rather than finding our own worth within ourselves*. Although times are changing and millions of women are helping support their families while others are the sole breadwinners, **we still place exaggerated value on the money and prestige a man can offer us and, in the process, neglect to discover what kind of heart and soul our prospective partner possesses.**

When a woman tells a female friend that she's involved with a new man, the friend's first response will most likely be:

"What does he do for a living?"

And when a woman meets another woman, and finds out that she has a boyfriend, or is married, she will probably ask:

"What does your husband do?"

I've heard women respond to this question apologetically, if they don't feel their partner's profession is prestigious enough. "Oh, he's just a salesman," or, "Well, right now he works in a clothing store, but he's taking classes to get into real estate." And how many of us have heard our parents or grandparents discussing a woman who *"married well,"* not meaning that she had found a caring, loving man but that she'd married a man with a good career, a prestigious job, or lots of money.

From the other point of view, although there are some guys who might attempt to marry a woman for her money, *most men care more about a woman's appearance than her bank balance*. When a man tells a male friend that he's involved with a new woman, the friend's first response will most likely be:

"What does she look like?"

Each time I lecture to men's groups I remind them that just as they hate being judged for what kind of car they drive or the size of their wallet, so women hate being accepted or rejected based on what we look like in a skirt and the size of our breasts!

The Dangers of Material Seduction

I have a thirty-four-year-old friend I'll call Robin who has had a string of unhappy and unfulfilling relationships, all because she makes the mistake of falling for material seduction. Robin is sweet and attractive, and I could never understand why she'd always end up with men with whom she wasn't compatible. Then I began to pay closer attention to the kinds of guys she chose, and I saw the problem. Robin *never* went out with a man who wasn't well off and living a flashy life-style. She looked for guys with fancy cars, high-profile jobs, and expensive habits. When I'd ask her how things were going with her latest date, her answer would always include what restaurant he'd taken her to or which lavish resort they were visiting that weekend. *In her mind, she was in a good relationship if she was spending time sunning in Palm Springs, skiing in Aspen, and playing in Mexico!*

Robin's material thrill would last for a month or two, and then the excitement would wear off and she would have to face her partner, who, in many cases, was incapable of making a commitment, or expressing real feelings, or caring about anything but how he looked and who he was seen with. She'd break off the relationship and go into a depression, wondering why she couldn't meet a wonderful man and fall in love. But a few weeks later, a friend would invite her to a fancy party in Beverly Hills and she'd start the cycle all over again.

Even if you are successful at finding a "good catch," the experience can backfire. I remember a call on my radio show from a woman who was falling apart. "I married my husband when he was a successful builder," she explained. "We didn't know each other for very long, just six months, but he really seemed to love me and swept me off my feet with exciting trips, expensive gifts, and romance. We had a huge wedding and a month-long honeymoon in Europe. But last year the bottom fell out of the building industry because of the recession, and my husband's business went bankrupt. *Barbara, I've lost my attraction to him.* I feel so guilty, because I know he loves me, *but I don't think I ever really loved him. I was in love with the life-style and the perks.* What do I do now?"

This woman learned about Mistake #5 the hard way.

▼

WHEN YOU CHOOSE A PARTNER BASED ON WHAT HE CAN OFFER YOU MATERIALLY RATHER THAN WHAT HE CAN OFFER YOU EMOTIONALLY, YOU WILL END UP IN THE WRONG RELATIONSHIP.

▲

I often meet single men who complain that although they are honest, loving, loyal, and looking for a committed relationship, women regularly pass them over because they don't have a lot of money or a prestigious job. "I'm a supermarket clerk (or shoe salesman or bank teller)," a man will explain, "and women are attracted to me until they find out what I do for a living. Then they run in the opposite direction. **These same women would rather go out with a guy who drives a Mercedes and is a doctor or a lawyer, even if he treats them like dirt, than have me pick them up in my nine-year-old VW and treat them like a princess.**"

I agree with these frustrated men: There are millions of potentially wonderful partners out there just waiting to share their love, but they may not fit your picture of what we've been programmed to believe is a "good catch." The same applies to men who complain they can't find women who are intelligent and caring, yet judge potential candidates solely on the basis of their physical attractiveness. **If you've been frustrated in your search for the right partner, consider getting to know people you would normally judge "not for you."** You may be pleasantly surprised.

MISTAKE

▼　　▼　　▼　　▼　　6　　▼　　▼　　▼　　▼

We Put Commitment Before Compatibility

The year is 1963. I'm sitting in my sixth-grade class, staring across the aisle at Robert Smith, the boy I'm madly in love with. He doesn't really know it, and if he did, I'm sure he wouldn't want anything to do with me—I'm skinny with pigtails and the ugliest glasses in the world. But it doesn't matter, because I'm committed to loving him. I'm not paying much attention to what the teacher is saying because I'm busy with something much more important. In my looseleaf notebook I am practicing writing:

> Barbara Smith
> Barbara Ann Smith
> Robert and Barbara Smith
> Mrs. Robert Smith
> Mr. and Mrs. Robert Smith

Here I was, only twelve years old, but I was already trying out my name with his, writing it over and over again until my hand got cramped. I'm certain Robert Smith never knew the extent of the plans I had for us. I guess he will now!

If you are a woman, you're probably laughing as you read this, because most likely you did the same thing. At a young age we learned to imagine ourselves happily married to—well, to someone. It was the married part of the fantasy that was most important. Whom we were married to was secondary.

This was my first experience of commitment before compatibility, and sadly, it was far from my last. I became an expert at *"falling in love with love,"* and like many men and women, **became seriously involved in relationships before giving much thought to whether this person was really right for me or not.**

How can you tell you are making this mistake? Here are some possible warning signs:

1. **You have sex with your partner within the first month of your relationship. (We'll talk about this in Chapter Ten.)**
2. **You and your partner begin living together within the first three or four months of the relationship.**
3. **You feel sure that this person is the one for you a few weeks into the relationship.**
4. **The intensity of your feeling for your new partner is proportionately much greater than the amount of time you have spent together.**
5. **Within the first weeks or month, you find yourself saying and doing things you have done before in relationships you thought would last forever.**
6. **Within the first weeks or month, you begin fantasizing, or even planning, the rest of your year or life and how you will spend it with your new partner.**

If you are in a new relationship and have experienced one or more of these warning signs, don't panic. It doesn't *necessarily* mean that you are going too fast, or that your relationship isn't meant to last forever. But there is a good chance that you are making an emotional commitment to your partner before you know him or her very well, and need to *slow down and take your time*.

▼

You may be prone to making Mistake #6—Commitment before Compatibility—if you:

▶ like being part of a couple much more than you like being single

▶ are tired of dating and trying out new partners, and long to settle down

▶ felt unloved or abandoned as a child

▶ feel lost when you are not in a relationship

▶ feel pressured by others to find a partner

▶ are a woman and feel your biological clock is running out

▶ are the only one of your group of friends who still isn't married

▶ have a lonely inner child who desperately wants to feel loved and belonging to someone

▶ are very idealistic and find it easy to see what is lovable in people

---
▲

BARBARA'S STORY

When I was a little girl, I watched my mother feel abandoned and alone because my father was out with other women instead of being home with his wife and family. I loved my father very much, and like most children caught in the middle of a bad marriage, I didn't understand why Daddy wasn't there when we needed him. When I was eleven, my mother called me and my brother downstairs to the kitchen and told us that she and my father were getting a divorce. My worst nightmare had come true. At that point, little Barbara made an unconscious decision: *When I grew up, I would love a man so much that he would never think of leaving me.*

Ten years passed. I was twenty-one years old, when I met a young man who told me he loved me and wanted to marry me. I'd only known him a few months and knew little about him, but no one had ever asked me to marry him before. So I blindly threw myself into this relationship and made the commitment. **I wasn't in love with this man. I was in love with loving.**

I spent the next few months crying my eyes out. I never stopped to ask myself why I was so miserable, because I was too busy planning the perfect wedding and the perfect honeymoon. I was on a mission. I was going to have the best marriage in the world and be the most loving wife anyone had ever seen.

I'll never forget my wedding day. I'd been trying to go without my glasses for the past year, and being severely nearsighted, I'd been walking around virtually blind. Now, as I stood wearing the perfect dress, I looked down toward the altar where I knew my fiancé was waiting, and all I could see was a blur. This was who I was marrying. The perfect music began, and I walked down the aisle toward the blur who would become my husband.

Within a year of my marriage, I was divorced. **Needless to say, I discovered that my husband was not the man I thought he was, or, more accurately, the man I wanted him to be.** I had been blind in more ways than one.

For the next fifteen years of my life I repeated this pattern in increasingly painful ways. I'd meet a man, make an instant commitment, and stay in that relationship for many years. The relationship would end suddenly when I'd wake up and realize my partner and I were wrong for each other. **I made a commitment to my partners unconditionally, without questioning whether they were the right mate for me.** That's why I kept getting involved—I wanted so desperately to make a relationship work with someone, just like the little girl I used to be so desperately wanted to help make her mommy and daddy's marriage work.

Five years ago, the last of these relationships ended, and my heart was broken worse than it had ever been in my life. And suddenly, through the darkness of my sorrow, all at once everything became clear:

► I saw that sad little girl within me who just wanted someone to love, whether or not they loved her back.
► I saw the woman with so much to give others who could not give to herself.
► I saw the teacher who encouraged everyone else to get the love they deserved, yet constantly settled for less than she deserved in her own relationships.

And in finally seeing the truth, I saw the way out of my pattern to freedom. For the past four years I've been in the most wonderful, healthy relationship of my life. My partner and I took a long time to make a commitment to one another, and during that time I made sure I was asking for what I wanted and getting it. *I've never been so careful, asked so many questions, or talked about so much before, but my patience and effort have paid off. I'm being loved more now than I could have ever imagined.*

I wanted to share my story with you so you would understand why writing this book has been so important to me. Everything I'm talking about, I've done. Every solution I'm offering you I use in my life every day. I am finding my way out of the darkness, and I hope that by sharing my journey, I'm helping you find your own path to freedom.

AVOIDING
▼
WHO'S
▼
WRONG

▼▼▼

This section of the book will teach you everything you need to know about *what doesn't work in relationships.* Chapter Five discusses ten types of love affairs that will end in pain and disappointment. Chapter Six presents some important "Fatal Flaws" to watch out for in your partner, since they lead to serious problems. Chapter Seven will educate you about "Compatibility Time Bombs," circumstances that exist in your relationship that can suddenly blow up and cause it to self-destruct. Once you read these chapters, I'm confident that you will be able to evaluate your past, present, and future relationships with much more clarity and honesty. Have fun!

▼

5

▼▼▼

THE TEN TYPES OF RELATIONSHIPS THAT WON'T WORK

▼▼▼

If I tried to count the number of relationships I've heard about in all my years of counseling, teaching, seminars, and hosting radio and TV talk shows, the figure would be astronomical. I've listened to every story you can imagine about every kind of problem you could invent. As I've worked with people to help them understand why their relationships turned out as they did, I noticed certain *patterns or types of love affairs that were destined to fail from the start*—So here they are, *the ten types of relationships that won't work*. As you read each one, think about your past love choices and your present relationships, as well as the relationships your family and friends have been involved in. The ten are:

▼

THE TEN TYPES OF RELATIONSHIPS THAT WON'T WORK

1. You care more about your partner than he does about you.
2. Your partner cares more about you than you do about him.
3. You are in love with your partner's potential.

4. You are on a rescue mission.
5. You look up to your partner as a role model.
6. You are infatuated with your partner for external reasons.
7. You have partial compatibility.
8. You choose a partner in order to be rebellious.
9. You choose a partner as a reaction to your previous partner.
10. Your partner is unavailable.

Important: If, after reading this chapter, you suspect that you are in one of these ten types of love affairs right now, reach out for some help: Talk with family or close friends, or seek professional counseling to help you decide whether it is wise for you to continue in this relationship, or whether you should end it.

RELATIONSHIP TYPE

▼ ▼ ▼ ▼ **1** ▼ ▼ ▼ ▼

You Care More About Your Partner Than He Does About You

You know the feeling: You're in love, but you're not sure how he or she feels; you think the two of you could be perfect together, but he doesn't seem to be that excited about the relationship; you can't stop thinking about him when you're apart, but he seems to be just fine without you. What does all of this mean? *It means you are in a relationship that is not going to work.*

In any love affair there are going to be moments, days, or even longer periods of time when one person is more focused on their feelings for their mate and seems to be more "in love." In a good relationship this polarity will periodically switch back and forth so that both partners "take turns" pursuing and being pursued. *When a relationship is healthy, this "emotional dance" takes place in a very subtle way,* like the tide slowly creeps up onto the shore and then gradually retreats back into the ocean. **However, a relation-**

ship is not healthy when one person is the emotional pursuer most or all of the time. *This is a relationship that is out of balance and therefore will not work.*

------------------------------▼------------------------------

HOW TO TELL IF YOU'RE NOT BEING LOVED ENOUGH

Here are some warning signs that you may be in a relationship in which you are loving your partner more than you are being loved. *For each statement that describes how you feel or behave* **most of the time,** *give yourself one point.* **Be 100 percent honest with yourself, even if it hurts.**

1. You are usually the one who reaches out first to be affectionate physically, (reaching for your partner's hand, offering a hug, giving a kiss, etc.).
2. You want to make love, to be intimate and loving when you are in bed, but your partner is into just having sex.
3. You go out of your way to be with him or do things for him, but your partner rarely goes out of his way for you.
4. In the beginning of the relationship you told your family about your partner before he told his family about you.
5. You are the one who makes most of the plans to do things together—restaurant reservations, weekend outings, romantic evenings—and your partner seems just to go along without showing a lot of enthusiasm.
6. You seem much more excited about being in the relationship than your partner, who doesn't show you how much it means to him.
7. On special occasions your gifts to your partner are well-thought-out and personal, while his seem last-minute and impersonal.
8. You initiate most of the contact in the relationship—phone calls, discussions, etc.
9. When you talk about your relationship, your future together, or your feelings for one another, your partner becomes very uncomfortable and unresponsive, or changes the subject.
10. You seem to be fitting yourself into your partner's life, habits, and schedule, and he doesn't make efforts to fit into your life and schedule.

------------------------------▲------------------------------

Now total your points:

▶ **0–2 points: Your relationship with your partner is fairly well balanced,** and you're probably getting back as much love as you give out. *Pay attention to those areas in which you scored a point, and make sure you are asking for what you need and want.*

▶ **3–5 points: You may try to convince yourself you are being well loved, but you aren't.** You are working too hard to get your partner's love, and he or she isn't working hard enough to get yours. *He's either emotionally lazy, or doesn't love you enough.* Stop rowing the boat so hard and see if your partner picks up the oars and does his share. If he doesn't, you know the relationship is not for you.

▶ **5–7 points: What are you doing in such an awful relationship?** Stop kidding yourself and face the fact that you aren't getting the love you deserve. Your self-esteem is so low that you are settling for crumbs and pretending it's enough. It's not! You are in a very unhealthy situation, and the longer you stay in it, the more emotional damage you will incur. *Give your partner an ultimatum immediately about the way you deserve to be treated, or get out.* Then do some work on learning to love yourself.

▶ **8–10 points: What relationship? You aren't in a relationship, you are in a fantasy.** You are giving everything and getting nothing in return. This isn't love, it's self-mutilation. *You aren't ready to have a relationship with anyone.* **Get out now before it's too late,** *and seek some professional counseling to help you reclaim yourself.*

Why You Would Settle for Loving Your Partner More Than You Are Loved

Here are several reasons why you would attract a relationship in which you were loving more:

▶ **You're repeating a childhood pattern.** If one or more of your parents didn't give you the love and attention you needed as a child, you probably made an unconscious decision that *"I have to work hard to get people to love me."* By attracting someone whom you love more, you are "going home" and repeating the pattern.

▶ **You're punishing yourself.** If your self-esteem is low, you will attract a partner who will validate your critical opinion of yourself by not loving you enough.

▶ **You're acting out one of your parents' role with the other.** If you watched your mother always pursuing your father, or vice versa, you may have concluded as a child that this is what relationships are like *and that it's "normal" for one person to love the other more.*

No matter what the reason for being involved with someone you are loving much more than they are loving you, the results will be the same:

▶ You will end up feeling controlled by your partner.
▶ You will end up feeling hungry for love.
▶ You will end up feeling angry.
▶ You will end up feeling cheated.
▶ You will end up feeling miserable.

Solution: When you first get involved in a relationship, watch for the warning signs we discussed. *Don't fall into the trap of making excuses for your partner about why he or she can't love you the way you want to be* loved. The sooner you're honest with yourself, the less likely you are to get your heart broken. If you are presently in a relationship and realize you aren't getting the love you want, read the remainder of this book to determine whether this relationship is worth saving.

RELATIONSHIP TYPE

▾   ▾   ▾   ▾   **2**   ▾   ▾   ▾   ▾

Your Partner Cares More About You Than You Do About Him

This is the opposite of type #1: Your partner is the one who loves you more than you love him or her. If you are in this kind of relationship, you are probably feeling guilty just reading these few sentences. You may deny it to your lover when he asks you about your feelings; you may try to convince yourself that you feel more strongly than you do. **But deep in your heart, you know you aren't loving your partner as much as he or she loves you. As in type #1, you are in a relationship that is out of balance and will not work.**

You can look at the quiz at the beginning of this chapter and reverse the questions to determine whether you are in this kind of relationship. For example, your partner calls you more; your partner initiates more of the physical contact, your partner says "I love you" more often. If you are in this type of relationship, you will probably also feel:

▶ defensive when accused of not loving your partner enough
▶ pressured or controlled by your partner's demands to be loved
▶ claustrophobic in a relationship, feeling you need "space" from your partner
▶ annoyed because your partner is too clingy and needy
▶ frustrated because your partner wants more than you can give

Here are several reasons why you might attract this type of relationship:

▶ **You're protecting yourself emotionally.** If you have ever been deeply hurt in a relationship by someone you really loved, you might make an unconscious decision that says *"I'm never going to get hurt like that again."* Then you find partners you don't love that much, so if they decide to leave you, you won't care anyway.

▶ **You're punishing one of your parents.** If you were not loved enough by one or both of your parents, or felt criticized or rejected by them, *you might attract a partner into your life whom you treat as your parents treated you.* You get to play the unloving one or parent, and your partner gets to play you, begging for love and not getting it. This role reversal is an unconscious way you punish your parent, even though it ends up hurting an innocent person in the process. It's as if part of you is saying, *"That's right—keep begging for my love, but you aren't going to get it, just like you didn't give it to me when I was little."* **Note: this is a very toxic pattern that you need to face and change if you ever want to have a healthy relationship.**

▶ **You need to be in control.** Whether you felt loved by your parents or not, if you felt very controlled as a child by one or both of your parents, you might choose to have a relationship with someone who loves you more than you love them as a way to always feel in control. When your partner is always wanting more from you and feeling more vulnerable than you feel, you have emotional power over them. *This false sense of power at someone's else's expense covers up your own deep sense of powerlessness,* which you must face if you want to have a truly meaningful relationship.

▶ **You're acting out one of your parents' roles with the other.** As I mentioned earlier, if you saw one of your parents being more aloof and distant than the other, you may think that this is what is "normal" in relationships. When you grow up and unconsciously choose which "role" you are going to play, *you choose to be the one who loves less rather than the one who loves more, since that partner doesn't get hurt as much.*

When you are in a relationship like this, you will never be truly satisfied, since you are not giving your heart completely. You may avoid getting hurt, you may convince yourself that you are in control, but you won't be happy. In addition, you will be hurting your partner by continuing to be with them when you cannot give them the love they deserve.

HOW MICHAEL LET GO OF CONTROL AND FOUND HIS TRUE LOVE

Last night as I was working on this chapter of the book, my friend Michael called me. Michael is thirty-five years old and a very talented film producer. We've known each other for many years and seen each other go through all kinds of personal and professional changes. Recently Michael ended a relationship with a twenty-five-year-old woman he'd been living with for several years, a relationship in which she definitely loved him more than he loved her. I had watched Michael agonize over his feelings for Nancy for the past nine months as she pressed him to set a date for their wedding, and he hesitated, so I wasn't surprised when he broke up with her.

Within a few months of leaving Nancy, Michael fell head over heels in love with Terri, a woman he'd known professionally for three years. I wondered if Michael would repeat the pattern he'd lived out with Nancy by holding back in this relationship and loving Terri less than she loved him, but I was happy that he had found someone new.

"Barbara," Michael said on the phone, "I have something to tell you: I've asked Terri to marry me." My mouth hung open in shock: Michael had only been seeing Terri romantically for four months. How could he be so sure that she was right for him?

"Michael," I began, "I'm sitting here at my computer working on the book, and all I think about day and night is what makes relationships work and what makes them fail. Tell me: What made you so sure about Terri after a few months when you lived with Nancy for two years and still couldn't make a commitment?"

Michael was quiet for a moment, and then he began to talk: "Barbara, I've been thinking about the same thing for the past few months. When I look at the women I've chosen in my life, I see a common theme in that **I became involved with women whom I could control.** I didn't see it this way, of course, but I've been attracted to women I would describe as 'soft and vulnerable,' when in truth they were women with low self-esteem who let me control them. Each of them loved me more than I loved them, and I guess part of me liked that—it made me feel powerful and safe. Even though I cared about Nancy, something inside me knew I could never marry her, but I couldn't put my finger on it until I left and met Terri.

"Terri is the only woman I've ever been with whom I could not control. She is powerful and confident, and I think the reason I was never attracted to her, although I've known her for a long time, is that she isn't weak and wimpy inside. Some part of me knew she'd never let me control her, and **I've always been afraid of what I can't control in my life.**

"I've always been afraid of being hurt, so I chose women who didn't have much power over me. But being with Nancy, I learned that when you know you can control someone, it doesn't work in the long run, because you're not happy.

"For the first time in my life I feel completely sure about loving someone. It's scary, because I'm not in control anymore. But I'm in love, and that's much more important."

Solution: When you first get involved with someone, be honest with yourself about whether you are taking more love than you are giving.

Important: Don't delude yourself into believing that your partner would rather have a little of your love than none at all, and use this as an excuse to stay in a relationship you do not belong in.

RELATIONSHIP TYPE

▼　　▼　　▼　　▼　　**3**　　▼　　▼　　▼　　▼

You Are in Love with Your Partner's Potential

"I know Fred has been out of work for a while, but he really is talented, and I know someone will come along and give him the chance he needs."

"I know Brad cares about me—it's just that he has a hard time showing his feelings. I think he needs a few more months with me to believe that I really care before he can open up."

"Sally's mood swings can be really difficult, but no one's ever taken the time to understand what a scared little girl she is inside. I just know that if I give her enough love and support, she'll get out of the depression she is in."

If these statements sound painfully familiar, you probably already know how it feels to be in love with someone's potential. **You aren't in love with who they actually are—you are in love with who you hope they could become.** Until several years ago this was my favorite type of relationship with which to frustrate and hurt myself. I'd find a man who had wonderful potential and then proceed to "help" him develop that potential, whether he asked me to or not. *These weren't really relationships—they were projects.* Was it any wonder that I didn't respect these men? Was it any wonder that after a while I'd find myself "falling out of love" with them? I didn't choose partners because we were compatible; I chose them for their "investment quality"!

These kinds of relationships are highly addictive, because you get hooked into what you wish would happen, and *then it becomes hard to break away.* After all, you never know when that miraculous change in your partner will occur. It's really not that much different from gambling.

------------------------------▼------------------------------

ARE YOU IN LOVE WITH YOUR PARTNER'S POTENTIAL?

Here are some symptoms that may indicate you are in relationship type #3:

▶ You tell yourself that your partner just needs a little more time to get himself and his life together.

▶ You tell yourself that no one has ever really loved your partner enough, that only you can love him enough to change him.

▶ You feel that everyone else misunderstands and underestimates your partner and that only you know the "real" person inside him or her.

▶ You make excuses to your family and friends for your partner's problems or the problems in your relationship.

▶ You feel you can't give up on your partner because it will just validate his feelings of worthlessness, and then he'll never change.

▶ You believe in your partner more than he believes in himself.

▶ You know you aren't getting the love you deserve, but you talk yourself out of your pain about it by telling yourself, "He's trying."

▲

Why You Would Fall in Love with Your Partner's Potential

Here are several reasons why you may be prone to making this relationship mistake:

▶ **You need to be in control.** When you are in a relationship to "improve" your partner, you get to feel superior, and feel some control or power over your partner. *Even if you don't behave in a controlling way, your **thought** that your partner isn't enough as he or she is puts you in a controlling position.* If you felt very controlled by people or circumstances as a child, you may attract partners as an adult to whom you are virtually saying, "You're not quite enough as you are—perhaps with a little work . . ."

▶ **You get to avoid your own life and your own dreams by focusing on what your partner needs to do and how your partner needs to change.** When you're busy looking at how someone else could improve, you don't have much time left over to face your own inadequacies. *Falling in love with someone's potential can be a highly effective method of procrastination.*

▶ **You made a decision as a child that you couldn't get what you wanted.** If you felt rejected or unloved as a child, you may have unconsciously decided that you can't get what you want from the people you love. *Thus you unconsciously seek out people who don't give you what you want—who aren't enough as they are—and you get to feel frustrated and deprived all over again.* This was my motivation in continually finding men whom I tried to fix and improve but who were never fixed enough to give me what I wanted—I got to replay my childhood experience of hoping my father would change and be there for me, and then getting disappointed when he didn't.

Obviously, every relationship between two people involves some hopes and dreams of how you'd like to see your partner grow and improve. The key is feeling satisfied with how your partner is today, not living for the future. As I said in my book *Secrets About Men Every Woman Should Know:*

▼

HAVING A HEALTHY RELATIONSHIP WITH A PERSON MEANS LOVING HIM FOR WHO HE IS NOW, NOT LOVING HIM IN SPITE OF WHO HE IS TODAY, OR IN HOPES OF WHO HE WILL BE TOMORROW.

▲

If you fall in love with someone's potential, you will probably end up feeling:

▶ angry at them for not becoming who you expected them to be
▶ turned off to them sexually since you are acting like their parent, not their lover
▶ bitter that you wasted so much time in the relationship
▶ hurt and let down because your dream of how it was supposed to turn out didn't come true

Solution: If you begin a realtionship with someone, make sure you love, respect, and enjoy that person as he or she is *today.* It's okay to have preferences of how you'd like to see him grow, but he should be enough for you as he is now. **If you keep hoping to change your partner so that you'll be happy with him, you aren't loving, you're gambling.**

RELATIONSHIP TYPE

▼   ▼   ▼   ▼   *4*   ▼   ▼   ▼   ▼

You Are on a Rescue Mission

▶ Do you find yourself feeling sorry for your partner more often than you'd like?

▶ Do you feel responsible for helping your partner get his or her life together?

▶ Do you feel afraid that, if you left, your partner would fall apart emotionally?

If you answered "yes" to any of these questions, you may be a "rescueholic" and not know it. **Rescueholics manage to get into relationships with partners whom they feel compelled to help, rather than partners with whom they feel compatible.** You find someone who seems wounded, fragile, unloved, and feel irresistibly drawn to caring for that person. They feel so grateful, and you feel so noble. Before you know it, you're in a relationship that looks more like a rescue mission than a healthy, balanced love affair. And once you're in it, it's *really* hard to get out.

Are You on a Rescue Mission in Your Relationship?
You may be if:

▶ You are with someone who has *serious emotional, physical, or financial problems*.

▶ Your partner frequently feels *confused, overwhelmed, helpless, or victimized*, and you console, calm down, and encourage.

▶ You often take a *parental role with your partner*—giving advice, warning him or her about possible problems, feeling frustrated when your advice isn't taken, etc.

▶ Your partner has been *mistreated or badly hurt in the past*, and you feel obligated to "make it up" to him or her.

▶ Your partner very *rarely acts as a support system or source of strength for you* as you do for him or her.

▶ You feel you have to *tiptoe around your partner to avoid upsetting him or her,* and consequently you avoid asking for what you want or confronting your partner with things that bother you.

▶ You *tolerate and excuse behavior in your partner* that you would never put up with from a friend or an employee.

▶ When friends and family question why you are involved with your partner, you feel they are picking on him or her, and you *become very protective,* as you would with a child.

▶ You feel like *no one else would understand or love your partner like you do,* and therefore you can't leave.

▶ You secretly wonder whether, if you ended this relationship, your partner would find anyone else or, as you suspect, *would end up unloved and alone.*

─────────────────────────────▲─────────────────────────────

If you can relate to even a few of these statements, you are prone to going on Emotional Rescue Missions. This kind of relationship is similar to type #3, falling in love with your partner's potential, because you hope that in time your partner will improve and change. And as with type #3, it is easy to get hooked into a rescue-type relationship because the *payoff is delayed—you don't know when your partner will get better, and you want to stick around to see it happen, especially after all your hard work!*

This type of relationship is also very different to end, since you will most likely feel you are abandoning your partner and hurting him or her terribly. *The same guilt that got you into the relationship in the first place can keep you in the relationship long after you know you should leave.*

Why You Might Go On Emotional Rescue Missions

▶ **You are completing unfinished business from childhood.** Remember in Chapter Two, when we discussed how we accumulate unfinished emotional business in our childhood that we then play out in our adult lives? If you are an "emotional Robin Hood," always finding partners in need of your help, you may in fact be attempting to rescue Mom, Dad, or another family member. **If you** saw one of your parents or siblings ignored, unloved, or mistreated when you were a child, you will find that person in the form of a partner in need, and will work hard to give him the love, support, and strength you feel you failed to give your family member.

▶ **You need to feel important and superior.** When you choose someone who is a mess, it automatically makes you look better, wiser, and more together. *By playing the hero in a relationship, you get to avoid your own feelings of inadequacy and powerlessness.*

▶ **You need to be in control.** When you are in a relationship with the agenda to "rescue" your partner, you feel some power over your partner. *Sometimes we forget that "helping" can be a very controlling way of relating to others.*

▼

PEOPLE WHO GO ON EMOTIONAL RESCUE MISSIONS OFTEN MISTAKE SYMPATHY FOR LOVE.

▲

HOW MARGO RESCUED HER HUSBAND AS AN EGO BOOST

When I first met Margo, twenty-nine, at one of my seminars, and heard her story, I felt sorry for her. "I'm married to an alcoholic who is in total denial," she stood and shared. "He can't keep a job; I'm the one who has been supporting us the last few years; and on top of that, he is a rageaholic. I don't know what to do."

I knew what Margo should do—leave her husband—and I told her so on the spot. "I know you're right," she said with her face all screwed up, "but if I left him, he'd think I was saying he wasn't good enough."

"Guess what, Margo: He's not good enough for you," I responded firmly.

"Well, he's trying, he really is," she replied with a weak smile.

Over the next few months as I worked with Margo, the situation deteriorated: Her husband spent the money she had saved for rent on an expensive stereo system; he would only talk about their problems if she threatened to leave him; and he would fly into rages. Finally Margo got the courage to ask him to move out to get his life together, and he left. "At last," I thought, "Margo will have a chance to blossom now that she is not taking care of her husband's mess."

That is just what happened. Margo became tremendously empowered living on her own. She looked and felt better than she had in a long time. So I was shocked when she called me one day and told me her husband was moving back in. "What happened?" I asked. "I thought you were going to give him a chance to take care of himself and become responsible." Margo hemmed and hawed and mentioned that her husband had been staying with a friend for a month, and now that the time was up, had no place to go. "We're really going to work on it this time," she insisted.

Margo's husband moved back in, and within days Margo's energy went from passionate and bubbly to tense and protected. I thought long and hard about Margo until I figured out what was going on: **Margo was a control freak. Feeling unloved, inadequate, and frightened of rejection, her method of feeling safe was to be in control. She needed to live with a man who chronically required rescuing because it made her feel competent, in command, and superior. Margo was using him as much as he was using her.**

Like many rescueholics, Margo kept herself busy trying to rehabilitate her husband to avoid her own pain and terror. The only way she will ever leave is if she finds the courage to face the emptiness she carries inside her.

Solution: If you find yourself attracted to someone who has big problems, *ask yourself if you are mistaking sympathy for love.* The key word to remember is **"RESPECT"**—you should feel respect as well as love for your partner, and be proud of who he or she is. Take time to get clear on what your needs are.

RELATIONSHIP TYPE

▼   ▼   ▼   ▼   **5**   ▼   ▼   ▼   ▼

You Look Up to Your Partner as a Role Model

► The young actress who falls in love with her director . . .
► The student in graduate school who falls in love with his professor . . .

► The new salesperson who falls in love with the Marketing Director . . .

► The paralegal who falls in love with the well-known trial lawyer . . .

All of these people may be making the same mistake: **They are putting their partner on a pedestal.** Theirs is not an equal relationship. *The balance of power is inequitable before the relationship even starts because of the lofty status their new partner has in their eyes.*

When you fall in love with someone who is your role model, it is difficult to have a normal relationship. You can act like you are equals; you talk as if you are equals. But if, in your mind, you have given your partner a heightened status, it will prevent you from ever feeling really empowered in the relationship.

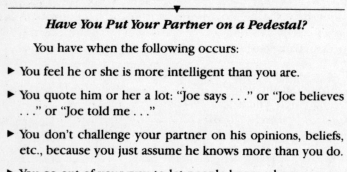

Have You Put Your Partner on a Pedestal?

You have when the following occurs:

► You feel he or she is more intelligent than you are.

► You quote him or her a lot: "Joe says . . ." or "Joe believes . . ." or "Joe told me . . ."

► You don't challenge your partner on his opinions, beliefs, etc., because you just assume he knows more than you do.

► You go out of your way to let people know whom you are involved with in order to impress them.

► You feel there is no way you could ever achieve as much or become as wonderful as your partner.

► You often do things not because you feel they are right but because your partner thinks you should.

► You often say "I am so lucky to be with (name), not just because you love him but because you feel it's some sort of fluke that he chose you!

► You would give anything to be more like your partner.

It's important to emphasize here that it's not the difference in the status of the two partners that makes the relationship fail, but *the **attitudes** of the two partners, one who looks to the other as the role model, and the second who willingly steps up onto the pedestal. It's to okay to be with someone who's smarter, more accomplished, or whatever, as long as both of you maintain your own sense of self.*

Why You Might Fall in Love with Role Models

▶ **You're falling in love with Mom or Dad.** If you never got the kind of attention or love you wanted from one of your parents, *you might attract an authority figure for a partner when you grow older, to finally get the sense of protection and guidance you missed out on as a child.* The opposite can be true as well: If you got a tremendous amount of attention from parents and *were perhaps too emotionally enmeshed with them, you might find it difficult to break away from the parent/child role, especially* **if you felt controlled by them,** and thus attract a powerful figure who treats you as less competent than he or she is and keeps you in a childlike role.

▶ **You are emotionally or spiritually empty.** We talked in Chapter Three about the dangers of choosing love partners when you are feeling empty yourself. *When you have a weak sense of self, you might be attracted to individuals with a particularly powerful sense of self and make them your role models.* But you aren't in love with the persons, and you are in love with their power and self-confidence.

Solution: If you realize you have put your partner on a pedestal, don't expect him or her to step down. You're the one who keeps your partner up there by not respecting your own opinion, not asking for what you want, and not loving yourself enough. **The only way your relationship can work is if you love and admire yourself as much as you love and admire him, and your partner is willing to relinquish his role as your mentor.**

RELATIONSHIP TYPE

▼　　▼　　▼　　▼　　6　　▼　　▼　　▼　　▼

You Are Infatuated with Your Partner for External Reasons

▶ "It was his blue eyes—they just pierced my soul, and I knew I had to have him."

▶ "When I first heard Sam play the guitar, I felt like he knew me inside and out, and our relationship started that night. I've always wanted to fall in love with a musician."

▶ "Ginger's hair was magic—it was long and blond and silky, and when I was with her, it made me feel like I was really a man. That's what made me fall in love with her."

▶ "Jennifer danced like I always imagined my soulmate would, slinky and sexy. When I watched her at that party, I knew we were meant for each other."

▶ "I've always had this fantasy about flight attendants, so when I met Christine, I felt like it was destiny that we got together."

Hair, eyes, dancing ability, musical talent—are these reasons to start a relationship with someone? The answer is obviously no, yet many of us become infatuated with partners because of something about them that has little to do with their true character, and more to do with their external qualities. These relationships usually don't last long. After all, how many hours can you spend staring at your girlfriend's hair, or listening to your boyfriend play the guitar before you want more? *But I've met many people who have gotten into this type of relationship for a night, a week, even a few months, only to discover that they were really kidding themselves.* Then they are stuck with someone they really don't want to be with and are faced with the unpleasant task of breaking this news to their partner. How do you tell someone you were infatuated with them without sounding like an idiot?

"Ginger, you are a really sweet person, but as much as I'm madly in love with your hair, it's just not enough to keep me interested in you for the next forty years."

THE SPELL OF THE JUGGLER

Here is a story from my own life I think you'll enjoy:

In 1974 I was living in Mill Valley, just outside San Francisco, finishing up my bachelor's degree. I was twenty-three and very excited to be living in a part of the country where there was so much artistic and psychological experimentation. One of my favorite yearly events was the Renaissance Faire, in which a forest is transformed into an Elizabethan village and everyone roams the grounds in costume. **It was on one such "faire" day that I came under the spell of the juggler.**

I was walking by a grove of trees when I saw a crowd forming around a young man who began to juggle balls, clubs, lit torches, and anything else he had with him. I stood spellbound as I watched his graceful sensuality, dancing and laughing as he entertained the crowd. He had long, dark hair and an earring in his ear—I was in love!

I spent the rest of that day following him around, mesmerized by his personal magic. I left the fair that night determined to find out who he was and to get to know him. I begged some of my friends who worked at the fair to introduce me to him, and the next day, they did. I felt like I was walking on air. We spent the afternoon together, and promised to meet again the next day.

For the rest of the summer and throughout the fall, I was his number one groupie. I went everywhere he went—I couldn't believe I was with this incredible artist, this sensitive soul who would understand me as I did him.

HOW THE SPELL WAS BROKEN

I won't go into the embarrassing details of my disastrous attempts to consummate my relationship with him except to say that *after spending one night with him I came back to reality really fast.* Driving home, I wept tears of anger and disappointment. How could my knight in shining armor, my sensitive artistic muse have been so cold, so uncaring? In my heart, I knew the answer: **I wasn't in love with him, I was in love with his juggling, his presence, when he performed. I took one special quality he had and** *projected other qualities onto him* **that I thought someone like him should have.** *He wasn't any of the things I'd imagined. I had been under a spell of my own making.*

Let me pass on this warning from one who's made this relationship mistake:

If you ever find yourself infatuated with one element of a new partner's personality, ask yourself: "if this person didn't have [blue eyes, gorgeous hair, a great voice] or wasn't [a juggler, a basketball player, a flight attendant, etc.], would I still want to be with him [or her]? Be honest with yourself. It could save you a lot of heartache and disappointment.

RELATIONSHIP TYPE

▼   ▼   ▼   ▼   7   ▼   ▼   ▼   ▼

You Have Partial Compatibility

Have you ever met someone with whom you didn't have much in common—except for one area in which you really connected? This kind of relationship can be very deceptive, **especially when the way in which you are compatible is so important to you that you mistake what is simply a powerful bond for love.**

Here are some examples of partial compatibility:

▶ **You meet your partner through a cycling club. You love cycling,** and are excited at first to share this hobby with a partner who feels the same way. You spend every weekend biking for hours on end. *But after two months of cycling and sex, you realize you don't have much else in common, and it's causing the relationship to be very rocky.*

▶ **You and your partner are thrown together on a project at work. The project requires long hours and teamwork, and in the middle of it you feel like you're falling in love.** For four months you have a passionate affair and spend most of your time talking about the project, sharing your ideas. Then the project is complete, and within a few weeks you begin to feel uncomfortable with one another. *Your common bond has been removed, and you are left alone with the fact that, outside of work, you don't share any of the same values or beliefs.*

▶ **You spend part of your summer renting a house with some friends by the beach in a resort town, and a few weeks into your vacation, you meet someone there.** For the next month you have a blast, taking long bike rides in the mornings and making barbecues on the grill at night. You've never felt so relaxed with anyone before, and when the vacation is over, you have no doubt that your relationship will continue back in the city. But you are wrong. Your first weekend away from the beach is a disaster. You can't agree on anything; you are getting on each other's nerves, and within a week you end the relationship. *Looking back you realize you'd never seen your partner under stress, and that once you did, he wasn't the same person you knew over the summer.*

You are susceptible to getting involved with this type of relationship when:

► You meet your partner under unusual circumstances that are different from those in your daily life or routine (stuck in an elevator, in physical therapy, etc.).

► You and your partner are thrown together with an activity or focus that is somewhat out of the ordinary (working on a special project, attending a seminar, serving on a committee).

► You meet your partner in an unusual environment (vacation, jury duty, etc.).

► You meet your partner during a time when you are both focused on an activity you don't participate in on a daily or frequent basis (skiing, ballroom dance classes, etc.).

You don't need a grasp of any great psychological secrets to understand the phenomenon of partial compatibility. *Like attracts like,* and it's natural for you to feel drawn to individuals with whom you have something significant in common, even if you share that bond for only a week or two. And often that initial connection *can* be the basis for what turns into a lasting and fulfilling relationship. Two cyclists won't necessarily lose interest after a few months— they may find out they are compatible in many other areas as well. Someone you meet on a ski trip or at the beach may not be just a vacation romance but also could turn out to have all of the qualities you are looking for.

The danger, however, is in becoming so infatuated with that area of partial compatibility that you don't pay attention to the rest of the relationship. This sets you up to get involved with people you normally wouldn't end up with at all, only to feel let down and disappointed when the relationship doesn't work out.

MY FRENCH FANTASY THAT FLOPPED

You may have figured out by now that the reason I know so much about these relationship mistakes is that I've made most of them myself. Here's another story from my past that is a perfect example of the problems that come with partial compatibility:

In 1975 I was still living in Mill Valley but was enrolled in a six-week meditation course in Avoriaz, France, in the French Alps. There, with about a hundred other men and women, I spent eight to ten hours a day meditating, doing Yoga and breathing exercises, all designed to purify my nervous system and expand my consciousness.

I was living in a hotel that had been turned into our meditation academy for the summer, and was run by a young Frenchman, Jean-Pierre. Three weeks into the course, I noticed Jean-Pierre for the first time—**he was handsome, friendly, drove a Jeep, and, most important of all, *he was French!*** What more evidence did I need to have the fantasy love affair with a Frenchman that I'd always dreamed about?

Jean-Pierre spoke some English, and I spoke fairly fluent French, so our communication was pretty good, though limited. It didn't really matter, because most of our time together was spent riding through the mountains in his Jeep or French kissing in the true sense of the phrase. We spent three glorious weeks together, and were both so sad when it was time for me to go back to the States. Jean-Pierre promised me he would come to visit the first chance he got, and I could hardly wait.

About a month after I returned to San Francisco, I received a letter from Jean-Pierre saying he had three weeks off and was coming to see me. I was so excited—the thought of my French boyfriend in California seemed too good to be true. It was.

I'll never forget what happened when I was at the airport gate, watching the passengers get off, and I spotted Jean-Pierre wearing the same green rubber raincoat he wore in the mountains. As he waved and started toward me, I thought, "That is the dumbest-looking coat I've ever seen." And as Jean-Pierre reached out to give me a kiss he'd traveled seven thousand miles to get, I had a sinking feeling that things weren't going to turn out the way I'd planned.

The closer we got to my apartment, the more panicky I felt. And as we sat on my couch and drank some tea, it hit me: *Jean-Pierre was here, but France wasn't. There were no mountains, no Jeep, no French shops and French culture.* **When Jean-Pierre was removed from his environment, my interest in him all but disappeared.**

I hardly knew Jean-Pierre. I wasn't in love with him; I was in love with France. I was horrified at my reaction, but try as I might, I couldn't get the feeling back. I'd left in Avoriaz along with the croissants and Camembert.

Poor Jean-Pierre! I tried explaining my feelings to him, but I'm sure I did a terrible job. Only years later, when I began to do some serious work on myself, did I realize that my relationship with Jean-Pierre was a perfect example of partial compatibility. Jean-Pierre was a really nice guy, but not what I'd imagined him to be. *The magic of my feelings came not from the person himself but from the circumstances surrounding our meeting.*

Solution: If you meet someone in one of the circumstances I described earlier, try to step back from the relationship and ask yourself the following questions:

► **"How much do I really know about this person aside from our area of partial compatibility?"**

► **"What are my needs and requirements for a partner? Does this person meet them?"**

► **"What possible problems could occur if my partner and I no longer shared this area of partial compatibility?"**

If you take the time to answer these questions, you'll be less likely to get hurt yourself, or unintentionally hurt your partner.

What if you are just looking for a summer romance, or a French fling? If that's your goal, then enjoy yourself, but be careful. And remember, in the end, there's nothing as magical or exciting as love that lasts.

RELATIONSHIP TYPE

▼　　▼　　▼　　▼　　**8**　　▼　　▼　　▼　　▼

You Choose a Partner in Order to Be Rebellious

Here's an exercise for you: *Make a list of all of the qualities your parents or family would want you to find in a mate. Then, next to that, make a list of all of the qualities in your partner.* **If the two lists are diametrically opposed, you maybe in a relationship as a way of rebelling against your parents, not because you are with the right person.**

This relationship type isn't as common as the others, but it can create tremendous drama in your life. Here's what I'm talking about:

► Your parents are *conservative white people* and you've had three *black boyfriends.*

► Your parents are Jewish and have always *insisted you marry a Jewish girl,* and you only go out with *Catholic women, or vice versa.*

► Your parents always emphasized the importance of *money and prestige,* and your partners are always *broke and anti-establishment types.*

► Your parents always insisted on order and discipline in your house, and all of the woman you get involved with are total slobs.

► Your father brought you up believing that the family lineage was everything, and you continue to fall in love with women who do not want or cannot have children.

► Your father is in the military, and all your boyfriends have been peace and environmental activists.

► You were brought up with strict religious discipline, and all your partners tend to be wild, immoral, and irreverent.

By now, you get the picture. **Some people choose partners based not on who is right for them, but on who is wrong for their family.** This will be especially true if:

You have a lot of resentment and bitterness toward one or more of your parents, or felt very controlled as a child.

You tend to choose the same types of "unacceptable" partners over and over again.

You stay in relationships that aren't particularly fulfilling rather than break them off and have your parents point out that they were right all along.

The point here is *not* that relationships between people of different backgrounds can't work. (Chapter Seven will talk more about some of the problems you might face in that situation.) **But if you have a pattern of choosing partners who not only don't fulfill you but also upset your family, you are probalby acting out of rebellion.**

HOW BRENDA USED THE MEN IN HER LIFE TO GET BACK AT HER PARENTS

Brenda's story is a classic case of this type of relationship. Brenda is a thirty-three-year-old art historian who comes from a conservative Jewish background. From the time Brenda was a small girl, her parents told her that she was "expected" to grow up and marry a nice Jewish boy. Along with this, Brenda's father was very strict and old-fashioned in his ways. Brenda loved her parents, though she feared her father's disapproval, and didn't date much in high school.

All that changed when Brenda left New York to go to college. Suddenly she found she was interested in men, and within two months had her first love affair—with a black law student. Brenda never even considered telling her parents about him, and when the relationship ended shortly, she felt tremendous relief. Her relief was short-lived. Three weeks later, she met a man at a fraternity party and ended up spending the night with him—another black man.

In four years of college, Brenda had several relationships, all with black men, none of whom was Jewish, and none of whom her parents knew about. After she graduated, Brenda moved back to New York to pursue her master's, and that's where she met Edward— a black art history major enrolled in the same program she was. This time it was serious, and soon Edward and Brenda moved in together. For two years, Brenda tried to hide the relationship from her parents, but finally gave up and blurted it out during a phone call. *Her parents reacted as she had expected them to—they stopped talking to her for three months, and when they finally restored contact, they refused to discuss "what's-his-name."*

A year later, Edward and Brenda broke up. Brenda threw herself into her work, landing a prestigious job at one of New York's finest museums. Her friends would try to fix her up with men, some Jewish, some not, but she'd lose interest after a few dates. On Brenda's thirty-first birthday, her coworkers from the museum threw her a party, and that's where she met Robert, an art professor who was *black, Baptist, and married.*

I met Brenda when she attended my Making Love Work Seminar. She'd read my books and desperately needed help. She was still in love with Robert; he still hadn't left his wife. And she'd written her parents a letter about him, which they responded to by pretending she hadn't mentioned it. "I'm so confused," she confessed. "I know I'm stuck in some kind of pattern, but I don't understand anything about it."

I asked Brenda to make a list like the one I mentioned earlier. This is what she came up with:

WHAT MY PARENTS WANT FOR ME	WHAT I END UP WITH
White	Black
Jewish	Catholic, Baptist, other Christian
Single	Unable to commit or married
Successful	Successful sometimes

"It's pretty transparent, isn't it?" she said with a wry smile.

"Yes, it is," I answered.

"You know, I've never thought it about this way, but if I'm honest with myself, I have to admit that I secretly like knowing that what I'm doing in my life drives my parents crazy. But I love them. So why am I trying to hurt them?"

"You're not trying to hurt your parents as much as you're trying to define yourself as separate and distinct from them. It may not even be a conscious decision to rebel. *If fulfilling your own desires would, in any way, make it appear that you had conformed to your parents' wishes, then, in your unconscious mind, you would have "lost" the power struggle.* **By unconsciously rebelling against them, you're declaring your autonomy (but in an unhealthy way)."**

Solution: If you suspect you have a pattern of choosing partners in order to be rebellious, you need to get to a place where you can reconcile your need to be independent from your desire to find a relationship that may be just what your parents want for you. Once you're free from your need to rebel, you may fall in love with whomever—black, white, Jewish, etc.—**but you'll be doing it out of choice, not out of compulsion.** I suggest you seek professional counseling to help you understand and release the deep childhood programming that is running your love life.

RELATIONSHIP TYPE

▼   ▼   ▼   ▼   9   ▼   ▼   ▼   ▼   ▼

───

You Choose a Partner as a Reaction to Your Previous Partner

I think we've all made this mistake at one time or another: **You end a relationship with someone and, for your next partner, you don't just choose someone different, but someone who is the complete opposite of your previous partner.** For instance:

▶ Your ex-husband was boring and predictable; your new boyfriend is wild and irresponsible.

▶ Your ex-boyfriend was unambitious and professionally passive; your new boyfriend is a workaholic who cares more about money than he does about you.

▶ Your ex-girlfriend was needy, clingy, and overly dependent; your new girlfriend has a hard time opening up and keeps you guessing.

▶ Your ex-wife was loyal, loving, but prudish and uncomfortable with her sexuality; your new girlfriend is an uninhibited, raunchy sex maniac.

This tendency to swing from one extreme to the other is the result of a sort of primitive way in which we communicate with our unconscious mind. It's as if you say to your brain, *"Boy, was I miserable with him. He never made any money; he never even worked hard. What a wimp! I never want to go through that again."* Your mind, like a faithful servant, takes in that information and reprograms itself:

"Old choice had no money, no drive, no aggression. New choice must have money, drive, aggression. Reprogramming complete."

Then you go out and find yourself wildly attracted to someone who is successful and materialistic, works twelve hours a day and is highly aggressive. For a while, you're in heaven. "My new boyfriend is so wonderful," you brag to your friends. "He's everything my ex wasn't." But one day you'll realize that your new love is too aggressive, too materialistic, and too work-addicted, and that you're not happy. That's when you feel like giving up on relationships and buying a dog.

There's nothing wrong with looking for qualities your last relationship was lacking. It's only natural that the most important things on your mind when selecting a new partner will be those areas you were most dissatisfied with in the old partner. **The mistake you make is in looking *only* for those missing qualities, rather than making them an important but incomplete part of an entire wish list of characteristics you want in a mate.**

FROM SWEETNESS TO SLEAZE: MARVIN'S STORY

Marvin, a forty-six-year-old salesman, epitomizes this relationship pattern. He met Shirley, his first wife, when he had just graduated from high school. Marvin was eighteen, Shirley seventeen. "My family loved Shirley," Marvin told me. 'She was perfect wife material—kind, loving, polite. I didn't have much experience with girls, and to tell you the truth, I felt flattered that Shirley seemed to care for me so much. Two years later we were married, and on my wedding day I was sure I'd made a great choice.

"The problems started on our honeymoon. Shirley was a virgin and didn't seem to enjoy sex that much. I didn't know much more than she did, and I figured with practice, she'd warm up. But she didn't. It's not that she refused to have sex with me—I don't think Shirley ever said no in her life. She was a devoted wife and a terrific mother, but as a lover, Shirley didn't satisfy me at all. *She even told me once that if we never had sex again, she wouldn't miss it!*"

"I hung in there for fifteen years and three kids, but finally I couldn't take it anymore. For years I'd fantasized about other women. I never cheated, but I came real close. Right after my fortieth birthday, something snapped, and I packed my bags and left. Oh, I felt sad, all right. *But I also felt like I could breathe again.*

"Four nights later I went out to a bar and met Darla. I couldn't take my eyes off her. She was the sexiest thing I'd ever seen. We talked and danced for a few hours, and then she invited me over to her place. We made love all night long. I felt like I'd died and gone to heaven.

"I was the happiest man alive. I felt bad for Shirley and the kids, but I was having such a damn good time. Darla was wild—she wanted me morning, noon, and night. Then one day Darla asked me what my intentions were. I figured she was kidding, so I grabbed her and said she could guess, but she pulled away and said she wanted to get married. I hadn't thought about it, but it made sense. We were happy, we had fun. What else was there? The next weekend, we flew to Vegas and got married.

"After that, everything started to unravel. It began the night I invited my daughters out to dinner to meet Darla. She'd picked an outfit I thought was a little provocative. 'You always loved this dress!' she yelled. And she was right. *But somehow because I was seeing her through my daughters' eyes, Darla suddenly looked cheap and trampy.* **I felt like I'd woken up from a dream.** Her party attitude and fun personality suddenly irritated me, and she seemed loud and disrespectful. Believe it or not, I started comparing her unfavorably to Shirley. That's when I knew I was in trouble. Two months later, I left.

"I've been alone since. I feel so confused. I don't know what I want. I even wonder if I was wrong to leave Shirley." *Marvin rebounded from Shirley, an asexual mother stereotype, to Darla, a whorish bad-girl stereotype.* **He was so intent on getting what he didn't get from Shirley that he looked only for that quality and no others.** His healing will come in learning to get in touch with what he really needs and wants, and looking for a partner who is balanced in what she can offer him.

Solution: *If you've come out of a particularly unsatisfying or frustrating relationship,* **be extra cautious about rebounding to a partner who is the opposite of the one you just left.** Discover *all* of the qualities you need in a mate, and look for a relationship that is balanced.

RELATIONSHIP TYPE

▼   ▼   ▼   ▼   **10**   ▼   ▼   ▼   ▼

Your Partner Is Unavailable

I've saved this type of relationship for last because in many ways, by definition, it's not a relationship at all.

The first requirement you should have for a partner is that *he is available*. For those of us who like to pretend we don't know what available means, here's a definition:

Available: Free to be in a relationship with you; not involved with anyone else; not married; not engaged; not going steady; not sleeping with another person; alone; single; all yours.

The following are *not* definitions of available:
▶ With someone, but promises to leave soon
▶ With someone, but he doesn't really love her
▶ With someone, but they're not having sex anymore
▶ With someone, but says he's just staying for the kids
▶ With someone, but she knows about you and it's all right
▶ With someone and isn't leaving, but wants you to stick around anyway
▶ Just left someone, but might be going back

In other words,

STAY AWAY FROM PEOPLE WHO ARE MARRIED OR IN OTHER RELATIONSHIPS!

I don't care what the circumstances or excuses are, the result will be the same: *You are going to get your heart broken.*

You may be prone to choosing unavailable partners if:

▶ **You felt abandoned by a parent as a child.** You repeat this pattern as an adult by *finding partners who can't be there for you either.*

▶ **You have low self-esteem.** If you came from a very dysfunctional home that left you with little self-esteem, *you may feel you don't deserve to have a mate all to yourself, so you'll take whatever you can get.*

▶ **You're afraid of intimacy.** Being in a relationship with a partner who is unavailable is a great way to avoid true intimacy. *If you were sexually of physically abused as a child and had your boundaries violated, or made a decision when you were young that you would never let anyone get close enough to hurt you again, you may find it "convenient" to choose partners with whom you can never have a truly committed relationship as an unconscious method of protecting yourself from pain.*

Solution: If you meet someone and feel strongly toward him, but he is married or involved, it doesn't mean you will never be together. It does mean you should say:

"I care about you very much, but I have a rule—I never get involved with someone who is with another person. If you leave the relationship, please let me know."

If you are involved with someone who is married or in a relationship, you should find the courage to say:

"I love you very much, but what we are doing is not healthy for anyone, and I love myself too much to let myself be treated this way. I can't see you anymore. If you leave your partner, call me and let me know."

Don't forget:

▼

WHEN YOU GET INVOLVED WITH SOMEONE WHO IS IN A RELATIONSHIP WITH ANOTHER PERSON, YOU ARE ACCEPTING THAT PERSON'S LEFTOVERS.

▲

You deserve better than that!

After reading about these ten types of relationships that don't work, you may be wondering if there are any kinds of relationships left! Take it from me, there are—healthy, loving relationships in which you love your partner not because you feel sorry for him, or want him to take care of you, or are in love with his potential, *but because he is fulfilling your emotional needs.* We'll talk more about how to tell it you're with the right person in Chapters Eight through Twelve, so you can create the kind of relationship that does work!

6

▼▼▼

FATAL FLAWS

▼▼▼

If you want to learn a great lesson in making sure you are with the right partner, spend a few hours in the produce section of your local supermarket watching the shoppers choose fruits and vegetables. A woman carefully examines the bananas: First she looks at their color—she wants to make sure they aren't too ripe, but they can't be too green, either. Then she turns them around to see if she can spot any bruises. Finally she holds the bunch in her hand and compares it to others, making sure she gets the right amount of bananas. Only then does she place it in her basket.

This shopper is taking her time buying her groceries because **she is trying to avoid buying flawed produce. She wants the best, and she's trained herself to notice the flaws so she can purchase better merchandise.**

This chapter is about flaws, not the kinds you'll find in fruits or vegetables, but the kinds you will encounter in people you choose for partners in a relationship. *I call these "Fatal Flaws," those characteristics in a person that can make a relationship anything from challenging all the way up to a nightmare.*

IMPORTANT: If someone you love has one or more of these traits, it does not necessarily mean he is incapable of having a relationship. It does mean that those "character flaws" will cause problems in your relationship that could be fatal to its longevity.

None of us is perfect, and it's obvious that we each have flaws or imperfections that affect our love life. But some of these characteristics are much more dangerous and destructive to our relationships than others, and those are the Fatal Flaws I'll talk about in this chapter.

▼

FATAL FLAWS TO WATCH OUR FOR IN A PARTNER

1. **Addictions**
2. **Anger**
3. **Victim consciousness**
4. **Control freak**
5. **Sexual dysfunction**
6. **Hasn't grown up**
7. **Emotionally unavailable**
8. **Hasn't recovered from past relationships**
9. **Emotional damage from childhood**

▲

FATAL FLAW

▼　　▼　　▼　　▼　　1　　▼　　▼　　▼　　▼

Addictions

Don't lie to yourself: When you get involved with a person who has an addiction, you are playing with fire, and you will probably get burned. Pretty strong way to start off a chapter, hmm? Well, let me explain. I have spent years listening to horror stories from people who loved someone with an addiction. I have watched them get their hearts broken and their families destroyed, and after a while I feel like saying, "I told you so: If you put your hand into a fire, you will get burned. If you walk in front of a moving car, you will get hit. *If you love an alcoholic or a drug addict or any other sort of user, you will get hurt.* It is inevitable." There's no polite or sensitive way to say it, and if you are an addict (we'll talk about what that is soon), I offer you no apologies for this section. **You need to hear it, because you are hurting the people you love.**

How Addictions Can Hurt Your Relationships

The physiological harm that addictive substances cause is well documented, but you need to understand the emotional harm as well. The first problem is:

▼

WHEN YOU LOVE SOMEONE WITH AN ADDICTION, YOU ARE IN A LOVE TRIANGLE—YOU, YOUR PARTNER, AND WHATEVER HE IS ADDICTED TO.

▲

If your partner has an addiction, he is in love with something other than you—the alcohol, the drugs, etc. **He is, in effect, cheating on you.** *That substance is your rival—it will take his time, his attention, and his spirit away from you.* You will end up hating it as much as you would hate another woman, or if you're male, another man.

Here's the second point: **Loving an addict also means loving someone who is a slave**—he is enslaved to drugs, alcohol, sexual addictions, gambling, or some activity that has become his master. Technically there are dozens of things one can get addicted to, from gambling to shopping to caffeine to cigarettes, which affect the individuals who use them but don't usually have as devastating an effect on relationships as drugs and alcohol, so I've chosen to focus on those two.

▼

WHEN YOU LOVE SOMEONE WITH AN ADDICTION, YOU ARE LOVING SOMEONE WHO IS NOT A FREE PERSON.

▲

You will have a hard time getting an addict to admit he is a slave, because he is controlled by the activity or substance that is his master, and he *will cover up that sense of impotence with **denial**.* To admit he is addicted would mean admitting he has been power-less, a frightening and humbling experience. This is what is so horrifying about addictions—they remove your desire to be addiction-free.

The third negative effect addictions have on your relationship is that they interfere with your partner's ability to be intimate with you. Addictive substances numb one's ability to feel. That's one of the reasons people drink the alcohol or smoke the joint—they don't like how they feel and want to feel better, only "better" means more numb. When one gets drunk or high, he's oblivious to much of what is happening outside and inside himself. This habit of emotional numbness will make it difficult for your partner to feel as much as you'd like him to.

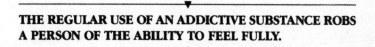

THE REGULAR USE OF AN ADDICTIVE SUBSTANCE ROBS A PERSON OF THE ABILITY TO FEEL FULLY.

Loving Someone Who Loves Alcohol

Alcoholics are not just people who stumble along the street with their liquor hidden in a paper bag. Alcoholics are not just people who get so drunk that it's obvious they have been drinking. *Alcoholics are people who need alcohol to function, and to whom alcohol is a consistent part of their life.*

An alcoholic may use alcohol all day long, but an alcoholic is also the person who has a few drinks after work every night. *Just because you don't drink during the day doesn't mean you are not an alcoholic.* And just because you don't drink hard liquor doesn't mean you aren't an alcoholic, either. Wine and beer count, too.

Then there are the **weekend alcoholics,** the most insidious group, because their behavior fits into what is socially acceptable. They don't drink during the week, but when they go out on weekends, consuming alcohol is a large part of their activity—the person who has several drinks every time she goes on a date or to a party; the guy who shares a few six-packs with his buddies watching sports on TV; the couple who shares a bottle of wine or champagne every Saturday night before they make love.

One beer on the weekend doesn't make someone an alcoholic. A few beers after work every night does. One glass of wine with dinner once or twice a week doesn't make someone an alcoholic. A few glasses of wine each evening does.

The problem with noticing that someone is an alcoholic is that *we live in a society where substance abuse is normal, even chic, and controlled alcoholism, in particular, is acceptable.* I cringe each time I get on an airplane and watch the flight attendants offer liquor to passengers along with soft drinks, as if they are the same thing. I watched part of a football game on TV with my boyfriend this past Sunday and counted dozens of beer commercials. At first it was hard to tell they were beer commercials at all—I saw shots of healthy places like the beach, the mountains, national parks, and good-looking young people engaged in athletic activities. Then they show the beer. And what do we bring friends when we visit their home? A bottle of wine or champagne. We even celebrate our friends when they reach the legal drinking age, as if they have achieved some wonderful feat!

You may be thinking, "Oh, come on, it's not that bad," but I couldn't disagree more. *I can't tell you how many thousands of letters I receive every year and how many phone calls I got on my radio talk show from people whose relationships were destroyed by their partner's drinking.* The majority of these people who drink are in such complete denial that **they don't even think they have a problem.** That's the scariest part.

If you love someone who drinks, be prepared to deal with the possibility of:

- ▶ inconsistent and unpredictable behavior
- ▶ outbursts of anger and violence
- ▶ consistent depression
- ▶ irresponsibility
- ▶ emotional deadness
- ▶ emotional unavailability
- ▶ lack of sexual desire or inability to perform properly
- ▶ fighting and bickering
- ▶ frequent "bad moods"
- ▶ lots of ups and downs in the relationship

GAIL'S BATTLE WITH HER BOYFRIEND'S BOTTLE

Gail, thirty-two, called me on my radio talk show seeking advice about her relationship with Danny, thirty-six. "Help me, Barbara," Gail cried on the phone. "I don't know what to do. I love Danny very much, but our relationship has gotten to be so painful, and I feel trapped." Gail explained that when she met Danny, "He was funny and warm and sensitive, and I felt like he was 'the one.' We fell in love right away. I couldn't believe how much we had in common. Everything seemed great until about six months into the relationship. Danny never drank that much, mostly on weekends, and it didn't really bother me. But all of a sudden he started drinking more on weeknights when we'd be together, and he'd get really irritable, and soon we'd be fighting. I've tried everything—walking out of the room; trying to reason with him; agreeing with him; fighting back. But in the end, he blows up and leaves. The next day he'll call and apologize and say he's under pressure at work, or worried about his bills, and he's so sweet I forgive him. But it's been going on for months now, and I can't take the verbal abuse anymore."

"Gail, do you realize that Danny is an alcoholic?" I asked.

"Well, I wouldn't say that. He doesn't ever really get drunk or anything," she responded sheepishly.

"Gail, I want you to listen closely. Danny is an alcoholic. *Unless he stops drinking, he'll continue to act this way. Nothing you can do will make a difference. You are not the problem. His drinking is the problem."*

Gail began to weep. "I've tried to talk to him about drinking less, but he tells me to stop policing his behavior, and says it's not the problem."

"That's called DENIAL, Gail," I answered. **"If you love him, you will insist that he get some help; if he doesn't, and you love yourself, you will leave."**

My heart ached for Gail. *Like many codependents who love someone with an addiction, she felt responsible for Danny's behavior and believed if she changed, he would stop drinking.* The only hope for their relationship was Danny going into recovery and facing his addiction. The saddest part was that **Gail could have avoided her pain if she had paid attention to Danny's drinking in the beginning of the relationship, instead of making excuses for it.** By not talking about it until it became a big problem, she missed an opportunity to prevent it from becoming worse.

What You Can Do

If you are single: When you meet someone, *determine his or her values and habits regarding alcohol from the very first date.* Watch his behavior carefully, and don't delude yourself or make excuses for him. *Don't compromise your beliefs or values to accommodate to your partner's addiction.*

If you are in a relationship and suspect your partner has a drinking problem: If, after reading this section, you suspect your partner is an alcoholic and realize you've been avoiding facing it, **deal with it** *now.* **Give your partner an ultimatum: Either he**

or she gets help and deals with the alcoholism, or the relationship is over. That may seem harsh, but any professional will tell you that patience, understanding, and love will not help someone stop drinking. No one is ever "ready" to stop. It is never "easy." There is no "right time." These are all *excuses; it's DENIAL talking.*

Think of it this way: If your partner had a sudden heart attack, you'd insist he get help. You wouldn't let him talk you out of it, because you love him. Well, your partner *is* sick. He needs help. **Love him enough to insist that he get it, and if he won't, love yourself enough to leave, because it is only going to get worse.**

Al-Anon, a twelve-step recovery group for families and friends of alcoholics, is a good place for you to get support for yourself as you go through this process.

If you are the one with the drinking problem: If, after reading this section, you feel ready to admit that *you* may have a problem, **your first step is to get some help.** Reach out to your friends and family and tell them you will need their support in your recovery. **Don't forget,** *facing the pain that caused the behavior is where your real healing begins.*

Loving Someone Who Uses Illegal Drugs

Everything I said about alcohol is also true about drugs, but even more so, for several reasons: **Drugs are illegal, and drugs are expensive.** Loving someone who uses drugs means you may have to face additional problems. I've seen a family's entire savings drained by a cocaine-using husband. I've seen a woman steal from her boyfriend to support her crack habit. I've seen a wife's dream shattered when the police came to the house to arrest her husband for using and selling amphetamines.

In many ways, drugs are more dangerous than alcohol because they affect your nervous system more powerfully. Alcohol disappears from your bloodstream within twenty-four hours. However, blood tests can detect traces of drugs in your system for up to three months. *That means, for three months after using a drug, it is still altering your body chemistry and therefore affecting your ability to think, behave, and feel.*

The one drug I want to single out is marijuana. **Don't kid yourself about pot: Consistent use will render you emotionally and intellectually dull and devoid of passion.** The problem with marijuana is it appears to be relatively harmless, and its proponents claim it is no different from having a drink. They are wrong. The long-term effects of smoking marijuana are subtle but powerful. *It can diminish memory, create lethargy, and interfere with communication from one part of the brain to another, which hinders clear thinking. Emotionally, long-term marijuana smokers have a sort of permanent "What, me worry?" attitude, which they may describe as being "laid back" but on closer inspection is actually emotional numbness.*

I'm not talking about someone who smoked pot a few times a month during college (although that will still create the other problems mentioned earlier). I'm talking about people for whom smoking pot is part of their life, something they do every day, or every weekend, for years.

HOW POT KEPT KARA'S HUSBAND FROM GROWING UP

Kara called me on the radio to get some guidance for her failing marriage. She was thirty-eight, and her husband, Nick, was thirty-nine. Nick was lazy and irresponsible, couldn't remember to pay the bills, hated working, continually lost his jobs, and was emotionally distant and detached. "I feel like Nick's mother," Kara complained. "I can't count on him for anything."

"Do you have any idea why Nick behaves this way?" I asked.

"Yes," Kara answered quietly. "I just haven't wanted to face it. *It's his pot smoking.* He smokes all the time. When we first met, in our twenties, we both smoked at parties and on weekends. I stopped when I enrolled in nursing school, but Nick never did. He says it relaxes him at the end of the day and that he does it for a treat on the weekends. *The truth is, it numbs him out completely.* I don't think he feels much of anything. And when he's high, I feel like he's far away. Our sex life is just about nonexistent. He doesn't care about sex anymore, or about anything else, for that matter. When I try to talk to him about our problems, he tells me to stop being obsessive and chill out. Well, I can't! For years I've tried to ignore it, but it's gotten to the point where I am so angry I could scream!"

Nick's addiction to marijuana had made him emotionally dysfunctional and kept him in a state of permanent lethargy, preventing him from growing up. I have seen this pattern many times. Some people, like Kara, are aware that chronic pot smoking is the source of the problem. Others are surprised when I make the connection, having believed, as many do, that marijuana is harmless.

Kara and Nick's story had a happy ending. Months later I

received a letter from Kara, telling me she had confronted Nick that night and threatened to leave unless he faced his addiction and got some help. He agreed, more out of fear than a desire to change, at first. But with professional help, he stopped smoking pot.

"I didn't notice a big change at first," Kara wrote, *"Then slowly, Nick began to come alive. He was sleeping less, working harder, and his sex drive was returning. That's when he realized how addicted he'd been, and after that he was like a changed man. Thank you, Barbara, for the kick in the pants I needed."*

UNFIT FOR LOVE

I feel fortunate that I have never had a relationship with someone addicted to drugs, but I've experienced the pain that comes from knowing drugs have stolen your partner's ability to feel and be present with you. Years ago I ended a very intense and difficult relationship, partially because I didn't feel my partner loved me the way I deserved to be loved. Months after we broke up, we met at a restaurant to talk about what happened between us and do some more healing. I remember sitting across the table from him, putting a forkful of pasta into my mouth, when he said, **"You know, Barbara, I smoked dope when we were together."** I went into complete shock. How could that be? I had lived with this man; he knew how I felt about regular drug use. How could he have been smoking dope without my knowing it?

He proceeded to tell me about the times we'd been away on vacation, and he'd procured marijuana from someone and been stoned, or the times he would smoke it for three straight days at home. *"You always knew something was wrong,"* he confessed. *"You'd accuse me of being distant and detached, and whenever I'd smoke I'd always pick fights with you and my sex drive would disappear."* All of a sudden, it made sense—the times when we'd be away at some beautiful beachside resort and he would be in a lousy mood for days on end; the sudden mood changes when he would become argumentative and difficult for no apparent reason; the feeling I had so often that he just wasn't there. I was relieved to know the cause of his behavior.

When I look back on this, I feel very angry. I'm angry that someone I loved was choosing to alter his consciousness without informing me. I'm angry that he used drugs to numb himself when I was begging him to feel more. I'm angry that I kept trying to understand his moodiness, his irresponsibility, and his temper—to get through to him—never dreaming he was stoned and unreachable.

Don't delude yourself: **Drugs make you unfit for love.** They interfere with your ability to be intimate on a consistent basis. And if you and your partner rely on doing drugs together as the way to create intimacy, you're fooling yourselves.

Loving Someone Who Is Addicted to Prescription Drugs

One day a few years ago, I was counseling a friend of mine I'll call Gordon, who was having a difficult time in his marriage. "Harriet is a mess," he told me. "She's always freaked out about something. She can't seem to handle any stress at all. She blows up at the slightest provocation. I feel like if this continues, I'll have to think about leaving."

I thought for a moment and said, "Gordon, what's your biggest complaint about Harriet?"

"Well, I guess it's those damn pills she takes all the time."

"What pills?" I asked. I knew Harriet well but didn't know she was on medication.

"I don't know—painkillers, Valium, a whole bunch of stuff."

I sat there in shock. *Harriet, a pill junkie? Hard to believe, but it explained all the symptoms Gordon described.* I urged him to confront his wife and beg her to get help immediately.

Several days passed, and I received a call from Harriet. "Barbara, I went to the doctor yesterday, and I'm on a three-week detoxification program. You were right: **I was addicted to prescription drugs, but I didn't even know it.** I've been taking so many pills for years—uppers, downers, painkillers, tranquilizers. I told myself I needed them, but before I knew it, it was *Valley of the Dolls* revisited! I have to tell you, I hated you when Gordon came home. I guess I was so embarrassed for you or anyone to know how I've been living. It's going to be hard, but I have to do it to save my marriage."

Harriet went through a very rough three weeks. All of the emotions she'd been trying to numb herself to with the pills came up at once, and her body went through an enormous purification once she gave it a chance to rid itself of the poisons she'd been putting into it. I saw her a month later and hardly recognized her. **She looked ten years younger!** "I feel like I just woke up from a long dream," she exclaimed. Two years later, Harriet is as beautiful and drug-free as she was then, and she and Gordon are a very happily married couple.

In our pill-pushing society, where we're told that the cures for headaches, stomach aches, acid indigestion, constipation, sleeplessness, and fatigue can all be found in pills, it's no wonder that millions of men and women are addicted to prescription drugs and don't know it.

If you are single and meet someone who takes a lot of pills, ask questions and get thorough information to make sure you aren't getting involved with a **"legal drug addict."** If you, like Gordon, are in a relationship with someone whom you suspect is abusing prescription drugs, insist they get help immediately, *and not from the doctor who is prescribing all that medication.* And if you are like Harriet, a slave to your tablets and capsules, *do yourself a favor and find a physician to help you determine what you really need and what is making you an addict.*

What to Do if Your Partner Has an Addiction

Relationships are difficult enough without knowingly getting involved with someone still enslaved by an addiction. Does that mean I don't think addicted people deserve to be loved? Of course not. It means that they need to get into recovery and free themselves of the addiction as well as understand the pain beneath it before they're capable of having a healthy relationship with anyone.

I guess what I'm saying is, if you're looking for a partner, don't get involved with someone who is still addicted, or freshly into recovery. That person needs to give himself 100 percent of his love and energy to heal. He won't be able to give you what you need right now. And if *you're* the addicted person, please love yourself enough to get the help you need, so you can be whole one day soon and have the relationship you deserve.

If you are already seriously involved with someone who has an addiction, and this chapter is helping you face facts, here is what I suggest:

▼

IF YOUR PARTNER IS AN ADDICT:

1. Tell your partner that *you refuse to live with an addict any longer.*
2. Tell him you will stay with him *only if he agrees to get some help and takes action IMMEDIATELY.*
3. Tell him that if he does not get help immediately, *you are leaving and not coming back.*

4. Stick to your word, and if your partner does not get immediate help, do not give him another chance. *LEAVE*.
5. DO NOT RETURN *unless your partner is clean and sober,* involved in a recovery program, and shows significant behavioral and attitudinal changes.

▲

FATAL FLAW

▼   ▼   ▼   ▼   2   ▼   ▼   ▼   ▼

Anger

► "My partner is a rageaholic. I live in fear every day."
► "The slightest thing sets him off. I have to tiptoe around the house."
► "She's wonderful and warm until she doesn't get her way. Then she turns into a screaming, raving bitch."

Living with an angry person is like living with a time bomb: You never know when it's going to go off, so you live in constant tension and fear. **When you love someone who has outbursts of rage, you feel controlled by his anger** and it keeps you from ever truly relaxing, since you don't want to be caught off guard.

Anger is a terrorist—it holds the people it comes in contact with hostage. If your partner has a problem with anger, you adapt your behavior to the situation, editing yourself so as not to upset your partner.

I'm not talking about normal, healthy expressions of anger: Your partner comes home an hour late and doesn't call, and you raise your voice to tell him you're angry; your wife neglects to tell you about an important phone call, and you bark at her in an annoyed tone of voice; your child spills nail polish all over the carpet, and you scold her with angry words.

The kind of anger that is a Fatal Flaw is anger that is out of the ordinary and inappropriate.

IS YOUR PARTNER A RAGEAHOLIC?

Here are some warning signs that your partner may have a serious problem with anger:

▶ Your partner gets very angry when little things don't go his way, and takes it out on the people around him.

▶ When you disagree with your partner, he responds with shouting, name-calling, threats, or other overreactive behavior.

▶ Your partner has very little patience, and becomes extremely annoyed if he has to wait for service, drive behind a slow vehicle, get put on hold on the phone, listen to you explain things, etc.

▶ When you ask your partner to do a simple task, he becomes defensive and rebellious.

▶ When you give your partner any feedback whatsoever about how his behavior affects you, he interprets it as an attack and viciously attacks back.

▶ Your partner acts out his anger by slamming doors, hanging up on you on the phone, storming out of rooms, leaving the house, sleeping on the couch at night, etc.

▶ Your partner can switch from a seemingly loving and warm mood to an angry mood within seconds.

▶ Your partner is quick to yell at you or put you down if you aren't doing what he wants you to do, or if he feels you made a mistake.

▶ Your partner often raises his voice or becomes angry in public places—restaurants, shopping malls, friends' homes, etc.

▶ Your partner expresses his anger physically, hitting or throwing objects, or shoving or striking you or your children.

Spotting someone who has potential problems with anger is one of the easier Fatal Flaws to detect. No one turns into a rageaholic overnight. You'll see signs of difficulty similar to the ones on this list in the beginning of the relationship—they're like sparks that tell you the fire is sure to follow. The most important point for you to remember is: **Don't ignore the warning signs that indicate your partner has an anger problem. Trust your gut instinct, and don't let yourself be intimidated or talked out of your feelings.**

If *a few* of these statements fit your partner, you need to take action immediately to confront the problem and insist your partner get help.

If *many* of these statements fit your partner, you are in a very dysfunctional relationship and should give your partner an ultimatum to *stop the abusive behavior immediately, or you will leave.* You need to face the fact that you've been playing the victim in the relationship, and need to get counseling for yourself as well.

If *most* of these statements fit your partner, *get out of this relationship now!* Even if your partner is willing to get help, it's going to take him a long time to work through his rage, and you shouldn't have to be mistreated one day longer. *Take care of yourself first, and work with a professional on recovering your self-esteem and self-respect.*

"Why Is My Partner So Angry?"

There are many reasons people grow up to become rageaholics:

▶ *They were physically, verbally, or sexually abused as a child* and stored up the rage inside, letting it out as an adult when they finally feel "safe."

▶ *They felt unloved or abandoned as a child,* either through divorce, an absent parent, or the death of a parent, and act out that childhood rage as adults when they meet people who love them (potential "leavers").

▶ *They felt powerless as a child*—they had alcoholic parents they couldn't save; they watched helplessly as one parent abused the other; they never had permission to express their feelings, and, as adults, they compensate for that powerlessness by controlling others with their anger.

We've already talked about how many of us were not given permission as children to put words to our feelings. If a child experiences any of the situations I just mentioned, he will naturally feel enormous sadness and grief. If he is unable to feel that grief at that time, it will surface years later as anger and rage.

▼

REPRESSED GRIEF FROM CHILDHOOD GETS ACTED OUT AS RAGE IN ADULTS.

▲

This is why trying to "control" one's angry behavior is a useless form of therapy. The anger is a symptom, albeit a totally unacceptable symptom, of the rageaholic's deep hurt and sadness. **Treating the anger without understanding the cause is a temporary and dangerous solution. Traditional talk or psychotherapy will not be an adequate form of help for someone suffering from chronic anger.** Experiential emotional work such as psychodrama, physical forms of release such as hitting punching bags, screaming into pillows, and using batakas to strike out, and inner-child work will all be essential ingredients in helping a person transform his anger into grief and finally into healing.

When I had my radio talk show, I heard questions such as, "Why is my partner so angry?" every day. "Why does my husband hit me? Why does my wife lose control and fly into uncontrollable rages?" And I would always answer my listeners with the same comment:

"You're asking yourself the wrong question. The right question is: 'Why am I putting up with this behavior?' Then ask yourself: 'What am I going to do about it?' "

Trying to understand your partner's anger is fine if:

1. Your partner has made a **commitment** to get serious help in healing his rage
   and
2. Your partner has taken **action** toward getting that help
   and
3. Your partner has made visible and significant **progress** in changing his behavior

But often, partners of rageaholics focus more on helping their angry mate than they do on dealing with their own feelings about being treated so badly.

Why You Might Attract an Angry Partner

No one consciously looks for a mate with a violent temper. As we discussed in Chapter Two, your unconscious emotional programming drives you to choose someone who is angry for several reasons:

► **You had one or more angry parents as a child, and you have anger and love closely associated in your mind.** If you grew up with a rageaholic and were accustomed to many of the symptoms I just listed, you may have an extremely high tolerance for angry behavior, since it was "normal" in your household. Your emotional programming may say: *"People who love me get angry with me."* So you meet a partner who yells a lot, or loses control, and although you may not like his behavior, you don't think he has a big problem. **Sadly, people who were physically or verbally abused as children often grow up to become battered spouses.** They can also become batterers, which we'll talk about later.

► **You have very low self-esteem and are an easy "victim" for an abusive partner.** If your self-esteem is low and you live with a high degree of powerlessness, you'll be a perfect partner for a rageaholic, since you're probably *easily intimidated and upset.*

► **You have a difficult time expressing your own anger.** *I believe that we often unconsciously attract our opposites as partners in order to heal the imbalances in our own personality.* The man who is emotionally shut down may attract a highly emotional woman who cries on a regular basis; the woman who can't express any anger or negativity may attract a man who is overly angry. In addition, as I explained in my first book, *How to Make Love All the Time,* **the emotions you suppress, your partner may express.** When you repress or deny your angry emotions, your partner picks those up, and they augment his own stored-up anger.

A LETTER FROM CLAUDIA

I know of no better way to sum up this fatal flaw than to share a letter with you that I received from one of my radio listeners:

Dear Dr. Barbara,

Let me tell you my story. I'm twenty-eight years old and have two small children, four and one and a half. I'm presently on public assistance due to the circumstances I'll explain, and I'm working as a housekeeper for two friends to try to support myself and my children. If you had ever told me I would end up living like this, I would have thought you were crazy.

My childhood was very lonely. My mother died when I was four, and my father remarried a year later. **My stepmother resented me from the start and her verbal abuse was constant, except when they were both ignoring me.** I felt very lost and hopeless.

I dated a little in high school but didn't have a lot of self-confidence. When I was twenty, I was working and going to school part time, and that's when I met Hank. He was a few years older, and the first guy who ever really paid attention to me. Hank and I started going out, and he really seemed to care. I started fantasizing about spending my life with him, and we began seeing more and more of each other.

I'll never forget the first night I saw another side of Hank. Driving home from the movies, Hank missed a turn, and I teased him about being forgetful and spacing out. **Hank slammed on the brakes, got out of the car, and pulled me out onto the road. "Don't you ever correct me like that, do you hear?" he screamed.** I was in such shock, I didn't know what to say or do. We got back in the car, and I cried the whole way home.

The next day, Hank called and apologized. He'd been tired and cranky and had "lost his temper." He was so sweet, and I was so stupid, I forgot the whole thing. Things were fine until a few weeks later, when he flew into a rage again. **I was so in love that I told myself he had a "fiery personality."** In a way I got used to the outbursts—scenes in restaurants, screaming arguments late at night in bed; and, Hank's favorite, the car fights. I hated this part of him, so I tried not to do anything that would get him upset.

When Hank asked me to marry him, I didn't even stop to think about the anger. I was so happy that someone wanted to be my husband! We got married a few months later, after a terrible fight the night before the wedding during which Hank pushed me up against the wall of our apartment and screamed in my face for ten minutes about how I didn't appreciate how much he sacrificed for me. I still didn't get it!

We had our first little girl a year later, and that's when I started to wake up. **It was one thing for Hank to take his rage out on me, but when I saw him do it to my daughter, I got scared.** I won't bore you with the gory details, but things got worse. **I couldn't wait for Hank to go to work each morning so I could at least have eight hours of peace. When I'd hear his car pull**

up, my stomach would get tied in knots. But as I've heard you say on your program so many times, part of me was in total denial, and blamed myself for the problem rather than facing the truth about Hank. **What made it even harder was that when Hank wasn't being angry, he was wonderful.**

Eight months ago, my daughter told me she had started praying that Daddy would die so we could all be happy. That night I told Hank I wanted him to leave, and he totally lost it. I grabbed the kids and ran to a neighbor's house, where we stayed until I found an attorney. Hank refused to leave the house, refused to give me any money, claimed I was an unfit mother, and we are still battling it out legally.

I'm on welfare and cleaning houses because I ignored all the warning signs in the beginning. That's why my children are afraid to go to sleep at night. That's why I am twenty-eight and feel fifty-eight. **Because I didn't pay attention, and now I am paying the price.**

I don't want you to get the idea that I'm a lost cause. I feel good that I have broken the chain of anger and abuse that began with my stepmother. I feel good that I get a chance to start over. And I feel good knowing I'll never let anyone treat me or my kids that way again.

—Claudia

FATAL FLAW

▼　　▼　　▼　　▼　　**3**　　▼　　▼　　▼　　▼

Victim Consciousness

Victim consciousness is an attitude some men and women adopt toward the events in their life, an attitude that blames others for their problems. It's often difficult to spot a victim because none of us really mind hearing our partner complain to us about his or her past relationships. If you meet a man, for instance, and he often tells you horror stories about his ex-girlfriend, you're secretly glad he's not missing her or comparing you to her unfavorably. After all, you certainly don't want to hear how wonderful she was. *But if your partner has a habit of blaming others for his* *circumstances and not taking responsibility for his part in problems,* **watch out: You will be the next person whose fault everything is.**

The tricky thing about victims is, in spite of their complaints about not having been loved or understood in the past, **they'll have a hard time receiving your love and support.** *Victims enjoy suffering: Holding on to their pain gives them the illusion that they have power over those who've hurt them.*

Therefore, when you love a victim, you may feel:

No matter how much you give, it is never enough.

No matter how much you try to console them, they refuse to be cheered up.

ARE YOU IN LOVE WITH A VICTIM?

Here are common traits your partner will display if he or she is a victim. See how many could apply to your mate (or yourself):

1. My partner rarely gets directly angry with me or others; instead, he complains or pouts about the situation.
2. When I make a suggestion or offer to help my partner with something he's upset about, he always seems to find a reason why my ideas won't work, and has an *"it's just no use"* attitude.
3. My partner won't come right out and tell me what's bothering him, but walks around looking miserable and makes me pull the information out of him.
4. Even when I try to love and comfort my partner, I feel like it doesn't help, and isn't even making a dent in his unhappiness, as if he is inconsolable.
5. My partner always seems to find something to be upset about in his life, and rarely has days or weeks go by without an event that puts him in a bad mood.
6. My partner often feels sorry for himself, and doesn't understand why unpleasant things happen to him.
7. My partner has a difficult time making decisions and often spends more time complaining about what might happen than taking action.
8. My partner still blames people in his past (parents, ex-mates, friends) for his misfortunes and the way his life has turned out.

9. My partner often feels trapped in circumstances that he feels are the causes of his unhappiness and can see no way out.

10. My partner is jealous of the success and happiness of others and frequently compares himself to them, resulting in either his feeling bitter or depressed.

———————————————————▲———————————————————

If you can relate to **one or two** *of these statements,* **your partner has a small victim streak** that you should talk about together. If you ignore these characteristics, you'll end up feeling angry and resentful.

If you can relate to **three to five** *of these statements,* **your partner has a serious problem with victim consciousness.** Make sure you aren't enjoying playing "rescuer," or setting yourself up to feel your efforts don't make a difference. This won't be an equal and healthy relationship until your partner gets some help and faces the victim inside himself.

If you can relate to **six or more** *of these statements,* **you are in love with a professional victim.** Good luck trying to discuss this with your partner: He will definitely feel attacked, become upset, and accuse you of not understanding or loving him—in other words, he will handle it just like a victim would! *This is not a healthy relationship, and if you don't already feel controlled, resentful, and turned off, you will soon. Your partner needs help now, and so do you.*

Here are the *symptoms* of victim consciousness:

▶ **Victims don't take responsibility for the events or circumstances in their life.** They feel sorry for themselves, they complain, eat, sleep, become depressed; they do everything but take action to improve the situation. Try suggesting to a victim what he or she should do to feel better or solve a problem and you will get a list of reasons why none of those things will work. Some victims will expect you to rescue them and solve their problems for them; *others don't expect anything but sympathy, since the only way they know how to get attention is to have someone feel sorry for them.* So, naturally, becoming responsible and autonomous wouldn't be practical. Who would pay attention to them if they didn't need help?

▼

VICTIMS SPEND THEIR TIME COMPLAINING ABOUT WHAT'S WRONG RATHER THAN DOING SOMETHING TO CHANGE IT.

▲

▶ **Victims are experts at blaming others for their problems.** From a victim's point of view, it's always someone else's fault that things are the way they are. Victims blame their parents, ex-spouses, children, friends, health, the economy, or whatever for the fact that they're not happy and fulfilled in their lives today. Some victims blame *overtly,* and are honest about their resentment. Some blame *covertly,* never actually expressing anything negative but simply not taking responsibility for fixing their own life. If this rationale doesn't make sense to you, and you say so, you'll be blamed for not understanding your partner.

▶ **Victims see life as an adversarial situation.** "It's the world against me," the victim thinks. *A victim perceives others as existing for the purpose of making him miserable, ruining his chances, interfering with his happiness, and disappointing him.* For many victims, this was true as a child, but when he projects that perception onto his adult relationships, he inevitably sets others up to fail him. Some victims go so far as to choose unsuitable partners who victimize them, only proving to themselves that they are, indeed, victims. Often victims will have only other victims as friends, since only they can truly understand.

▶ **Victims express their anger covertly.** Victims are rarely direct with their anger. *They would rather make you feel guilty by looking upset and hurt than lose your sympathy by confronting you with their true hostility.* **They may make statements that don't sound angry or hostile, but indirectly communicate their hostility while still allowing them to maintain the appearance that they're not angry.**

For instance, a woman is upset with her partner for not making her birthday more special. She says, "I guess we were just brought up differently. Some families teach their children to care about other people's feelings and some don't." When her boyfriend accuses her of calling him insensitive, she responds with disbelief: "Sweetheart, I didn't say you were insensitive, did I? I'm just making a point about how people are different." She would be a lot more honest if she said, "I'm pissed off at you for giving me one lousy card for my birthday and making me feel like I'm not special to you."

▶ **Victims think of themselves as powerless and helpless.** They're experts in negativity thinking. "I can't," "It won't," "I'll never" are common phrases you'll often hear from a victim. *Victims often procrastinate because they don't trust themselves enough to take action.* They may appear to be leaning on you for support until you realize it's not support they want, it's rescuing. **Adult victims may have been victimized as children, either sexually, physically, or emotionally. The powerlessness they experienced then prompted them to make an unconscious decision about themselves: "I am powerless. Others have power over me."**

▶ **Victims repeat the same negative patterns in relationships and in life because they don't attempt to find the source of the patterns.** When faced with a problem, the powerful person asks:

"Why is this happening, and how can I change it?"

The victim asks:

"Why is this happening to ME?"

When a victim focuses on the persecution aspect of a crisis rather than understanding how this crisis occurred and what can be done to avoid creating it next time, he robs himself of the opportunity to learn from his mistakes.

What to Do If You Are in Love with a Victim

All of us have a secret victim inside us. But when this pattern dominates someone's personality, it becomes toxic to their own mental health and their relationships. **If you become involved with someone who possesses this Fatal Flaw, it's essential that you confront this issue with him or her, even though it will undoubtedly make your partner very uncomfortable.** As with all of these Fatal Flaws, victim consciousness can be successfully combated with commitment and perseverance if your partner is willing to change. But don't kid yourself: If you ignore this pattern, it won't go away. *People involved with victims learn the hard way that, in time, your sympathy for them turns into apathy.*

FATAL FLAW

▼　　▼　　▼　　▼　　*4*　　▼　　▼　　▼　　▼

Control Freak

▶ Does your partner always have to have things his way, and if he doesn't, becomes very upset?

▶ Do you live in fear of displeasing your partner by doing things the "wrong way"?

▶ Do you feel criticized, judged, and constantly scrutinized by your partner?

If you answered yes to any of these questions, you might be in love with a control freak. I've chosen this name for the fourth Fatal Flaw since I have heard it used so often over the years by clients and friends to describe *someone who is addicted to being in control.* A control freak is virtually the opposite of a victim. While a victim often avoids making any decisions, **a control freak must make all the decisions himself.** A victim looks to others for help and rescuing; a **control freak almost never asks for help, since he tells himself he can handle it.** A victim often wants you to tell him what to do; **a control freak tells you what to do.**

Most human beings like to feel in control of their lives and feel uncomfortable being out of control. The difference is that **control freaks must be in control of their lives, and they *will do anything to avoid feeling out of control.*** This presents serious problems in relationships:

▶ *Control freaks have a difficult time opening up* and showing you their vulnerable and emotional side.

▶ *Control freaks don't like to admit that they need you,* or . . .

▶ Control freaks need you so much they *want to control all your time, becoming highly possessive and jealous.*

▶ *Control freaks can become easily upset,* expressing either anger or hurt when they don't get their way or feel out of control.

▶ *Control freaks can be compulsive* about their living habits, routine, work, etc., and therefore be very difficult to live with.

▶ *Control freaks can attempt to control the choices and habits of those around them*—coworkers, friends, children, and *you!*

▶ *Control freaks don't like being told what to do*—it makes them feel out of control.

▶ *Control freaks may have sexual problems*—either a difficult time letting go in bed, an attachment to a particular idea of how sex "should" be, a need to control you but a resistance to losing control himself.

▶ *Control freaks have a hard time relaxing,* whether after work, on weekends, or on vacations; they may be workaholics.

▶ *Control freaks can be very impatient and irritable.*

▶ *Control freaks may become very domineering and critical parents,* since by definition, babies and young children are beyond their control.

Partners who as children felt controlled by adults or by circumstances that rendered them powerless may make an unconscious decision that, when they grow up, they'll never be out of control.

▼

Why You Might Be Attracted to a Control Freak

Here are some reasons why you might find yourself attracting control freaks into your life:

▶ You had a very controlling mother or father, and therefore *you associate LOVE with CONTROL.*

▶ You feel somewhat powerless yourself and *mistake your partner's addiction to control for power and purpose.*

▶ *You are a victim,* looking for someone to tell you what to do and take charge of your life for you.

▶ *Your last partner was passive, weak, and wimpy,* and you've made the mistake I talked about in Chapter Five, choosing a partner in reaction to a previous partner.

▶ *You were physically, sexually, or verbally abused as a child* and only see yourself relating to others when they're in control and you're afraid of them.

▶ *You are a control freak yourself* and have attracted your own mirror image.

▲

This Fatal Flaw is one of the most difficult to cure, since by definition a control freak hates being out of control, and that includes admitting he has a problem, and especially being given an ultimatum by a partner.

If you're in love with a control freak, don't kid yourself: If left untreated, the situation will only get worse with time. Your partner must acknowledge the problem and take action to improve it, or you should reconsider the relationship.

FATAL FLAW

▼   ▼   ▼   ▼   5   ▼   ▼   ▼   ▼

Sexual Dysfunction

► *"My husband is addicted to pornographic magazines and X-rated movies, and it's ruining our relationship. What should I do?"*

► *"My wife couldn't care less about sex. I have to practically beg her to do it. Now I'm feeling like having an affair. How can I help her?"*

► *"My boyfriend has always been a terrible flirt, making comments about women's bodies, coming on to my friends. Now I just found out he's been sleeping with this girl he knows from work. Is there any hope for our relationship?"*

Every day on my radio talk show, I heard questions like these from people in love with partners who exhibited Fatal Flaw #5: sexual dysfunction. Despite what you might think, sexual dysfunction does not simply mean problems with sexual performance, such as impotence, or inability to have an orgasm. For the purpose of our study of fatal flaws, I've divided sexual dysfunction into the following categories:

1. **Sexual addiction and obsession**
2. **Lack of sexual integrity**
3. **Sexual performance problems**

▼

Sexual Addiction and Obsession

Here are some warning signs to look for that indicate your partner might have a problem with sexual addiction or obsession:

▶ When you and your partner have sex, he almost always includes some form of fantasy (pornographic materials, verbal play-acting, films, etc.).

▶ Your partner is an avid reader of pornographic magazines.

▶ Your partner rents pornographic videotapes and watches them alone.

▶ Your partner needs you to dress up in sexual costumes on a regular basis in order to get turned on.

▶ Your partner calls 900 sex numbers for phone sex.

▶ Your partner frequently goes to topless bars, strip clubs, or other types of sex-related facilities, alone or with friends.

▶ Your partner is addicted to masturbation, and engages in it many times a week or even daily, in spite of your active sex life.

▶ Your partner is compulsive about a particular sexual fantasy (being tied up, having pain inflicted upon him, being raped, raping, etc.), which he uses to become aroused.

▶ Your partner needs to have sex one or more times a day, every day, regardless of whether you're in the mood or not.

▶ Your partner enjoys seeing you engage in sex acts you find humiliating (anal sex, sadomasochism, etc.).

▶ Your partner has sexual feelings for children that he acts on or fantasizes about.

▲

If you know that one or more of these statements describes your partner, don't hide from the truth any longer: **your partner has a problem with sexual addiction.** These are not healthy behaviors, and they will definitely affect your relationship in a negative way.

There are several problems you might face when identifying and confronting someone with this Fatal Flaw:

1. **You mistake your partner's sexual addiction for sexual interest in you.** It's easy, especially in the beginning of a relationship, to get seduced and flattered by a partner's excessive sexual interest, rather than seeing it for what it is: obsession with sex.

Cindy, twenty-eight, described it this way: "Charlie wanted to have sex every day, which I thought was great at first, and he seemed so turned on to me that I didn't mind when he wanted to watch films together or have me act out his fantasies. But after about three months, I began to get uncomfortable when I realized *it wasn't me he couldn't live without, it was sex,* and kinky sex to boot."

2. **Your partner makes you feel that your discomfort with his habits is "your problem" and that you have sexual hang-ups.** I've had so many women ask me if I thought there was something wrong with them because they minded the fact that their partner wanted sex three times a day, or watched porno films whenever the wife left the house, or masturbated every morning in the shower while refusing to have sex with her. In each case, I would reassure these women that, no, there was nothing wrong with them, but there was something wrong with their mate. The sighs of relief I heard were unbelievable, because *each of these women had been told by their partners that they were too conservative, too frigid, or too sexually boring and that their concerns were unfounded.* **Women who are used to being victims or to giving up their power often find themselves being talked out of their feelings in this way.**

3. **You're embarrassed or frightened to confront the problem because you don't want to rock the boat.** It's not easy to say to your husband, "Honey, I think you're a masturbation addict," or "Sweetheart, the fact that you have to watch porno films to get turned on really frightens me and I won't put up with it anymore." However:

IF YOU DON'T FACE THE TRUTH ABOUT YOUR PARTNER'S SEXUAL ADDICTIONS, YOU'LL DESTROY YOUR RELATIONSHIP.

It's not that people with sexual addictions are "wrong" or "bad," but their behavior is disruptive to the intimacy and safety in the relationship:

▶ You'll feel "cheated on" by your partner because he needs something other than you to become aroused.

▶ You'll feel insecure about your body, your sexuality, and your ability to satisfy your partner.

▶ You'll feel emotionally distant from your partner during sex, as if he's not completely "there" with you.

▶ You'll feel sexually used and manipulated rather than loved.

▶ You'll feel angry and resentful toward your partner for not respecting your feelings.

▶ You'll eventually feel turned off to sex, since for you it's associated with humiliation, control, and a feeling of inadequacy.

WHY PORNOGRAPHY DESTROYS INTIMACY

Recently I was asked to be a guest on a national TV show. When the producer called me to talk about the show, I told him that I had very strong views on fantasy and pornography, and he responded by telling me that's why they wanted me as an expert. The evening of the taping arrived, and I met the other guest, a man who believed sexual fantasy was harmless and should be enjoyed by everyone. I sat there listening to him and the host of the show talk about how "normal" it was to be in bed with your partner and fantasize about making love to someone else, or what "innocent fun" it was to leave your wife at home and go to a topless bar and become aroused by the waitresses.

As I watched the faces of the audience members, I noticed something very interesting: When the host would ask, "Come on, don't you all fantasize about making love to other people while you're in bed with your partner?" there would be applause and nervous laughter. But the women, in particular, looked very uncomfortable. I knew what was going on in their minds. *They were feeling pressured to be sexually open and "hip" by pretending they weren't bothered by their partner's interest in fantasy or pornography, when the reality was that it upset them.*

Finally the host turned to me and asked my opinion, and I let loose. **"If you're making love with your partner and fantasizing about having sex with someone else, you're cheating on your partner!"** I wasn't surprised when all the women began applauding wildly. **"Indulging in sexual fantasy about other people, in your mind, through reading magazines or watching films, is a form of infidelity,"** I continued. **"You've made a commitment to be sexually monogamous with your partner, and you're breaking it by deliberately focusing your sexual attention on someone else."**

The guest next to me responded with a smirk on his face: "How can you make such a broad statement?" he asked. "There's nothing wrong with fantasizing or looking at naked women as long as you don't do anything about it. It's harmless."

"Harmless?" I responded. "Tell that to the thousands of women who've called me in tears because they found out their husband watches porno movies each night after their wives go to bed alone. Tell that to the woman making love to her boyfriend, not knowing he's imagining that she's his secretary. Tell her it shouldn't bother her. Tell that to the man who feels sexually inadequate because his girlfriend can get turned on only when she fantasizes about her ex-husband. And while you're at it, try convincing the woman whose husband looks at pornographic magazines while lying in bed with her that she shouldn't feel upset because it's harmless."

My response pretty much shut this guy up for the rest of the program. I wasn't coming on strong because I wanted to be right but because I feel so passionately about this subject. *As someone who works with couples in crisis, I have heard thousands of stories, mostly from women, about how their partner's obsession with pornography and sex is ruining their relationship.* I have seen women burst into tears during my women's seminars when they finally give themselves permission to express the rage and humiliation they feel because of their partner's sexual addiction. It's a problem often overlooked and minimized because of the sexist attitude in our society that supports milder forms of pornography such as the *Sports Illustrated* Swimsuit Edition or commercials selling beer by using bikini-clad women and claiming to disapprove of so-called hard-core pornography.

Intimacy is the shared experience of closeness and connection by two people. Sexual compulsion and addiction destroy intimacy because, by definition, they introduce a third element into your relationship: the thought or picture or video of another person or sexual situation. Although some couples claim they both enjoy sharing pornography together, I strongly doubt that it creates more intimacy. **What it does create is more eroticism, which many couples mistake for intimacy.**

HOW TO PROTECT YOURSELF

It's not as easy to spot this Fatal Flaw on the first few dates as it is with other problems we're talking about. But it's important for you to find out as much as you can about your partner's sexual history, habits, and taste to make sure you're not getting yourself into something you'll regret later. Obviously, each person must define for herself what she's comfortable with sexually and what she finds unacceptable. My advice would be: **Trust your instincts.** If something bothers you, don't let yourself be talked out of your feelings about it. It's not a question of what's normal and what's not. It's a question of what's healthy or unhealthy for *your* relationship.

If your partner has a problem with sexual addiction, encourage him to get professional help. Sexaholics Anonymous has support groups throughout the country that are helpful, and for a serious "sexaholic," psychological counseling is essential in understanding and breaking free from the addiction. *If your partner is willing to work on the problem, there is hope for your relationship. If not, get out while you still have some self-esteem left.*

Lack of Sexual Integrity

This is the second of the sexual Fatal Flaws, and it's related to the first in that *your partner doesn't honor the sanctity of your monogamous relationship—in this case, by "leaking" his sexual energy in someone else's direction.* This includes:

▶ flirting with other people
▶ constant staring at other people's bodies
▶ making sexual comments about your friends, strangers, etc., to you
▶ making sexual comments to your friends, strangers, etc.
▶ inappropriate touching of other people
▶ actual sexual infidelity

Here are some of the ways in which you might be in denial about this Fatal Flaw:

1. **You dismiss your reactions by telling yourself, "I'm just being paranoid."** None of us likes to appear overly possessive, so often, if you notice your partner behaving in a way that makes you uncomfortable, you might ignore it rather than confront your mate. This may especially be true if, based on your emotional programming, you don't trust your own feelings or perceptions. *Your partner may even minimize your feelings by calling you jealous and insecure.*

2. **You rationalize your feelings by telling yourself your partner's behavior isn't that bad.** "He never really does anything but look." "She doesn't ever cheat—she just flirts with guys." These are comments from people attempting to talk themselves out of their discomfort. If you're afraid to confront your partner about his lack of sexual integrity, you might convince yourself that what he's doing really doesn't bother you that much. This may be especially true if you dislike conflict and have a difficult time expressing anger.

3. **You tell yourself your partner will grow out of this behavior in time.** "He's probably just acting this way because we've only been together for a little while—if we're married, I'm sure he'll change." Don't kid yourself—**if your partner doesn't treat you with respect in the beginning of the relationship, he won't suddenly learn respect later.**

All of these reactions are dangerous when it comes to lack of sexual integrity, because:

▼

WHAT STARTS OUT AS A PARTNER WHO FLIRTS AND OGLES MAY VERY WELL END UP AS A PARTNER WHO CHEATS.

▲

HOW ︎Y CHEATED HERSELF OUT OF HER OWN HAPPINESS

Jody was a thirty-five-year-old mother going through a marital crisis with her husband, Ned. "Ned's flirting ruined our marriage and destroyed my family. I met him eight years ago through work, and we clicked right from the start. Ned was very outgoing, and he told me he'd never really had a long-term relationship before because commitment scared him. Like most women, my first thought was, 'I'll fix that,' and I decided he was the man I wanted to spend my life with. My only real complaint about him was his flirting. *He looked at every woman within twenty feet,* and not just looked, mind you, but stared. I used to hate it! We'd be out to eat, and I'd be talking to him, and suddenly I'd see his eyes shift to the left and I'd know he was staring at some girl. *Whenever he met any female, even my friends, he would have to get them to pay attention to him, joking, telling them they looked nice, or something.*

"Every time he did things I felt awful, but when I'd try to talk to him about it, he'd accuse me of being insecure and controlling. I didn't want to be a controlling bitch—that's how my mom treated my dad—so I tried to ignore it. Looking back, I realize I just didn't want to face the truth. Ned and I got married a year and a half later, and even at our wedding he was flirting with one of my bridesmaids. I kept looking at the ring on my finger, telling myself he was mine now.

"Once we got married, Ned's behavior seemed to get worse. We started fighting more, and I became increasingly insecure. Then, I got pregnant. I thought having a baby would force Ned to grow up a little, but I was wrong.

"One night last year while Ned was supposedly out with his friends at a hockey game, the phone rang and a woman's voice said, 'Ned?' When I asked who was calling, she hung up. My heart started pounding a mile a minute. When Ned came home, I confronted him and we had a terrible fight. He told me I was crazy, and he denied everything. I was desperate, and the next time he went out, I put the baby in the car and followed him. *When his car pulled into a cheap motel, I felt like my world had collapsed.* **And I'm having a hard time forgiving myself for being so blind. If I'd paid attention in the beginning, maybe I wouldn't have to be feeling this pain."**

Jody cheated herself by ignoring the Fatal Flaw she noticed when she first met Ned. *By overlooking the problem in Ned's personality, Jody set herself up for much bigger problems later.*

A person who exhibits a lack of sexual integrity almost always had a childhood in which he didn't feel he received enough love and affection. This individual has a voracious appetite for attention from the opposite sex, almost like an addiction. With some good counseling, this Fatal Flaw can be healed, but only if you spot it and deal with it. **IF YOU IGNORE IT, IT WON'T GO AWAY.**

Sexual Performance Problems

I've saved this until last because it's often the least "fatal." Sexual performance problems can be resolved with some honest communication and hard work by both you and your partner, but the first step is admitting you have a problem. Although none of us has a perfect sex life, some sexual problems can be serious enough to create tremendous tension and unhappiness in a relationship. They are:

1. Impotence: Many men experience periods of less sexual potency at certain times in their lives. *However, if you're just beginning a relationship and encounter this problem from the start,* **don't ignore it, no matter how embarrassed you feel discussing it with your mate.** Impotence, or the inability to achieve and maintain an erection, can be caused by the following:

▶ *Suppressed anger and resentment:* If your partner is carrying around a lot of unexpressed rage toward women, his mother, or an ex-lover, he may have difficult performing sexually. I think of it as if his penis is "on strike"—*"I refuse to get excited or satisfy you."* Your partner may be totally unaware of this unconscious anger, but I've found this to be the case with most impotent men. The impotence may also be a form of "getting even," or retaliation, if your partner feels you've hurt him deeply (i.e., you cheated on him, etc).

▶ *Feeling controlled or overly mothered:* If your partner feels "emotionally impotent" in your relationship, or felt this way in the past, his body might reflect that powerlessness by not being able to get an erection. This will also occur if he has set you up as his mother or if you treat him like a child—a man can't sleep with his mother, so his body unconsciously refuses to perform.

▶ *Extreme fear of intimacy:* Most of us battle with fear of intimacy, but in extreme cases a man might be unable to perform sexually. It's as if his penis is saying, *"I don't want to be engulfed by her. It's too frightening for me to be that close to someone else."*

▶ *Physical causes:* Anyone experiencing regular sexual impotence should immediately see a physician. There are many physical causes for impotence, including complications from medication, a diet extremely high in fat, etc. However, if no physical source is found, your partner should investigate the emotional sources I've mentioned.

2. Premature ejaculation: As I mention in my book *How to Make Love All the Time* most men experience difficulty with premature or "early" ejaculation at some point in their lives. If the problem is chronic, it can be a source of frustration to both partners. Here are some common causes of early ejaculation:

▶ *Improper lovemaking techniques:* Early ejaculation occurs when a man is too tense physically, mentally, or emotionally. This can be due to poor lovemaking habits, such as trying to get turned on much too quickly, tensing the buttocks to intensify the pleasure, or rushing to get to orgasm. There are many excellent books that discuss techniques for handling the sexual tension during lovemaking so it doesn't release too soon. I would also suggest you read *How to Make Love All the Time* and learn about "gourmet sex" verses "greedy sex." It'll help both partners enjoy their sexual experience much more.

▶ *Withholding emotions from a partner:* If your partner is holding back feelings of anger, guilt, or fear when he's making love to you, or has a secret he hasn't told you, he'll have more of a tendency to ejaculate quickly. The holding back creates tension that makes lasting longer difficult. Men who have a hard time communicating or sharing their emotions often have problems with premature ejaculation.

▶ *Fear of or dislike for sex:* If your partner was ever sexually molested, or taught that sex was dirty, he may "rush" through lovemaking to get it over with. It's as if his penis says, *"Let's come and get out of here in a hurry."*

▶ *History of having sex with women he didn't love:* If your partner has a history of sleeping with women he didn't care for, or visiting prostitutes, he may find it difficult to take his time making love to you. His penis is in the habit of making "quick departures."

▶ *Fear of intimacy:* As in the reasons for impotence, premature ejaculation can be a way your partner's body responds to fear of getting too close during sex. Coming quickly ensures that he won't spend too much time loving you.

3. Difficulty experiencing orgasm for women: When I teach women's seminars, this topic comes up all the time. Statistics tell us that over half of all women have difficulty achieving orgasm, and a smaller percentage of women have never experienced it. Aside from having an unskilled man make love to you, the reasons for "female impotence" are similar to those I mentioned earlier regarding male impotence and premature ejaculation.

▶ *Anger:* I would say that suppressed anger and rage is the main cause for a woman's inability to achieve orgasm. Anger doesn't allow us to feel pleasure. Women who've been molested or raped, abandoned, unloved, or cheated on may have anger locked inside them that prevents them from feeling joy and passion.

▶ *Fear of being controlled and going out of control:* Being in control is the opposite of orgasm, which is a total letting go. If a woman has a problem with control, is feeling controlled by her partner, or has felt victimized by men in the past, she may have a difficult time "losing control" enough to have an orgasm. Like impotence, withholding orgasm from your partner is an unconscious way of saying, *"See, you can't even turn me on. You don't have any power over me."*

▶ *Dietary causes:* The same link between a high-fat diet and male impotence applies to nonorgasmic women. Sexual excitement is caused by blood flow, and if your diet is too high in fat, you may have a sluggish circulatory system, making it difficult for you to experience sexual arousal and orgasm.

4. Lack of interest in sex: The fourth kind of sexual performance problem is no performance at all! If you meet a partner who seems to have a very low sexual desire and who tells you he or she could easily live without sexual contact, don't convince yourself this won't create conflict in your relationship. Asexuality is more complex than it appears. *While it may look like a disinterest in sex, it usually covers up an aversion to sex.* I've heard so many sad stories from men or women who've complained that their partner never really enjoyed sex, and after they were married, lost all desire for it so that, much to the dismay of their mate, the marriage was celibate. Disinterest in sex can stem from the same problems mentioned earlier, such as fear of intimacy, anger, etc., **but more often it can be traced to serious trauma such as sexual molestation, incest, rape, or other violent forms of abuse.**

Whether your partner is addicted to pornography, flirts too much, can't perform sexually, or isn't sexually interested, **DON'T IGNORE THESE SEXUAL FATAL FLAWS!** I know they aren't fun to talk about or deal with, but avoiding them won't make them disappear. As I mentioned at the beginning of this section, sexual disorders can be easily treated with some professional counseling and good communication between you and your partner.

SEXUAL PROBLEMS DON'T HAVE TO BE FATAL TO YOUR RELATIONSHIP, BUT THEY WILL BE IF YOU AVOID DEALING WITH THEM.

FATAL FLAW

▼　　▼　　▼　　▼　 **6** 　▼　　▼　　▼　　▼

Your Partner Hasn't Grown Up

▶ *"He never remembers where he puts things; he's always losing his wallet or car keys; he constantly forgets appointments—honestly, I feel more like his mother than his wife."*

▶ *"I think my girlfriend wants a sugar daddy more than a boyfriend. She promised me she'd get a job over nine months ago, but she really doesn't make an effort to look. All she does is shop, watch TV, and eat. I wish she'd wake up and start acting like a grown-up."*

▶ *"My boyfriend is very sweet, but his finances are a mess. He owes money to people all over town; his credit is awful; he never balances his checkbook; and he doesn't pay his bills on time. When I ask him why he lets things get this bad, he just laughs and tells me he 'lives in the moment.'"*

All of these comments are from people in love with partners who possess fatal Flaw Flaw #6—they haven't grown up. I'm not talking about a person who has a healthy relationship with his own inner child, allowing him to be playful, joyful, and adventurous. **The men and women with this Fatal Flaw have an adult side that refuses to behave in a responsible, mature manner, forcing you, as the partner, to take on the role of parent.**

Here are some of the warning signs to look for in determining whether your partner hasn't fully grown up:

1. Financial irresponsibility. I hate to admit it, but I've been in several relationships with men who were financially irresponsible, and like a typical rescuer, I didn't see it as a Fatal Flaw, but convinced myself my partner just wasn't a "practical" person. Practically infantile was more like it!! *Financial irresponsibility is a strong indicator that your partner has some deep Emotional Programming that needs to be changed in order for you to have a healthy relationship.*

▼

Is your partner financially irresponsible?

Here are some specific signs that indicate your partner might have Fatal Flaw #6. Watch for someone who:

- ► bounces checks
- ► never balances his checkbook
- ► frequently needs to borrow money from you or from others
- ► doesn't pay bills on time and waits until he receives collection notices
- ► doesn't plan ahead financially and spends all his money on luxury items (clothing, stereo equipment, jewelry, etc.) rather than saving for expenses
- ► has a poor credit record
- ► can't seem to keep a job for any length of time
- ► waits until all of his money runs out to make more
- ► counts on you to bail him out of financial trouble
- ► has owed people money for quite some time without paying it back

---
▲

If any of these sound familiar, don't ignore them. Your partner's financial irresponsibility not only affects him or her but you as well, since you usually end up footing the bill or feeling responsible to "help." And don't make the mistake I did, of convincing yourself your partner is just "not good with money." The truth is, he neglects the financial portion of his life because he doesn't want to grow up and take responsibility for himself. **Your mate's carelessness with his finances will be reflected in his carelessness toward how he treats you, and his unreliability will prevent your relationship from growing into a healthy, mature partnership.**

2. Undependable. We don't expect a small child always to be on time, keep all his promises, remember all the rules, or do everything he says he will. A patient parent knows that her child is learning what it means to be responsible and that at three or four the concept is still sinking in. *But you should expect your adult partner to be dependable, and if he isn't, you're in love with someone who hasn't grown up.*

Lack of dependability means:

▶ Your partner constantly *makes promises to you and then breaks them.*
▶ Your partner is frequently *late* for dates, events, etc.
▶ Your partner is *forgetful* of important information you've told him.
▶ Your partner agrees to do things for you (pick up some food for dinner, make reservations at a restaurant, etc.) and often *forgets.*
▶ Your partner is a *procrastinator,* putting off doing things for as long as possible.
▶ You are hesitant to count on your partner, since *he's let you down* so often in the past.

When you're in relationships with someone who's undependable, you begin to act like a parent, reminding them of things they should remember themselves, doing things for them they should be doing for themselves, and making excuses for their lack of dependability to your friends and family. You don't have much trust in or respect for your partner and will inevitably store up a great deal of anger and resentment.

3. Unmotivated.

▶ Does your partner seem to have no direction or purpose in his life?
▶ Is your partner waiting for something outside himself to motivate him to take action?
▶ Does your partner have a difficult time making plans for the future?
▶ Does your partner put off making decisions of any kind?
▶ Is your partner still trying to figure out what he wants to do when he grows up, but he's over thirty years old?
▶ Does your partner have significant problems he's unwilling to face?
▶ Is your partner waiting for someone to give him his "big break"?

If you answered yes to any of these questions, you're involved with someone who isn't taking responsibility for the quality of his life, but, like a child, is waiting for someone to figure it out and do everything for him. We all go through stages in our life when we examine how we're living and question whether or not we should continue doing what we're doing. But when this stage lasts for years, it's not a stage—it's an immature state of mind.

Why People Resist Growing Up

If you're in love with someone who hasn't grown up, you're in love with a complex person. The resistance to responsibility isn't simply a bad habit, like reading pornographic magazines, that can be put aside. Rather, **it's an unconscious response to circumstances that left your partner feeling robbed of his childhood.** Your partner might exhibit this Fatal Flaw if:

▶ **He had to grow up too fast.** Sometimes children are thrust into adult roles too soon by tragic events: A mother dies, and the oldest daughter takes on her role in the household; a father abandons the family, and the only son assumes the responsibility for his mother; a parent is unreliable due to alcoholism, and a child becomes like a parent to his or her siblings. These people may grow up feeling unconsciously resentful that they missed out on childhood, and resistant to acting as responsible adults now. It's as if their mind is saying, *"I had to be grown up when I was little. I'm tired of it, and now I want to play."*

▶ **He felt very controlled as a child.** *If your partner grew up in a family with lots of rules and strict discipline, he may rebel as an adult by ignoring the rules.* For instance, a little boy always told exactly how to behave and punished for acting like a "kid" might grow up into a rebellious man who doesn't pay his bills on time, forgets to do things you ask him to do, etc.

CHILDREN WHO ARE ANGRY AT THEIR CONTROLLING PARENTS OFTEN GROW UP INTO ADULTS WHO REBEL AGAINST ALL AUTHORITY FIGURES, RULES, PROTOCOL, LEGAL SYSTEMS, ETC.

▶ **He felt neglected as a child.** If your partner didn't get enough caretaking when he was small, *he might act out irresponsible and*

*childish behaviors as an adult as an unconscious way to say,
"Take care of me."* If you're always reminding him to remember
his appointments, helping him find his keys, or motivating him to
do well, you're "mothering" (or "fathering") him in a way he was
never parented as a child.

Parenting Your Partner Kills the Passion in Your Relationship

No matter how helpful you tell yourself you're being, parenting
your partner will create an unhealthy relationship. You'll end up
feeling:

▶ angry
▶ taken advantage of
▶ manipulated
▶ disrespectful toward your partner
  and
▶ sexually turned off.

As I said in my book *Secrets About Men Every Woman Should
Know,* how turned on can you get to a man when you just spent
fifteen minutes looking for his wallet, or when he acts like an
irresponsible six-year-old? How attracted can you be to a woman
who can't make simple decisions, or spends money without keeping
track of it like a thirteen-year-old? **The more your partner behaves like a child, the worse your sex life will be.**

Of course, if you've attracted someone like this into your life,
it's important that you look at your role in the relationship. You're
playing rescuer; you get to feel superior and avoid your own life by
constantly helping your partner. You need to stop the role-playing
and let your partner confront the consequences of his irresponsibility.

FATAL FLAW

▼　　▼　　▼　　▼　　## 7　　▼　　▼　　▼　　▼

Your Partner Is Emotionally Unavailable

I could write an entire book on this Fatal Flaw, defining what it means, how to spot it, and what causes it. All you really need to know is:

STAY AWAY FROM PARTNERS
WHO ARE EMOTIONALLY SHUT DOWN!

There are so many people in the world eager to love you and receive your love in return. Why choose someone who has a hard time opening up and spend your time trying to pry open that person's heart?

Naturally, there are varying degrees of emotional unavailability. We all have emotional walls that hide parts of us we're afraid of showing others, and part of the purpose of a healthy relationship is to learn ·to become increasingly open and trusting. **But some people aren't ready to have a relationship because they're too emotionally blocked.** They need to do some serious healing before they are capable of giving and receiving love.

I've talked a lot in this chapter about symptoms of emotional damage, but let me sum up by listing some warning signs to watch for in spotting an emotionally unavailable partner:

1. Your partner cannot show emotions.

"I know John is a very sensitive person inside—it's just hard for him to show any feelings because he's been so hurt in the past."

What's the point of being in a relationship with someone if he can't show you how he feels? Why not just be alone? The very definition of relationship means interaction between two people, not one person trying to interact and the other doing nothing. If your partner can't share his feelings with you, your relationship will be shallow and frustrating. You'll become a "human can opener," trying to get your partner to open up all the time. **THAT'S NOT YOUR JOB—IT'S HIS.** You should expect your partner to be *capable of demonstrating basic emotions* such as happiness, sadness, disappointment, excitement, desire, and love. If he or she can't, they're not ready to be in a relationship with anyone.

Remember: There's no such thing as someone who "just isn't an emotional person." We were all emotional infants. Have you ever seen a baby who couldn't express his feelings? There's such a thing as someone who's emotionally damaged from childhood and has lost his ability to feel and show emotions.

2. Your partner cannot or will not talk about feelings.

"I know Lawrence loves me. He just isn't the kind of person who can talk about feelings."

Once again, the purpose of a relationship is not just to keep each other company, but also to *relate.* That means to share feelings, ideas, and insights with your partner, and in order to do that, you have to speak. Nothing saddens me more than hearing someone say, "My husband can't talk about his feelings." I feel like saying, "Then why do you pretend you're even in a relationship? You're living in the same house, but you aren't relating."

▼

IF YOU'RE MARRIED TO SOMEONE WHO WON'T COMMUNICATE WITH YOU ABOUT EMOTIONS, YOU AREN'T IN A RELATIONSHIP—YOU HAVE A LIVING ARRANGEMENT.

▲

We've seen that, for many people, talking about feelings is difficult, especially if they were taught not to express their emotions as children. But if your partner refuses to even try learning to express himself, or is just noncommunicative, your relationship is going to be awful. *Communication is one area where couples can really make a difference in their relationship if they are willing to learn how.* Reading books, taking workshops or classes, and going to marriage counseling are all effective methods of learning to talk with one another. **But both partners need to work on this problem.**

3. Your partner can't open up or trust.

"Andy says he doesn't want to lose me, but he refuses to let me in emotionally."

As I said earlier, there are some people who are not capable of having a healthy relationship because they are too emotionally shut down. They may want to open up but not know how, or need to do some intense healing before they're willing to relinquish their emotional armor enough to let you in. **When it comes to having a**

**lasting relationship, good intentions don't count for much—
you need to find someone willing to do what it takes to knock
down their own protective walls.** Otherwise you'll get into an
emotional tug-of-war, you pushing your partner to open up and him
pushing you away.

If any of these descriptions sounds familiar to you, go back and
read the beginning of Chapter Five, where I talk about why you'd
choose someone who doesn't love you as much as you love him. You
need to understand your own emotional pattern that got you involved in a relationship with someone emotionally unavailable.

FATAL FLAW

▼   ▼   ▼   ▼   **8**   ▼   ▼   ▼   ▼

Your Partner Hasn't Recovered from Past Relationship(s)

We all carry emotional baggage from our past relationships into
each new one. But sometimes that baggage can be so overwhelming
that it's fatal to your love affair. If you meet someone who hasn't
recovered from a past relationship, you're in for heartache and
disappointment. Here are some specifics to watch out for:

1. **Your partner still carries tremendous anger and resentment toward his previous mate.**
   One of the questions I always advise singles to ask prospective
partners on a first date is: *"How do you feel about your ex-lovers?"*
If your date launches into a tirade about what a bitch his ex-wife is,
or bitterly denounces his ex-girlfriend as a slut who cheated on him,
I would think long and hard before going out on a second date. As
we saw earlier, that unresolved anger and blame will eventually be
projected onto you. Your partner may not have recovered from his
previous relationship enough to have a healthy relationship with
you. He may need time to evaluate the events of the past and to take
responsibility for his part in what occurred.

▼
_____

THE MORE ANGER TOWARD THE PAST YOU CARRY IN YOUR HEART, THE LESS CAPABLE YOU ARE OF LOVING IN THE PRESENT.
_____
▲

This flaw isn't permanently fatal. The passage of time combined with some good therapy can eradicate this problem. **Note:** It's *possible* to work on this while you're in a relationship, but it's much more difficult and *can backfire by creating anger in you if your partner's healing takes longer than you feel it should.*

2. **Your partner still feels guilty and responsible for his previous mate.**

▶ Does your partner call or receive calls from his ex, claiming it's only because he's worried about her?

▶ Is your partner continually talking about his ex and allowing his concern for her to interfere with his being happy in his new relationship?

▶ Do you feel your partner hasn't set up proper boundaries to his ex about appropriate and inappropriate behaviors?

▶ Do you feel your partner is "leading his ex on" by not making it crystal clear that there's no hope of reconciliation in their relationship?

▶ Does your partner try to "protect" his ex from being hurt by lying about his relationship with you, hiding it from her and his children, or procrastinating about confronting her with the truth?

If you answered yes to any of these questions, you're involved with someone who hasn't completely let go of his past relationship. This behavior is acceptable only if you and your partner got together very close to the time of his breakup and it's been only a few weeks or months since then and your partner is still adjusting to the sudden change. *Even under these unusual circumstances, this behavior shouldn't continue for longer than a month or two at the most.* But if it's been a while since your partner ended his relationship, and one or more of these warning signs is still present, you've got a problem.

If your partner is feeling guilty or sorry for his ex-mate, it will interfere with his ability to surrender to the new relationship. It also creates a triangle even if he has no direct contact with his ex, so there are three people in the relationship, not two. **If you meet someone who fits this description, give him your phone number and tell him to call you when he has resolved his feelings about this ex.** Otherwise you'll be in competition with her, and it's impossible to compete with a memory, especially a sympathetic one.

3. **Your partner is still traumatized from being hurt or abused in his or her past relationship.**

▶ Does your partner seem emotionally fragile?

▶ Is your partner afraid to trust you?

▶ Does your partner frequently cry on your shoulder about how terribly her previous partner hurt her?

▶ Does it seem that no matter what you do or say, you can't make your partner happy?

If these sound familiar, be careful. You may be with someone whose heart is not healed enough to love yet.

Rescuers, beware! You'll be tempted to become involved with people who've just come out of a painful or unloving relationship, and to act as the healer who repairs their broken heart. Go back and read the part of Chapter Five where I talk about Rescue Missions as one of the wrong reasons to get involved in a relationship. **If someone is that damaged, give them time to heal themselves.** If you step in too soon, you'll be setting up a negative pattern in your relationship from the start.

Remember what I said in Chapter Five about getting involved with people who are not emotionally available: It can be a way for you to avoid intimacy, or to deprive yourself of love by choosing someone who can't love you in return. **If you always seem to find partners who haven't let go of the past, get some help in looking at your own fear of commitment.**

FATAL FLAW

▼ ▼ ▼ ▼ 9 ▼ ▼ ▼ ▼

Emotional Damage from Childhood

All of us carry emotional baggage from our childhood into our adult relationships. We are formed, to a large extent, by our past. If you want to meet someone who doesn't have some emotional damage from childhood, good luck! We all do. When looking for Fatal Flaws, however, we need to ask ourselves three questions:

1. **How *severe* was the emotional damage incurred by my potential partner when he was young?**
2. **Is my partner *aware* of this emotional damage and how it affects his ability to function in a relationship?**
3. **Is my partner *actively working* on himself to repair this emotional damage (reading, therapy, seminars, etc.)?**

The answers to these questions will determine whether your partner's past will be "fatal." The truth is, you could meet someone who had a relatively happy childhood but was totally spoiled by his mother, and because he is unaware of this pattern, always insists on having his way to the point where he is incapable of having a good relationship. And you could meet someone who was sexually molested and beaten as a child but is totally aware of the emotional trauma and working on healing it and is therefore capable of having an excellent relationship.

▼

YOUR PARTNER'S WILLINGNESS TO FACE HIS EMOTIONAL PROGRAMMING AND TAKE ACTION TO HEAL IT WILL GREATLY DIMINISH THE EFFECT ANY FATAL FLAWS MIGHT HAVE ON YOUR RELATIONSHIP.

▲

All of the Fatal Flaws discussed in this chapter can be symptoms of painful events from childhood. But it's important to look for a history of certain more serious childhood traumas in your partner so you can better understand him, or if the traumas are so severe and his recovery from them is insufficient, so you can avoid getting involved in a very painful and disappointing relationship. I've broken down emotional damage from childhood into the following categories:

1. **Sexual abuse and sexual trauma**
2. **Physical or verbal abuse**
3. **Parental abandonment: divorce, death, adoption, suicide, emotional distance**
4. **Eating disorders**
5. **Parental addiction to alcohol, drugs, pills, etc.**
6. **Religious fanaticism**

Because we're talking about things that happened in the past, emotional damage may be more difficult to spot than a present problem with addiction or some of the other Fatal Flaws. For each category I've included some questions about your partner; it's important to know the answers to these questions to determine whether there may be severe emotional damage. **Obviously I'm not suggesting you discover the answers to all these questions in your first few months. And I'm not advising you to make a psychological diagnosis of your mate, since you're probably not a mental health professional, and aren't qualified to do so.** But within the first few weeks of your relationship, and *before you become sexually involved,* it's important to get some idea of whom you're dealing with.

▼

IMPORTANT: **DON'T FORGET ALSO TO ANSWER THESE QUESTIONS ABOUT *YOURSELF,* TO GAIN INSIGHT INTO YOUR OWN PERSONALITY.**

▲

Sexual Abuse and Sexual Trauma

1. Does your partner remember being sexually molested or abused as a child? Was it by a family member, friend, authority figure such as a priest or teacher, or stranger? Has your partner been in recovery or therapy? Has she told family members or confronted the abuser?

2. Is your partner aware of other family members who were sexually abused? Have they been in recovery?

3. Was your partner ever caught masturbating or having sex and punished for it?

4. What attitudes and values was your partner taught about sexuality?

5. Was your partner aware of a parent having inappropriate sex (affairs, multiple partners, prostitution)?

6. Has your partner ever been raped? Has she worked with a rape crisis center or support group, or received individual counseling to help heal the trauma?

Possible Problems

▶ **Sexual addictions or dysfunction.** Victims of sexual abuse often develop either an obsession with their sexuality, which we'll discuss later, or an aversion to it, losing sexual desire and becoming dysfunctional. I've received hundreds of calls over the years from frustrated husbands, telling me they've just discovered their wife, who dislikes sex, was molested as a child but has never received any help. **It's very difficult to have a normal sex life and love life if you've been sexually abused and haven't received professional counseling to help you deal with the powerlessness and rage. Recovery work is essential.**

Even if there was no physical molestation, but your partner grew up with inappropriate sexual behaviors going on around her, similar problems can develop.

▶ **Difficulty being intimate.** Victims of sexual abuse may have a difficult time with emotional boundaries, either becoming too passive with no boundaries, or very protected and closed with rigid boundaries. Often partners who were sexually violated will not let you in emotionally.

Adults who were taught to feel shame about sex as children, either through religious teachings, parental discipline, or having been caught in sexual activity and punished, can also have a hard time opening up emotionally and sexually.

▶ **Weight problems.** One of the first questions I ask people who seek my help and are very overweight is whether they were abused as a child. Over two thirds of them answer yes. Violated individuals often unconsciously protect themselves by building a physical shell around their damaged inner child, insulating themselves from further pain.

► **Deviant sexual behavior.** We'll discuss this more later in this chapter. It's important to note that adult survivors of childhood sexual abuse may often turn to fantasy, pornography, and promiscuity to act out their confusion about sex.

Physical or Verbal Abuse

1. Was your partner or one of his family members ever physically hit or beaten as a child? How often and how severe was the abuse?
2. Was your partner physically terrorized in other ways (locked in the basement, starved for a day, had hands put in burning hot water, etc.)?
3. Did your partner grow up in a home where there was a lot of expressed rage in the form of constant fighting, shouting, name-calling, etc.?
4. Did your partner have a parent he was afraid of or hated?
5. Was your partner verbally abused as a child (told he was no good, screamed at, constantly criticized and humiliated, or simply made to feel nothing he did was ever quite good enough)?
6. Did your partner feel there were an unusual and unreasonable amount of "rules of behavior," either expressed or unexpressed, in his home, and that if he broke any of those rules he would be severely criticized, rejected, or punished?
7. Did your partner witness one of his parents verbally abuse the other?
8. Has your partner ever physically hit any of the people he's been in relationships with as an adult?

Possible Problems

► **Acting out stored-up anger and rage.** Children who grow up being physically or verbally abused usually carry tremendous rage inside them. *Without professional help they'll act out that rage by becoming rageaholics, just like their parents, abusing you in the process. This acting out may take the form of being highly critical, difficult to please, and moody, or may manifest itself in actual physical abuse of you or your children.*

► **Addiction (Substance Abuse).** If people who were physically abused decide to repress their rage, *they may be susceptible to taking on an addiction that will help them "numb" themselves to their suppressed feelings.*

▶ **Controlling behavior.** When a person feels out of control as a child, he may grow up to be very controlling in his relationships.

▶ **Inability to handle conflict or problems.** Some children from homes with tremendous anger and turmoil grow up with an intense aversion to conflict. *In their adult relationships they hate discussing problems, avoid conflict at all costs, and refuse to tell you what's bothering them.*

▶ **Addiction to drama.** When a child lives in a home in which there's constant drama, he grows up associating love with drama. *If your partner lived in a chaotic, unpredictable environment, he may unconsciously create drama in his adult life because that's the way "home" is supposed to feel.*

Parental Abandonment: Divorce, Death, Adoption, Suicide, Emotional Distance

1. Were your partner's parents divorced? Did your partner remain in contact with both parents afterward? Was it a friendly or a nasty divorce?
2. Did your partner's parents fight for custody of the children?
3. Did your partner's parents bad-mouth one another after the divorce, or use him as a go-between to manipulate each other?
4. Did your partner's parents remarry? What were his relationships to his stepparents, if any, or his parents' dates?
5. Did one or both of your partner's parents die when he was a child? What were the circumstances (illness, sudden death, suicide, etc.)?
6. Was your partner adopted? Does he know anything about his birth parents?
7. Were your partner's parents emotionally cold and distant? Is it hard for him to remember being told "I love you" as a child? Did his parents have a difficult time showing love and affection?

Possible Problems

► **Fear of commitment.** If your partner felt abandoned as a child due to divorce or death in the family, or lack of love, he may find it difficult to make emotional commitments. *Not committing is a way he unconsciously protects himself from getting abandoned again.* (See Chapter Eleven for more on commitment.)

► **Premature commitment.** We talked about this earlier in the book. *Often adults who felt cheated out of a "normal" family as a child may rush into relationships and commitments, hoping to create what they never had.* They are in love with the "idea" of being committed vs. being ready to commit.

► **Insecurity, possessiveness, and mistrust.** The more abandoned and rejected your partner felt as a child, the more likely he is to have a problem with *insecurity, possessiveness, jealousy, and mistrust.* It may be hard for you to convince him that you really love him, won't cheat on him, or betray him in some way.

► **No picture of a healthy relationship.** When a child grows up in a home where the parents' marriage did not stay intact, he doesn't have a healthy role model of what a lasting relationship should look like. *He may have a difficult time with romance and affection if he never saw his parents demonstrating love and affection toward him or one another.*

Eating Disorders

1. Did your partner have a weight problem as a child? Was he too thin or too heavy? Was he teased about his weight? Was food used as a reward or withheld as a punishment?
2. Has your partner ever had an eating disorder—anorexia, bulimia? Did she receive professional treatment?
3. Does your partner use food to cover up feelings? Does he have food addictions to sugar, or salty foods, that he can't control?

Possible Problems

► **Suppressed anger:** Eating disorders often cover up anger and resentment a person doesn't feel safe expressing. This person could be a time bomb waiting to go off.

▸ **Self-esteem problem:** People with food issues very often have a low sense of self-esteem due to childhood events, and the food problems make the self-esteem even lower, creating a vicious circle.

▸ **Control issues:** Your partner is probably a control freak. *Eating is about control and power,* and anorexics and bulimics are especially addicted to control.

▸ **Hidden sexual abuse:** As I mentioned earlier, an eating problem might be covering up sexual abuse from childhood.

Parents were Addicted to Alcohol, Drugs (Prescription or Nonprescription), Pills, Etc.

1. Did one or both of your partner's parents drink or do drugs excessively? Did your partner see them drunk or high? Did they become abusive when under the influence? Did they ever get clean and sober?
2. Did their addiction cause financial, marital, or legal problems?
3. Is your partner in denial about his parents addiction? Was he in denial as a child?
4. Did your partner feel responsible to take care of his parents or the family because of their addiction?
5. Did your partner feel deprived because his parents couldn't be there for him due to their addiction (sleeping, hangovers, spacing out, etc.)?

Possible Problems

▸ **Codependency:** The biggest problem all adult children of addicts have is the tendency toward codependent behavior. Much has been written on this subject, but in simple terms, *the codependent person has learned to make someone's else's reality more important than his due to traumatic events in childhood. Your partner may be codependent if he:*
   1. has difficulty setting boundaries with you and others (can't say no, etc.)
   2. has a hard time knowing what he wants and asking for it, and is more concerned with your needs

3. doesn't trust his own instincts, perceptions, and feelings and often gives his power away to others
4. is dependent on others to make him feel good about himself

► **Tendency toward addictive behavior:** Children of addicts learn how *not* to cope with feelings by watching their parents numb themselves with drugs, alcohol, food, etc. Your partner may have a tendency to become easily addicted in order to numb himself to unpleasant emotions.

► **Difficulty communicating:** Children of addicted parents often didn't have permission to communicate at home, and *become adults who have a hard time expressing their feelings or talking about problems.*

► **Difficulty trusting:** If your partner grew up in a home where a parent was addicted, he most likely didn't have a stable, safe environment in which to grow. *He may have difficulty trusting you and your love, and letting you in emotionally.*

Religious Fanaticism

1. Did your partner grow up in a home with extremely strict religious values and no room for questioning those beliefs?
2. Was your partner told he was "evil," "bad," or "a sinner" as a child and that if he didn't obey, would go to hell? Was your partner afraid of God as a child?
3. Did your partner's parents profess to be godly people, yet were cold, unaffectionate, and physically or verbally abusive?
4. Was your partner taught that sex was dirty and sinful?
5. Was any expression of "unholy" thoughts or feelings such as anger, hurt, or disappointment prohibited in your partner's home?

Possible Problems

► **Sexual dysfunction or obsession:** When a child makes early associations with sex as evil and sinful, he'll either have to make sex dirty as an adult to participate in it, or will have a strong aversion to sex.

► **Inability to communicate emotions:** If your partner wasn't given permission to feel or express "unholy" emotions, *he'll grow into an adult who has a hard time recognizing, let alone verbalizing, all but the most loving feelings.*

► **Low self-esteem:** If a child is told God thinks he's bad, *he'll grow up as an adult who has a difficult time loving and accepting himself just the way he is.*

WHAT'S NORMAL AND WHAT'S NOT?

I hope you've learned a lot from this list. *My purpose in pointing these patterns out to you is NOT to scare you away from having relationships with anyone with a flaw. All of us have emotional baggage we carry with us.* My intention is to make you aware that **it's important for you to learn about the emotional background of your partner, as well as your own, so you can know what to expect in the relationship.**

So if you meet someone whose parents were divorced, you shouldn't say, "Sorry, you have a Fatal Flaw. I can't go out with you." However, you should discuss your partner's life with him, and if, a month or two into the relationship, you notice he has difficulty expressing his feelings or making a commitment, be extra cautious before getting more deeply involved.

Remember those three questions I presented earlier?:

1. **How *severe* was the emotional damage incurred by my potential partner when he was young?**
2. **Is my partner *aware* of this emotional damage and how it affects his ability to function in a relationship?**
3. **Is my partner *actively working* on himself to repair this emotional damage (reading, therapy, seminars, etc.)?**

The bottom line is: There is no such thing as a normal person, or normal problems. *None of us is normal—we are all unique.* And understanding our uniqueness and its history is the key to emotional freedom. **Out of the greatest pain can come the most powerful lessons, and with some hard work, you and your partner can turn your emotional baggage into emotional building blocks, helping to create a foundation for a loving and healing relationship.**

When I finished this chapter on Fatal Flaws, I gave it to a single friend of mine, who'd been begging me to show her this information as soon as I could. The next day she left a message on my answering machine that she needed to talk to me right away. When I returned her call, she said, "Barbara, I stayed up all night reading your chapter, and I learned things I wish I'd known years ago. But I'm worried about something: I met this guy last week who I really like, but he had a bad marriage, and he told me he's working on learning to express his feelings more. Does that mean he has Fatal Flaws? Should I tell him I can't see him anymore?"

She was relieved when I reassured her that, yes, she could keep dating her new man. But, listening to her, I realized that I needed to add something to the end of my chapter. So let me repeat something I said when I first started my discussion of Fatal Flaws:

IMPORTANT: If someone you love has one or more of these traits, it does not necessarily mean he is incapable of having a relationship. It does mean that those "character flaws" will cause problems in your relationship that *could* be fatal to its longevity.

Human beings are capable of tremendous personal transformation. Flaws are fatal only when we refuse to face them and run away from the exciting challenge of healing ourselves.

7
▼▼▼

COMPATIBILITY
TIME BOMBS

▼▼▼

Two households, both alike in dignity,
In fair Verona, where we lay our scene,
From ancient grudge break new mutiny,
Where civil blood makes civil hands unclean.

From forth the fatal loins of these two foes,
A pair of star-crossed lovers take their life;
Whose misadventured piteous overthrows,
Doth with their death bury their parents' strife.

FROM THE INTRODUCTION TO *ROMEO AND JULIET*
BY WILLIAM SHAKESPEARE

▼▼▼

In the late 1960s, the famous Italian filmmaker Franco Zefferelli brought the most famous star-crossed lovers in history to life in his beautiful movie *Romeo and Juliet*. I'm sure you won't be surprised to discover that I saw the film at least ten times, weeping just as much with each viewing for the tragic romance the innocent couple endured, and moved, as millions of other people have been, by the ill-fated love William Shakespeare so compellingly created when he wrote *Romeo and Juliet* almost four hundred years ago.

The tragic relationship may be wonderful entertainment as an artistic fantasy, but when it becomes a reality in your own life, you're sure to get your heart broken. Sadly, too many people end up having love affairs that are doomed to fail because of what I call *Compatibility Time Bombs* (CTB).

Unlike Fatal Flaws or Emotional Programming, Compatibility Time Bombs have very little to do with obstacles in your *inner world,* but rather are obstacles in your *outer world* that make having a lasting relationship with a particular partner difficult.

For this reason, Compatibility Time Bombs may often be impossible to change, whereas Emotional Programming or Fatal Flaws can be worked on. For instance, if you meet someone who has a hard time expressing his feelings, you'll have problems in that relationship. These problems can disappear, however, if your partner gets some counseling, or if you work on learning to communicate together. On the other hand, if you fall in love with someone who's a devout Catholic and you're Jewish, your problems are more serious: You can't change or improve the situation as if it's a bad habit or an unhealthy emotional pattern. *You may be able to compromise or adjust, but the situation itself will always remain.*

Remember in Chapter One where I talked about the Love Myths that give us a low Love IQ? One of myths was "True love will conquer all," and the reality was that love alone isn't enough to make a relationship work. This truth is never more sadly apparent than with a couple who love one another but have been hit with a compatibility time bomb. **In spite of their strong feelings, circumstances, mostly beyond their control, turn them, like Romeo and Juliet, into star-crossed lovers. Their love isn't enough to overcome the obstacles in their path and make their relationship last.**

Here are seven Compatibility Time Bombs that can destroy a relationship:

1. **Significant age difference**
2. **Different religious background**
3. **Different social, ethnic, or educational background**
4. **Toxic in-laws**
5. **Toxic ex-spouse**
6. **Toxic stepchildren**
7. **Long-distance relationships**

I call these obstacles Compatibility Time Bombs because *the problems they present to a relationship usually emerge over time rather than in the beginning of a love affair.* When you first meet someone with whom you share a CTB, you're too busy falling in love to pay attention to what's probably an uncomfortable issue for both of you. *"It doesn't bother me." "We'll deal with it when it comes up." "We'll love each other so much that it won't matter."* These are the kinds of things you tell yourself to avoid facing what you suspect could potentially be an insoluble problem. But one day the realities you've been ignoring explode in front of you, and you're forced to deal with them.

As you read about these Compatibility Time Bombs, I hope you'll learn about what to watch for in your present or future relationships, and gain an understanding of what may have contributed to the failure of your past relationships.

IMPORTANT: DON'T FORGET WHAT I'VE EMPHASIZED THROUGHOUT THIS SECTION OF THE BOOK: IF YOU RECOGNIZE A POTENTIAL PROBLEM IN YOUR RELATIONSHIP, WHETHER A FATAL FLAW OR COMPATIBILITY TIME BOMB, **IT DOES NOT MEAN YOUR RELATIONSHIP IS DOOMED.** IT DOES MEAN YOU NEED TO PAY CLOSE ATTENTION TO THE PROBLEM RATHER THAN IGNORING IT AND HOPING IT JUST GOES AWAY.

COMPATIBILITY TIME BOMB

▼　　▼　　▼　　▼　　**1**　　▼　　▼　　▼　　▼

Significant Age Difference

▶ Eric, fifty-eight, and his wife, Janelle, thirty-two, are having the same fight they've had for the past nine months. Eric wants to spend the weekend relaxing at home, and Janelle wants to go out to a friend's party and dancing. "You used to like going out," Janelle says accusingly. "But since we've gotten married, every time I want to go out, you make excuses about being too tired or just wanting to stay home."

"We've gone over this before," Eric answers bitterly. "My idea of a good time isn't being around a bunch of people in a room with music so loud I can't hear myself think. What's wrong with wanting to stay home with my wife?"

"What's wrong is that it's boring," Janelle complains. "After working all week, I like a little fun on the weekend."

"Well, after working all week, I like a little peace and quiet. I'm sorry I'm not exciting enough for you anymore. Maybe I'm too old for you after all."

"Oh, don't start again, Eric," Janelle pleads. "And don't lecture me as if I'm your daughter."

▶ Andrea, thirty-nine, is arguing with her boyfriend, Don, twenty-six, about the same issue they always argue about—his fear of making a commitment. "We've been together for almost a year, Don, and I feel like we need to take things to a deeper level. But every time I bring it up, you react like a rebellious teenager."

"Don't start pulling that age thing on me again," Don retorts angrily. "I've told you over and over again that I'm just not ready to tie myself down and start a family right now—I don't feel financially stable enough in my business yet, and I just need more time."

"Well, if you worked a little harder, you'd be ready by now. Maybe you've got all the time in the world, but I haven't."

"Stop telling me how to run my life, Andrea, you sound like my goddamn mother. Just let me do things in my own time, okay? I'm only twenty-six, and I'm just not ready yet. If you want to marry me, you're just going to have to wait."

Significant age differences between partners can cause serious problems in relationships. The word "significant" is important here: If your partner is four or five years older or younger, it won't make much of a difference. **However, if your partner is ten or more years older or younger than you, it can cause difficulties depending on your ages and other aspects of your personalities.**

Eric and Janelle love each other very much, but there's a twenty-six-year difference between them, and after less than a year of marriage, they're discovering that this age gap is posing a lot more problems than they ever expected it to. Janelle, in her early thirties, has different social needs and interests than Eric, who is almost sixty. Eric has been married before and has three grown children. He's worked very hard for most of his life in a fast-paced profession, and while he was dating Janelle, was willing to endure the fast times and whirlwind social life she loved. Now that he's married again, he wants to slow down and enjoy life in a simpler way. Janelle has never been married before and has a fantasy picture of what the social life of a married couple should look like—dinner parties with other couples, dancing, etc. Neither of them is right or wrong; they just have some incompatible needs. *Like many couples with Compatibility Time Bombs, Janelle and Eric weren't aware of their conflicts in the beginning of the relationship. Dating didn't give them an accurate picture of what their partnership would feel like once it settled into a routine.*

Andrea is thirteen years older than her lover, Don, and insisted when she got involved with him that their age difference wouldn't have an effect on their relationship. In the beginning, it didn't. Andrea and Don started off with a very passionate sexual affair filled with excitement and romance. Nothing seemed to be lacking, and Andrea had never felt more loved in her life. But six months into the partnership, when the initial sizzle began to quiet down, the problems emerged. *Andrea began feeling impatient with the way Don was handling his life, and in spite of herself, had a hard time not pressuring him to "catch up" to where she was, and began offering advice, judging him and feeling resentful that he wasn't more prepared to make a commitment. And although Don's crazy about Andrea, at his age he's just not ready to give her the things she wants: marriage, children, stability.*

I've found that age differences mean less as both partners get older. For instance, a fifteen-year age difference between a thirty-five-year-old man and a twenty-year-old woman will probably create more potential hazards than that same fifteen-year span between a sixty-five-year-old man and a 50-year-old women. The age difference will affect the first couple more, since their maturity and experience levels are usually much more dissimilar than the second couple's. There are common life experiences that mold us that most people pass through from ages twenty to forty-five, a softening and mellowing-out process. A forty-year-old woman and a fifty-five-year-old man will have more of these life experiences in common than a twenty-year-old woman and a thirty-five-year-old man.

I'm obviously making generalizations about age here. There are, after all, fifty-year-olds who have never grown up and are totally irresponsible, as well as twenty-four-year-olds who are mature and wise way beyond their years. Nevertheless, significant age differences between partners are too important to be dismissed as inconsequential.

Although you may recognize some of these characteristics in other types of relationships, here are some potential problems to watch out for with this Compatibility Time Bomb:

IF YOU'RE THE OLDER PERSON IN THE RELATIONSHIP

1. You can become impatient with your partner.

If you are significantly older than your mate, *you may begin to lose patience with his level of immaturity, lack of life experience, and learning process.* This will be especially true if your mate is twenty to thirty years of age. After all, you've already gone through a lot of what he's dealing with: You've learned how to ask for what you want and take charge of your life; you've realized it's not the end of the world when you go through a crisis; you've made mistakes and figured out how to do things the right way. So it's not easy watching your younger partner stumble through these same life experiences. In fact, it can be quite exasperating watching someone you love go through life lessons you're glad to have left behind.

One of the reasons that Andrea and Don fight so much is because she's becoming impatient watching Don "grow up." She's been a successful marketing consultant for over ten years, but Don is just beginning to do well as a writer. He doesn't make that much money yet, and is still learning a lot about selling himself and his work. Don's self-doubts are normal for a twenty-six-year-old guy just starting out, but they drive Andrea crazy, and she feels like he's taking too long to make a lifelong commitment to their relationship. **What Andrea forgets is that the confidence and easy expertise that come so naturally to her now took years to develop.** And her impatience is only making it more difficult for Don to feel good about himself and move confidently forward. *She's not wrong, and Don isn't right—they're just in very different life phases.*

2. You have a tendency to act like a parent to your mate.

When you have ten, twenty, or thirty more years of life experience than your partner has, you'll find it next to impossible not to offer advice, correct, and direct him or her. After all, you've been through this before—you know the best way to do it. Your intentions are loving; you're only trying to help. But the effect can be very destructive to your relationship. **YOU BEGIN ACTING LIKE A PARENT AND TREATING YOUR PARTNER LIKE A CHILD.** Naturally, your mate feels as if you don't trust or respect him, and responds just like a rebellious teenager would—he becomes resentful and pulls away. And this parent-child game will quickly destroy the passion in your sex life.

Sometimes if your partner has been looking for a parental figure, you will unwillingly find yourself playing this role, desperately longing to get out of it but unable to as long as your mate continues to be irresponsible and overly dependent on you. These relationships can be very toxic and usually end up with the older person feeling let down and disappointed, and the younger person feeling abandoned.

3. You may be much more financially successful than your partner.

Most older partners have more financial stability, and therefore more power in the relationship. You've had many more years to build up your income, purchase property and other possessions, etc. This financial superiority can create tension between you and your partner in numerous ways: You may feel resentful about being the one who provides more, especially if you're a woman: You may feel like you should make the important decisions (what to spend, where to live, what kind of vacation to take) because it's your money, and your partner might not feel this is fair. You may have difficulty lowering your standards of living to accommodate to your mate's.

When Leslee, a thirty-eight-year-old film editor, met Martin, a twenty-seven-year-old fitness trainer, they fell head over heels in love. Three months into the relationship, their troubles began when they started planning a vacation together. Leslee wanted to go to a resort in Mexico for a week, and Martin, knowing he could barely afford to leave town at all, suggested they go on a camping trip. "I don't mind paying for the vacation," Leslee insisted. "I've gone to Mexico for the past five years, and look forward to it for months."

"I know you'll pay," Martin responded angrily, "But that makes me feel really humiliated. If we go somewhere, it has to be a place I can afford to split with you."

"Why should I stop taking the kinds of trips I'm used to just because you don't have the money to go? I've worked hard for the past fifteen years to be able to afford these vacations. It's stupid for me to pretend I'm having a great time camping just so you don't have to feel bad," Leslee complained.

4. You may be tempted to control your partner because you hold more of the power in the relationship.

All of the warning signs above add up to this one—it's easy when you're much older than your partner to get into a power trip and become controlling. You have more money, success, and experience, and therefore it's tempting to "pull rank" on your mate.

5. **You may be tempted to compromise or sacrifice your interests, friends, and activities to appear more compatible with your partner.**

If your mate is much younger, you may give up interests he or she doesn't appreciate and take on habits that make you appear younger. I knew a man once who met a young actress when he was in his fifties. This guy loved to play bridge, listen to classical music, and watch old movies on television. I bumped into him at a restaurant with his new girlfriend and was shocked at what I saw. He was dressed in leather from head to toe, had pierced one of his ears, and told me he was on his way to a Madonna concert. Now, I'm not saying that leather and rock music are not for people over thirty, but this man was trying so hard to bridge the age gap between himself and his lover that he looked ridiculous.

If you're involved with a much younger person, here are some questions to ask yourself to avoid Compatibility Time Bomb #1:

▶ "Do I respect my partner?"
▶ "Am I proud of my partner?"
▶ "Do I trust my partner?"
▶ "What am I learning from my partner?"

IF YOU'RE THE YOUNGER PERSON IN THE RELATIONSHIP

1. **You may put your partner on a pedestal and give up your power because of his or her age.**

If your mate is much older than you, he or she is probably more successful, experienced, and financially secure. This may influence you into unconsciously feeling your partner is "better" than you are, and tempt you to idealize him rather than see him for who he really is. **When you allow yourself to feel less important because of your mate's chronological advantage, you give up your power. You take his advice rather than trusting your own; you blindly believe his criticisms rather than questioning whether he's correct; you invalidate your own needs and feelings out of deference to your partner.** You tell yourself:

▶ "He's the one who's paying for it, so we'll do it his way."
▶ "I'm sure he knows what he's doing. After all, look how successful he is."

▶ "He knows much more about these things than I do because he's older."

Even if your partner doesn't want to play this role with you, you may be tempted to fall into this pattern simply because of the age difference. And if your partner happens to enjoy his role as the older, wiser one, or actually uses it to control you, watch out: Your relationship won't be very healthy.

2. You may set your partner up to be like a parent.

Another consequence of being the less experienced, less worldly one in a relationship is that you may be tempted to re-create a parent/child dynamic with your partner. **If you're always asking his advice, counting on him to help you, depending on him for money, using his connections to your advantage, or allowing him to make decisions for you, you are, in essence, behaving like a child** and giving him the authority to be your father (or if you're the younger man, your mother). This prevents you from truly growing up and opens the door for all kinds of emotional programming to run itself out.

Even when your partner doesn't control you, you may *feel* controlled and intimidated just by virtue of the fact that he or she is that much older. You may react by becoming rebellious, withdrawn, or difficult. Perhaps this is the relationship you had with your own parents, or you may be acting out the anger you never had the courage to express to them when you were growing up.

3. You may be tempted to compromise or sacrifice your interests, friends, and activities to appear more compatible with your partner.

If you are involved with a much older person, here are some questions to ask yourself:

▶ "Does my partner respect me?"
▶ "Does my partner treat me as an equal?"
▶ "Do I feel like an equal with my partner?"

When It Can Work

A relationship between two people of very different ages can work if both partners avoid falling into the patterns we've just talked about.

The more you have in common and the more committed

you are to working on the relationship, the better your chances for survival.

If you use the challenge of your situation to grow as individuals, your age difference can actually serve as a great teacher to you both.

Remember Andrea and Don? Their relationship ended up working despite the thirteen-year age difference. Andrea realized that she was trying to control Don by wanting him to run his life according to her plan, and that she needed to give him a chance to follow his dreams. Don saw that he was avoiding taking responsibility for their relationship by putting Andrea off. They agreed to give things another chance, and within six months their relationship radically changed for the better. Don's career started to take off, and he was able to give Andrea more of what she wanted because she wasn't breathing down his neck all the time. And Andrea learned that Don could be trusted to be responsible and committed to their relationship. **From Andrea, Don learned more about commitment, and from Don, Andrea learned more about trust and letting go of control.**

When It Can't Work

Some couples never recover from the Compatibility Time Bomb of their age difference. Eric and Janelle, twenty-six years apart, didn't make it, **because their ages created too much incompatibility in their relationship.** The longer they lived together, the more unhappy they became. Eric realized that although he loved Janelle, he'd been so physically attracted to her that he'd neglected to ask himself what kind of life she expected. Once the sexual intensity calmed down, Eric found himself feeling that Janelle just didn't fit into his life as he'd hoped she would. She expected him to keep up the active social pace they'd set when dating, whereas he wanted a more mellow life-style. Eric didn't like Janelle's friends, and she wasn't crazy about his, either. To make matters worse, Eric was very close with his grown children and enjoyed spending time with them, but Janelle couldn't get used to the fact that Eric had a family whom he loved—her picture of a marriage was more traditional, and although she tried, she couldn't ever quite accept the reality that Eric had had a life before her. As their dissatisfaction with one another grew, their fighting escalated until they split up.

A significant age difference between partners can be a wonderful inspiration for growth, stretching each person's ability to love and understand the other, or it can be the cause of consistent tension and unhappiness that ultimately make staying together impossible.

COMPATIBILITY TIME BOMB
▼　　▼　　▼　　▼　2　▼　　▼　　▼　　▼

Different Religious Background

One of the most painful types of telephone calls I used to take on the radio came from the people who wanted my advice on the religious conflicts they were facing in their relationship: The Jewish man whose fiancée was a practicing Catholic; the born-again Christian who'd fallen in love with an agnostic; the Unitarian girl whose boyfriend was a Mormon. Many of these couples were discovering the hard way that differing religious backgrounds is one of the most difficult and deadly Compatibility Time Bombs. At least when there is an age difference, you know that your age and the characteristics that go with it will change over time, but for most people, religious preference stays the same. Many time all I could offer these broken-hearted lovers was a shoulder to cry on.

Compatibility Time Bomb #2 often makes a surprise attack on the relationship, simply because, for most of us, our spiritual beliefs and values aren't topics of discussion in the early days of a relationship. You don't need to share the same religious philosophy to enjoy a date with someone; you don't need to know his feelings about God to have a good time at the movies. Even if you do know you come from different backgrounds, you're tempted to put the information aside and focus instead on what you have in common. *Unfortunately, you only begin to notice the problems when your relationship has matured and become more serious, but by then your feelings for one another are so strong that it's very difficult to separate, even if you know it's inevitable.*

Here are the areas where different religious backgrounds create conflict in a relationship. *Remember, as in all Compatibility Time Bombs, the more extreme the differences, the worse the explosion!*

Customs and holidays.

This is usually the first place where religious differences become uncomfortable. Everything is fine until the Christmas season rolls around, or Passover comes, and suddenly the issues you've been unconsciously ignoring are thrust into the limelight. Holidays and special occasions reveal much about our religious and spiritual beliefs, and accentuate differences two people might be telling themselves aren't that great.

Beth, twenty-nine, and John, thirty-one, are a couple in a compatibility crisis. Beth and John have been in a serious, committed relationship for eight months, and are very much in love, but there's one problem: *Beth is Jewish, and John is Protestant.* Although neither consider themselves devoutly religious, they both enjoy the customs and teachings of their respective faiths. They've spoken about their backgrounds before, but never really had to face the effect it would have on their life until their first holiday season together.

Beth frequently spent the night at John's apartment, and often stayed the whole weekend. Even though she had no immediate plans to move in with John, she considered his place like a second home. Three weeks before Christmas, John picked Beth up after work and asked her to help him pick out his Christmas tree. He noticed that Beth seemed unusually quiet as they walked through the lot and on the ride home. When he finished setting up the tree in his living room, he asked Beth if there was anything wrong. "I feel strange telling you this," Beth confessed, *"But I don't feel comfortable having a tree in the house.* We never had one growing up—my parents felt very strongly about keeping our Judaism pure. I didn't think it would bother me that much, but it does."

John didn't really know how to respond to Beth. "I can understand how you feel, honey, but I've always had a tree. Christmas is my favorite holiday, and I love everything that goes with it. *I can't just give up what I believe in, even though I hate making you uncomfortable."*

"I'm not asking you to give anything up," Beth answered defensively. "I just don't know if I feel right staying here during the holidays. How can I light my menorah and celebrate my heritage with a Christmas tree staring me in the face?"

Beth and John are arguing over more than holiday traditions: They're confronting a major difference in their spiritual belief systems. **If they discover that their belief systems are too dissimi-**

lar and that those conflicts in customs and attitude interfere with their happiness together, they'll have to end their relationship.

Children.

If you want to flush out any hidden religious incompatibility with a partner, just ask him what religious or spiritual background he'd like to pass on to his children; then tell him your preferences and watch the sparks fly! **Nothing forces us to examine our values and beliefs more honestly than thinking about raising our children.** We all know someone claiming to be quite liberal and nonreligious who, upon having a child, suddenly becomes ultraconservative and rushes to sign his son or daughter up for Sunday school. Unfortunately, this pattern can cause tremendous pain to couples in love. When they discuss marriage, becoming pregnant, or having a child, they suddenly discover that they have very different and rigid religious views after all.

What to Do if You're in This Situation

If you and your partner have very different religious backgrounds, here are some suggestions:

1. Be honest about your feelings in the beginning of the relationship.

It's very tempting to downplay your religious convictions or spiritual beliefs when you suspect that standing by them might alienate your partner. Don't give in to the temptation to be dishonest. If you have strong religious affiliations, share these with your mate when you first begin dating, rather than waiting until you're closer or more serious. The longer you wait, the more painful a possible realization of incompatibility will be.

2. Don't avoid talking about the future.

Make a point of discussing how you want to bring up your children, celebrate holidays, and integrate spirituality into your life with your partner *early in the relationship.* Don't use the excuse that discussing these topics will put pressure on your mate, or make the person feel you're asking him or her to marry you, etc. You can have a philosophical exchange of ideas that'll help you discover whether you and your partner may be sitting on a Compatibility Time Bomb without promising to spend your lives together. **If you** aren't sure of your feelings about this, take some time to explore your own religious and spiritual beliefs. Don't wait until it's too late.

3. **If you're serious about pursuing your relationship, seek advice from clergy or other interdenominational couples.**

Don't attempt to explore the hazardous waters of interdenominational relationships by yourself. There are support groups available for couples in this situation, and clergy of all faiths are available to give you advice and guidance.

When It Can Work

The more flexible you and your partner's religious beliefs are, the greater your chances of avoiding this Compatibility Time Bomb. Even if your differences aren't extreme, it'll still take a lot of compromise and commitment for your relationship to adapt.

Maybe you have a strong relationship with God but not a strong connection to organized religion. You rarely attended church services and are more attracted to a loose interpretation of your faith, emphasizing loving values rather than doctrine. Maybe you don't even care about bringing up your children in a particular faith; you just want them to understand and hopefully experience a relationship with a Higher Power.

In this case you may discover that you would be comfortable sharing in the traditions of your partner's religion while acknowledging your mutual belief in God. *If you're not a strict adherent to your faith, it's quite possible you'll be able to find enough religious compatibility to make a relationship of differing faiths work.*

When It Can't Work

The stronger your own religious beliefs, the more difficult it will be to avoid this Compatibility Time Bomb.

It's not easy to walk away from someone you love because of differing religious beliefs, but the longer you wait, the harder it becomes. I know a woman who believes in God but doesn't follow any particular religion, and who fell in love with a wonderful man who was everything she wanted in a partner except for one thing: He was a born-again Christian. They dated for three months, and even though he didn't try to push his beliefs onto her, she knew how strongly he felt. They weren't even talking about a future together, but she realized that one day they would, and she would have to tell him she was unwilling to embrace the life-style he wanted for himself. *She decided to stop seeing him, and as hard as it was for her, it was a lot easier than it would have been if she'd waited six months or a year.*

▼

DON'T LET THIS COMPATIBILITY TIME BOMB BLOW UP IN YOUR FACE—CONFRONT THIS ISSUE BEFORE YOU BECOME SERIOUSLY INVOLVED WITH SOMEONE.

▲

COMPATIBILITY TIME BOMB

▼　　▼　　▼　　▼　　**3**　　▼　　▼　　▼　　▼

Different Social, Ethnic, or Educational Background

In 1990, one of the most popular films of the year was *Pretty Woman*, in which Julia Roberts played a hooker who fell in love with millionaire Richard Gere and got him to marry her. For three quarters of the movie the audience sees the extreme differences between the backgrounds of the two characters. Richard Gere's character is well educated and well bred, highly intellectual, and an expert on everything from opera to wine. The hooker never graduated from high school, comes from the seedy side of town, and has probably never even seen a copy of *The Wall Street Journal*. Toward the end of the film they both decide their relationship would be impossible, only to realize in the movie's last few minutes that they can't live without one another, and they reunite in a wonderfully romantic scene and supposedly live happily ever after.

Pretty Woman is certainly not the first film, play, or book to depict lovers from different sides of the tracks. Who can forget Tony and Maria in the Broadway musical *West Side Story* singing "There's a Place for Us," dreaming of a time when it wouldn't matter if one of them was white and one Puerto Rican, as long as they loved one another, or Professor Henry Higgins in *My Fair Lady* falling in love, in spite of himself, with Eliza Doolittle, the flower seller he'd plucked from the ghettos of London? I think one of the reasons we enjoy seeing these fictional lovers survive against all odds is because, in our everyday reality, different social and educational backgrounds can be a very painful Compatibility Time Bomb.

In many countries around the world this problem doesn't even exist, because marrying out of one's social class is unacceptable. America, however, is the melting pot of the world, and especially in large urban areas, each of us is exposed to people from all financial, social, and ethnic backgrounds as part of our daily existence. *And as much as, in principle, we'd like to believe we accept all people regardless of how they were brought up or who their ancestors were, those beliefs get challenged when we or one of our children falls in love with someone "different."*

A healthy relationship is based in part on the commonality you share with your partner—mutual interests, beliefs, tastes in style, and reference points. All of these serve to make living together comfortable rather than full of friction. **It's not that you and your partner have to agree on everything and have gone through all the same experiences. But there's a point beyond which** *too many differences will create too much tension, and make a harmonious relationship next to impossible.*

This Compatibility Time Bomb is one of the most difficult to detect until you're actually living with someone, because you may be unfamiliar with their habits or life-style unless you make a point of finding out what their values are. This sounds easier than it is, because many people are hesitant to talk honestly about these sensitive issues. For instance, it's hard to admit to yourself, *"I'm embarrassed by my partner's lack of education and poor habits,"* or *"I love my girlfriend, but when I think of having racially mixed children with her, I become upset."* It's even harder to tell your mate, "You're not sophisticated enough for me, and I don't feel comfortable introducing you to my friends," or the reverse, *"I feel like your family makes me feel inferior because of my background, and I don't think they'll ever accept me."*

I believe that in a perfect world, we all would be able to love enough to transcend these differences. What's important for you to know is this: **If you suspect that you have strong feelings and preferences regarding background in a partner, don't deny them, even if you don't approve of your own judgments.** I've seen so many couples get into trouble by telling themselves their differences *shouldn't* matter, when in reality, right or wrong, *they did.*

Trying to accept something you aren't comfortable with in your partner will only hurt that person more in the end, when your true feelings emerge.

As usual, I'll remind you that the *more extreme the differences, the more likely they'll be to cause problems.* And depending on what those differences are, in some cases even small ones will be big problems, while in others, major differences can be accepted.

Possible Problems Different Backgrounds Will Create

1. You may not have enough in common.

Olivia, a forty-six-year-old physician, met Ted, a forty-eight-year-old gardener, at an Alcoholics Anonymous meeting. Both were in recovery, and immediately hit it off. "You're dating a gardener?" Olivia's friends at the hospital would remark. "What do you talk about?" Olivia would laugh and tell them how happy she was to be in a healthy, sober relationship for a change. In the back of her mind, she wondered about the differences between her and Ted. Olivia was very involved with the arts, and most of her friends and activities revolved around concerts, theater, and creative pursuits. Ted was the complete opposite. He'd never gone to college, and had worked all his life outdoors. *"I don't think I've worn anything but blue jeans for twenty years,"* he'd boast proudly. It was part of what Olivia loved about him—he was so unlike many of the pretentious men she'd dated.

For the first few months of their relationship, Ted and Olivia got along wonderfully. They spent most of their time alone together, or going to AA meetings. The problems began when Olivia asked Ted to attend a benefit gala she'd helped to organize for the hospital.

"I'll only go if I don't have to wear a tuxedo," Ted insisted.

"Look, it's only for one night," Olivia pleaded. "And you'll love my friends. I've told them all about you." Ted reluctantly agreed.

The evening was a disaster. Ted was bored to death by Olivia's friends and their talk about this artist and that opening, and hardly said a word all night. Olivia felt torn in half—one part of her wanted to enjoy the gala she'd worked so hard to put on, and the other wanted to make Ted comfortable. By the end of the evening, she was in tears.

Over the next few months, the problems between Ted and Olivia escalated. Ted tried introducing her to his friends at a bowling party, and she felt just as out of place as he had at the gala. "Your friends are very warm and good people," she explained at the end of the evening, "but I had a hard time finding anything to talk to them about." That night, as she lay in bed, Olivia knew she couldn't run from the truth anymore: It would never work out with Ted. They were too different. *She thought about the gentle, sleeping man she loved, and she wept for what could never be, and for the love that wasn't big enough to bridge the gap between them.*

Some couples make their differences work for them. They learn from each other, and each becomes more well rounded. But if the differences are too extreme, they'll only produce conflict and alienation.

2. You may have very different values.

Each of us forms our value system based on our upbringing, our ethnic background, and our educational and life experiences. *If your background is radically different from your partner's, you'll probably find your values greatly differ as well.*

▼

COUPLES WHO SHARE SIMILAR VALUES HAVE A MUCH GREATER CHANCE OF CREATING A HAPPY, HARMONIOUS, AND LASTING RELATIONSHIP.

▲

Your values determine many aspects of your personality, including:

▶ how you treat other people
▶ how you treat yourself
▶ how you spend money
▶ how you raise your children
▶ what kinds of goals you set and how you go about achieving them
▶ your political opinions
▶ your attitude toward those less fortunate than you
▶ your health habits

Your values effect you every day of your life. **When your values and your partner's are very different, you'll experience tremendous tension in the relationship on a consistent basis.** This can turn your relationship into a battleground.

Mark, thirty-six, and Juliana, twenty-nine, were newlyweds when they came to me for help in their relationship. "All we ever do is fight about money," Mark complained. "Juliana acts like we're living on welfare, and I'm tired of her telling me how to spend the money I make."

"Well, if you wouldn't be so extravagant, we wouldn't fight so much," Juliana insisted with tears in her eyes. "All I'm trying to do is get you to save for our future, but you're so used to doing whatever you want that it's impossible to talk to you about it. I'm tired of you blaming me for doing what any good wife would do."

You can understand how this Compatibility Time Bomb hit Mark and Juliana if I tell you about their backgrounds. Mark came from a fairly wealthy family. His father was a self-made man who owned a chain of clothing stores and prided himself on giving his children everything he didn't have himself as a child. Mark spent each Christmas skiing in Colorado, and went to Europe every summer. He attended a very expensive private college and came back home to work for his father. *He didn't consider himself financially reckless— he simply liked to enjoy the good things in life.*

Juliana's past was quite different. She was the oldest of four children raised by a single mother—her Dad left when the kids were small and only sent money sporadically. There was a lot of love in Juliana's house, but not much of anything else. Her mom worked in two jobs to support the kids, and as soon as Juliana was old enough, she went to work after school to help pay the bills. "Thrift" was the motto she lived with. *Money was something you worked hard to get, then spent on practical things such as food, rent, and doctors' bills.*

When Mark met Juliana, he was instantly attracted to her down-to-earth practicality. "She wasn't like all the other girls out husband-hunting," he told me. He knew about her upbringing, but he couldn't understand why she wouldn't buy herself new clothes, or why she'd become upset when Mark gave her expensive jewelry for special occasions. "I spent weeks looking for the right bracelet for our first anniversary," he said angrily, "and all she could say when she opened the box was, 'Mark, you shouldn't have spent so much money on this. I won't feel right wearing it.'"

Juliana shook her head. "He doesn't even ask me when he makes big purchases. I feel so left out, like he's hiding something from me."

When It Can Work

When both partners are willing to compromise their values and find a common ground together, they can overcome this Compatibility Time Bomb. Mark and Juliana are a couple who had enough in common to give them a foundation for working through their area of incompatibility. They were successful in saving their relationship because *compromising didn't mean sacrificing, but rather enhancing their needs.*

Many of Juliana's values were due to emotional programming, and not simply preferences. She'd learned to be financially conservative as a child out of necessity. In going through counseling, she realized that she was still operating out of "poverty consciousness" and wasn't giving Mark a chance to prove that he could spend money without putting them into financial jeopardy. Mark saw that he was still spending money as if he were single and not consulting Juliana about big purchases or including her in his decision-making. He promised to be more sensitive to her feelings, and she committed herself to trusting him more. **By working together, Mark and Juliana created new, healthier values for themselves as individuals and grew even closer in the process.**

CAUTION: I do not suggest that you even consider compromising values you feel are part of you. Sacrificing what you believe in to keep the peace in a relationship will only backfire later. For instance, if you're committed to taking good care of yourself, and your boyfriend eats junk food, smokes, and isn't interested in changing, you should not start abusing your body to become more like him. Reexamining your values is always a good idea, and if you find room for change, great. *But do it for yourself, not to make your partner happy or keep the relationship going.*

When It Can't Work

Some couples are just too far apart in their thinking and background to live together compatibly. This was the case for Shelly and Ali. Shelly was a soft-spoken, beautiful woman from Arkansas farm country who moved to Texas and met Ali, a handsome and successful Persian. At first he was everything Shelly imagined a lover should be—charming, well educated, and very polite. He courted Shelly with fervor, showered her with gifts and exciting trips, and when he proposed, she was ecstatic.

From the moment they got married, though, everything changed. Ali seemed to become much more conservative and demanding, expecting Shelly to work full-time, do all the housework, and shop and cook, too. And *as she became familiar with Ali's family traditions, she became truly uncomfortable.* They began to see his family several times a week, segregating the men and women in separate rooms.

Shelly didn't understand what had happened to Ali, but Ali really hadn't changed that much. Now that they were married and living together, his values about marriage and family had begun to emerge, and she just hadn't realized how different their backgrounds were. She tried talking about it with Ali, and they ended up having an enormous argument during which he told her that *he was the man of the house and his desires were more important.*

Shelly tried to ignore her increasing discomfort but became more and more unhappy in the process. Desperate to save their marriage, Shelly went to a counselor by herself. After a few sessions she began to face the painful truth that she and Ali had very different value systems and came to understand more about his cultural background. "All this time I've been blaming him," she told me on the phone, "making him the bad guy. Ali is just being who he is. **This is the way he lives; this is how his family is. Women have a very different role in his culture, and it's not wrong—it's just very different from how I was brought up.** I never took the time to talk about these things before we got married because I was too swept up in all the romance."

Shelly had to come to terms with the fact that not only was Ali not going to change, he didn't want to change. He had the right to live as he wished. It just wasn't how Shelly wanted to live.

Shelly learned an important if painful lesson from Ali: She needed to find out more about the values of a prospective partner *in the beginning of a relationship.*

COMPATIBILITY TIME BOMB

▼   ▼   ▼   ▼   **4**   ▼   ▼   ▼   ▼

Toxic In-laws

▶ "My mother-in-law is driving me crazy. She calls my husband ten times a day and criticizes me every time we are together."

▶ "My wife's family decided I wasn't good enough for their daughter when we first met, and have never accepted me. My wife won't confront them, and I'm starting to resent her for it. What should I do?"

▶ "Why won't my husband stop rescuing his mother? He runs over to her house the minute she calls him to change a light bulb, or if she has a headache. We fight about her all the time. I'm at the end of my rope."

These are the kinds of phone calls I got on the radio and letters I've received from frustrated men and women who'd been hit with Compatibility Time Bomb #4, **Toxic in-laws.** If you're fortunate enough to be unfamiliar with this phenomenon, you're probably laughing at the phrase. But for the thousands of people who've come to me for help, there's nothing amusing about having in-laws who are ruining your relationship.

Before I talk more about this CTB, I want to emphasize the following point:

IF YOUR PARTNER HAS TAKEN A STAND WITH HIS PARENT OR PARENTS, COMMUNICATED HIS FEELINGS, AND SET CLEAR BOUNDARIES AS TO WHAT BEHAVIOR HE WILL ACCEPT, YOU WILL NOT HAVE A PROBLEM REGARDLESS OF HOW TOXIC YOUR IN-LAWS MAY TRY TO BE.

You may not particularly like your in-laws. But if your mate refuses to tolerate any unloving or disruptive behavior from them, your relationship won't be in jeopardy. **You *will* experience a Compatibility Time Bomb when your partner refuses to ac-**

knowledge or confront his parents on behavior or attitudes that are negatively affecting your relationship (of course, the same applies to you if you're the one with the toxic parents driving your mate crazy).

The term "toxic" comes from the Greek word *toxicon,* meaning "poison." Poison is something that harms whatever comes in contact with it. And that's what a toxic in-law is—a parent of your spouse whose contact with you is harmful to your happiness.

Toxic in-laws make great CTB's because of their delay factor in striking:

▶ **You may not know much about them until you're part of the family, and then it's too late.** If your partner is in denial about his parents, or tries to avoid the problem, you may have been presented with a very different picture of your in-laws until you got to know them personally.

▶ **You may not have been a threat before you were married.** I have a male friend whose mother adores all his girlfriends—that is, until he tells her he's thinking of marrying them. Suddenly she turns into Attila the Hun and makes life so miserable for the prospective brides that they get out of the relationship as quickly as possible. If you aren't this lucky, your in-law will wait until you're already married to reveal his or her true vicious self.

▶ **You may not experience the full impact of the problem until you become pregnant or have children.** Some women in couples report that only after they have a child do the in-laws start to meddle heavily in their lives and cause all sorts of tension.

▼
DO YOU HAVE TOXIC IN-LAWS?

Here's a brief quiz to help you determine whether you have toxic in-laws.

▶ If the statement applies to you **almost always,** give yourself **2 points.**

▶ If the statement applies to you **frequently,** give yourself **1 point.**

▶ If the statement applies to you **rarely or never,** give yourself **0 point.**

NOTE: If you suspect that your parents are Toxic in-laws for your mate, answer the questions as he would, or better yet, ask him to take this quiz!

1. Sometimes I feel like I'm sharing my partner with his mother (her father).
2. My in-law calls our house more than anyone else in our lives.
3. My partner and I argue about his parent(s) at least once a week.
4. I dread visits to or from my in-laws.
5. When we are around my in-laws, my partner and I almost always fight.
6. I have never felt totally accepted by my in-law(s).
7. I often feel nothing I do will ever be good enough for my in-law(s).
8. I sometimes fantasize about my in-law(s) dying, and how much easier our life would be.
9. I don't feel like my partner takes a strong enough stand with his parent(s).
10. When I try to talk about my in-laws to my partner, he becomes defensive, or tells me it's my problem.

———————————————▲———————————————

Now total your points:

▶ **0–4 points: You're safe for now!** You have some of the normal problems people have with their in-laws. Try working on those areas in which you scored highest.

▶ **5–9 points: Your in-laws are causing too much tension in your relationship.** Does your mate know how hard it is on you? What may seem tolerable now will get worse over time. Start asking for what you want and insist on some action.

▶ **10–14 points: Warning! You have a full-blown case of Toxic in-laws.** Are you really willing to live this way for the rest of your life? Either your partner needs to grow up and stand up to his parents, or you need to get out.

▶ **15–20 points: EMERGENCY! TOXIC IN-LAW FATALITY WARNING!** I'm surprised you are even alive to read this. Stop fantasizing about their funeral and face reality: Your partner isn't married to you, he's married to his parents. When you finish reading this section, put the book down and talk to your partner immediately. If he won't listen, call your attorney.

Some of the Problems Toxic In-laws Can Cause

Toxic in-laws do not respect the boundaries of your marriage and the boundaries between them and your spouse. Here are some of the ways this can manifest:

1. They become "time and energy vampires."

Toxic in-laws think the purpose of your life is to be there for them. *They'll call your house incessantly, making feeble excuses or none at all. They'll feel offended if you don't have time to talk with them.* "Dan's mother must call him several times each day at the office and call the house four or five times, often after ten o'clock at night," complained Susie. "She very rarely has anything to say, but she talks nonetheless! If I tell her I'm busy, or have to put the kids to bed, she'll sound dejected, and Dan will hear about it the next day when she calls him at work. 'Your wife isn't being very nice to me,' she'll begin. Not Susie, but 'your wife.' Then he comes home and gives me the 'Be nice to my mother lecture.' It's at the point where I dread answering the phone."

Toxic in-laws drain your time by insisting that you see them constantly. Naturally, an ill or very aged parent will demand a lot of time and energy from the children. **But Toxic in-laws simply haven't let go of their kids and don't respect the autonomous life they're trying to lead.**

2. They attempt to interfere in your life.

You can spot a Toxic in-law by how much *unsolicited advice* they give you on raising your children, decorating your house, investing your money, choosing your wardrobe, and everything else under the sun. Toxic in-laws don't know the meaning of the phrase "mind your own business." They'll pull you into arguments, get you to lose your temper, force you to become rude, and raise your blood pressure, all by interfering in what you thought was your private, personal life.

3. They may refuse to acknowledge you or your relationship.

A favorite pastime of Toxic in-laws is to punish you for taking their child away from them either by acting as if you don't exist or treating you like dirt. There are many ways in which they do this:

▶ addressing cards or letters to your spouse and not to both of you
▶ calling and asking for your spouse without speaking to you
▶ asking you to wait on them when they visit as if you're the maid

▶ forgetting your name, or, better yet, calling you by the name of your spouse's ex

▶ talking about you in the third person when you're present: "If your wife would cook more, maybe you wouldn't be so thin"

▶ fawning over your spouse when they see him and ignoring you completely

▶ treating the children as if they belong solely to your spouse and his side of the family

▶ inviting your partner to family events without you

▶ criticizing you in front of your spouse or your children

Even when these tactics are used in a seemingly unconscious manner, as if your in-law made a simple mistake or oversight, the results are the same: *you feel rejected.* Sometimes in-laws will behave this way to express their disapproval of their child's choice of you as a partner—if you are of a different religion, for instance. *But often they do it because they can't accept the presence of someone their child loves. Perhaps they've made their child into a "pseudospouse," looking for the love they aren't getting from their own partner.*

4. They may attempt to drive a wedge between you and your partner.

If you and your mate seem to fight all the time about his parents, and you suspect it's harming your relationship, your Toxic in-law has succeeded in creating dissension in your relationship and driving a wedge between you. It works like this: Your mate's parent does something to upset you. You naturally react with anger or annoyance. Your in-law then goes to your spouse and complains about the way you've treated him or her. Your spouse comes to you and says things like:

▶ *"Why can't you learn to get along with my mother?"*

▶ *"All I ask is that you be nice to her."*

▶ *"I refuse to get involved. You two work it out together."*

▶ *"Look, she's old, she may not be here soon. If she wants to be this way, why upset her by getting angry?"*

You feel unsupported and misunderstood by your partner and even more furious at your in-law who is manipulating your spouse to see you as the bad guy.

When It Can Work

If you have a Toxic in-law, you only have one choice if you want your relationship to survive: **YOU MUST INSIST THAT YOUR PART-NER CONFRONT HIS PARENT AND SET BOUNDARIES IN THEIR RELATIONSHIP.** *As long as your spouse thinks it's your problem and refuses to get involved, you'll continue to grow farther and farther apart.*

I believe that when you marry someone, you make that person number one in your life. They're now your family, your priority. That doesn't mean you ignore everyone else, but it does mean that the demands on your time and energy change. If your partner is allowing his parent to interfere with your happiness, he doesn't have his priorities straight. And the same goes for you if you're allowing your parent to be a Toxic in-law to your spouse.

Sons and daughters who tolerate hurtful and harmful behavior from their parents toward themselves and their spouse are children who've never grown up and taken their power back from their parents. They're still being controlled by their need for approval from Mom or Dad.

The child of a Toxic in-law needs to communicate the following information to their parents if they want to save their marriage:

1. **I have chosen my spouse to be my lifelong mate, and I expect you to treat her (him) with total respect, courtesy, and warmth. We're a couple, and when you criticize or hurt my partner, it's the same as hurting me.**

2. **If you can't bring yourself to behave with respect around my spouse, then I do not wish to see you. You'll either see us together and treat us with love, or not see us at all.**

3. **My home is mine, not yours. When you come over, you'll call first, and if we want to see you, we'll tell you. When you do come over, you will not tell me or my wife how to run our lives, raise our children, arrange our furniture, etc.**

4. **You need to respect our time and privacy. That means**

I do not wish you to call my house five times a day. Give us the space to want to call you. Naturally, I will be here for you if there's a real emergency.

5. I know this may be difficult for you to understand, but that's the way it is. I want you in my life, but not if you can't accept my marriage and respect our relationship.

I'm not suggesting you use these exact words or this tone. At first, try sitting down and having a serious talk with the parent. **However, if you've done that over and over again and the problem persists, your spouse needs to give your parent an ultimatum.** I've found that the in-law is often upset, and may even refuse to talk to you for a while, but often they come back and comply with your requests without actually admitting they're doing so.

There really is no alternative. Your partner (or if it's your parent, you) needs to grow up and take a stand. You won't believe the positive difference this will make in your relationship. I used to give this advice on the radio at least once a week to sufferers of Toxic in-laws, and I still get letters thanking me for giving them the push to confront their husband or wife, and sharing the wonderful change it made in their marriage.

When It Can't Work

If you discuss this with your partner and he repeatedly refuses to confront his parent, you can try suggesting marriage counseling so he can get a third opinion. If he refuses that, you need to ask yourself why you're staying in this relationship. It isn't going to get any better, and you know it's already tearing you apart. **You are married to someone who has some heavy-duty emotional baggage about his parents and isn't ready to have a grown-up relationship, because he hasn't ever emotionally left home.** You deserve better than this.

COMPATIBILITY TIME BOMB

▼　　▼　　▼　　▼　　**5**　　▼　　▼　　▼　　▼

Toxic Ex-Spouse

Jerri, a thirty-eight-year-old photographer, is dating Herb, a forty-five-year-old recently divorced real-estate appraiser. "I've never been in such a wonderful relationship," she gloats. "Herb is sensitive, faithful, and caring. I think this may be it. We've been talking about marriage, and I'm secretly hoping Herb asks me on my birthday next month. Well, there is one small problem: Herb's ex-wife, Marlena. *I don't think she's let go of Herb yet.* She still calls him all the time, sometimes after midnight when we're asleep, and she's usually crying and depressed. Twice she showed up at his apartment without calling and threw herself at him. Herb says she's unstable. *I'm hoping that when we get engaged, she'll finally realize it's over between them."*

Boy, is Jerri in for a surprise. Not only will Marlena not get better when she hears they're engaged, she'll get worse. She'll barrage Herb with hysterical phone calls, make him feel guilty for abandoning her, and find all kinds of problems with their children that she needs his advice on. Why? **Because Marlena is a Toxic ex-spouse.** Like Toxic in-laws, Toxic ex-spouses don't respect the boundaries of their relationship with their ex. They exhibit all of the same behaviors we discussed in the last section:

▶ **They don't respect your privacy.**
▶ **They use guilt to try to drive a wedge between you and your mate.**
▶ **They become "time and energy vampires."**
▶ **They don't acknowledge your relationship.**

In addition, they can:

▶ **Financially blackmail your mate by threatening to ask for more money as a way of punishing him for being with you.**
▶ **Emotionally blackmail your mate by threatening to ask for total custody of the children if your relationship becomes serious.**
▶ **Turn the children against you.**
▶ **Continually come on to your mate sexually as a way to interfere.**

I hope none of these sounds familiar to you, but if any does, you're probably already feeling the painful effects of this Compatibility Time Bomb. Toxic ex-spouses are less common than Toxic in-laws but no less deadly. I'm not talking about an ex-wife who's upset that your partner isn't paying his child support on time, or an ex-husband who's angry that your partner is saying bad things about him to the kids. **Toxic ex-spouses are partners who've never really let go of their mates and will hang on for dear life, all the while destroying your relationship.**

If your partner has a Toxic ex-spouse, **you're in an emotional triangle, a threesome.** And don't blame it on on the ex. Unless he or she is really mentally ill, your mate is just as guilty because he hasn't made his boundaries clear. What I said for children of Toxic in-laws applies to mates of Toxic ex-spouses:

IF YOUR PARTNER HAS TAKEN A STAND WITH HIS EX-SPOUSE, COMMUNICATED HIS FEELINGS, AND SET CLEAR BOUNDARIES AS TO WHAT BEHAVIOR HE'LL ACCEPT, YOU WON'T HAVE A PROBLEM REGARDLESS OF HOW TOXIC HIS EX-SPOUSE MAY TRY TO BE.

People with Toxic ex-spouses have often never really broken off those relationships. They're still emotionally married to their ex, and have a difficult time doing anything that would hurt them. It's also possible that your mate *has* let go, but his ex really is disturbed, and becomes obsessed with getting him back, as depicted in the frightening film *Fatal Attraction,* starring Glenn Close and Michael Douglas. If this is the case, make sure your partner isn't in denial about his ex's mental problem, and don't accept excuses such as:

► *"Give her time. She'll get used to it."*
► *"Oh, I know he can be dramatic, but he'd never really do anything to hurt you."*
► *"If we just ignore her, I'm sure she'll stop bothering us."*

How You Tell if Your Partner Has a Toxic Ex-Spouse

If you suspect your partner has a Toxic ex-spouse, take the quiz in the previous section, and instead of asking the questions about in-laws, ask about his ex-spouse. Except for questions 4–7, the others all apply.

Just like Toxic in-laws, Toxic ex-spouses may not emerge as a problem in the beginning of your relationship. The ex may not start the disturbing behavior until he or she realizes your partner is serious about you. You may also not see how much of a problem it is until you move in with your partner. Perhaps he never told you about the phone calls and visits because he didn't want to upset you. But once you live together, it may become apparent that his ex is much more in the picture than you believed her to be. **It's important to pay close attention and asks lots of questions *when you first meet someone* whom you suspect may have a Toxic ex-spouse.**

If you're in love with someone who has a Toxic ex-spouse, it is normal to feel:

▶ **angry that your partner seems to be more concerned about his ex's feelings than about yours**

▶ **angry when he accuses you of being jealous instead of understanding how you feel**

▶ **frightened that the problem won't get better with time (it won't)**

▶ **impatient with his excuses about feeling sorry for his ex**

▶ **suspicious that your mate is using his ex as a way to avoid becoming more intimate with you and going forward in his life (quite possible)**

▶ **resentful that your partner never brings you along when he sees his ex, picks up the kids, etc., because he "doesn't want to upset her"**

People with Toxic ex-spouses often have emotional programming that makes letting go of the past very difficult. Your mate might feel guilty abandoning his ex if one of his own parents left the other, or *he may feel guilty for leaving if he was left by one of his own parents, and be punishing himself by unconsciously sabotaging his new relationship with you.*

When It Can Work

If your partner has a Toxic ex-spouse, you must insist that he honor his commitment to you by letting go of his ex and relinquishing his responsibility for her. He needs to set boundaries for their relationship and stick by them. If the problem has been chronic, a period of no contact whatsoever will be necessary. If there are children involved, this still needs to be enforced. That means the kids run out to the car when he picks them up, and not that he comes in for ten minutes and let's his ex do her number. *It's up to your partner to break the pattern. Don't wait for the Toxic ex to do it.*

IMPORTANT: If your mate has a friendly relationship with his ex that is *not* toxic, and you have a real problem with jealousy, don't give your partner this ultimatum and say you read it in my book! Get some help on your jealously, or better yet, attend some counseling sessions together.

Sometimes your mate might need you to give him a bottom line to realize what he's been doing and to change his behavior. In these cases your relationship will become even closer after you confront your partner.

When It Can't Work

If you discuss this with your partner and he repeatedly refuses to confront his ex, you can try suggesting counseling so he can get input from a professional. If he refuses that, you need to ask yourself why you're letting yourself be treated in this way. **Until he makes a complete commitment to you, you're going to be miserable. Your partner isn't emotionally available because he's still involved with his ex.** Tell him you're leaving, and to call you when he's finished with his other relationship.

COMPATIBILITY TIME BOMB

▾ ▾ ▾ ▾ **6** ▾ ▾ ▾ ▾

Toxic Stepchildren

You meet a wonderful man at a party, and spend the evening getting to know one another. He seems to be everything you're looking for, and you're thrilled when he asks you out for Saturday night. "By the way," he says, "I forgot to mention that I have two children from a previous marriage. They'll be staying with me this weekend, so you'll get to meet them." "Great," you think. "He's a devoted father, too. I love children. I bet his are terrific."

Saturday evening finally arrives and you drive over to his house. He greets you at the door enthusiastically and explains that he needs to make a quick phone call. "Kids, come meet my new friend and talk to her while I make a phone call," he says. Suddenly two boys, ages nine and eleven, tear into the room, punching and kicking each other.

"Are you Dad's new girlfriend?" the older one asks in a sarcastic voice, looking you up and down.

"No, I'm just a friend," you answer.

"Are you and my Dad going to have sex?" the younger one says, shrieking with laughter.

"Shut up, Brian." Punch.

"Ouch. DAAADDD, Larry hit me."

"You little asshole, I'm going to get you."

"DAADDD!!!"

Suddenly your fantasies of romantic evenings by the fire and quiet mornings in bed change into scenes of "STEPCHILDREN FROM HELL."

This story describe the first glimpse of Compatibility Time Bomb #6: Toxic stepchildren. Now, before I upset anyone, let me make myself clear: I'm not saying children are toxic, and I'm not saying stepchildren are toxic. **I _am_ saying that some stepchildren can make their new stepparent's life so miserable that they can actually threaten the future of your relationship with your mate.** If you don't know how to handle these kids, you'll be in for a rocky ride.

Why am I so sure of this? _Because I was a "Stepchild from Hell."_ Just ask my stepfather, Dan. Although I didn't bite his leg or ask him embarrassing questions, I did treat him so terribly that I made my mother miserable and, no doubt, caused him to question whether he wanted to move in with a thirteen-year-old brat. Looking back, I realize that he must have loved my mother even more than I knew in order to put up with me.

What was I trying to accomplish by my obnoxious behavior? The same thing any potential stepchild is hoping to achieve—I **wanted to scare him off so I could have my mother all to myself, and maybe preserve the slim chance that my parents would get back together.** Of course, now I'm thrilled that my nasty plan didn't work. He and my mom have been married for twenty-seven years, and we are all very close.

Toxic stepchildren are really kids in a lot of pain. They feel let down by their parents, possibly rejected by the one who left, and frightened of being hurt again. Many times they are also misunderstood children whose emotional turmoil was underestimated or overshadowed by the drama their parents were going through. Suddenly they're expected to welcome a stranger into their lives to take the place of the missing parent, and everyone gets angry at them when they don't feel like being nice to this stranger. Out of this explosive mix of emotions comes the rebellious behavior that can make stepchildren a compatibility time bomb.

The problem, however, is not the stepkids, but the parents and stepparents who don't want to deal with the situation. I have a saying,

"Guilty parents make bad parents."

When a parent feels guilty about divorcing (and who doesn't?), they may have a tendency to overlook a problem with their children, hoping it will go away, or be too lenient in dealing with a problem, frightened that setting boundaries for the children will traumatize them even further.

This guilt interferes with their ability to see their children realistically. Josh, the father of Larry and Brian, is an example of a lenient dad. He sees his kids once every other weekend, so when they're visiting, he tends to let them do whatever they want. Josh knows his children are behaving terribly, but is afraid to punish them out of the fear of alienating them even more. In the case of a single mom whose kids live with her, this guilt may take the form of allowing the children to interfere with her ability to start a new relationship by manipulating her in some way (sleeping in her bed, criticizing her new mate, etc.).

When a parent of a Toxic stepchild gets into serious relationships or remarries, the new spouse will have to deal with these Compatibility Time Bombs and will probably go through problems similar to those caused by all Toxic stepchildren:

▶ You and your partner argue about the kids.
▶ You feel your partner takes the kids' side and not yours.

▶ **You feel like the kids are ruining your relationship.**

▶ **You feel your partner is too lenient with the kids.**

▶ **You feel like you can't talk to your partner about the kids without her becoming defensive.**

When It Can Work

With over half of all American children growing up in families different from their one of origin, it's essential that we all find ways to make stepfamilies work. Here are some steps you can take if you fall in love with someone who has children:

1. Work on your relationship with the kids as much as you work on your relationship with your new spouse.

Talk honestly about your feelings, acknowledge theirs, and don't pretend everything is fine when it's not. Kids will respect and accept you more if they feel you're being real with them.

2. Discuss all potential problems with your new partner while the relationship is developing.

Don't tiptoe around the issue of your potential stepchildren. If you're dating someone and feel there are some issues they aren't facing about their kids, talk about it. If your partner refuses to discuss it with you, or remains in denial, you may want to reconsider going further with this relationship. *Don't wait until you move in together or get married to deal with it—it'll be too late, and the time bomb will explode!*

3. Agree with your partner about how you'll treat the children and how they'll treat you.

Consistency and solidarity are two important keys in dealing with children, especially stepchildren. *You and your partner must present a united front to the kids.* If they suspect they can create a crack in your relationship, they'll be relentless. Have family meetings in which you can discuss the guidelines and air grievances.

4. Get outside support.

The Stepfamily Association of America is a wonderful network of specially trained counselors and support groups designed to aid stepfamilies in the challenging process of blending together. They can be contacted c/o *STEP FAMILY ASSOCIATION, 215 Centennial Mall South, Suite 212, Lincoln, NE 68508; tel. (402) 477-STEP.* Another good organization is the *The Stepfamily Foundation;* tel. *1-800-759-7837.* Remember, you're not alone! Reach out to other families in your situation. (Experts estimate that it takes five to seven years for a stepfamily to come together harmoniously! Hang in there!)

When It Can't Work

Stepfamilies will only be as healthy as the parents who create them. **If you're in a relationship with someone who doesn't seem to know how to parent his or her kids, and refuses to get help or face the issues even when you give them an ultimatum, I suggest you end the relationship.**

COMPATIBILITY TIME BOMB

▼   ▼   ▼   ▼   **7**   ▼   ▼   ▼   ▼

Long-Distance Relationships

Have you ever examined your face closely in the mirror? You start seeing all kinds of things you didn't know were there—tiny scars, discolored areas, pores that suddenly look gigantic. Yet if you stand back a few feet, you can't see any of the imperfections, just a smooth face. The point I'm trying to make is that *things look different close up than they do from a distance—faces, paintings, and even relationships.*

This brings us to our final Compatibility Time Bomb, long-distance relationships. There's nothing wrong with the long-distance relationship—in fact, many happy marriages began as commuter romances. However, there are hazards in this arrangement that many unsuspecting people overlook until they get hit with the Compatibility Time Bomb months or even years later.

▼

A LONG-DISTANCE ROMANCE MAKES IT EASY FOR YOU TO THINK THE RELATIONSHIP IS MUCH BETTER THAN IT IS BECAUSE YOU DON'T SPEND CONSISTENT QUALITY TIME TOGETHER.

▲

The very same factors that make a long-distance relationship romantic also make it hazardous:

- ▶ the distance that separates you
- ▶ the fantasizing about seeing your partner
- ▶ the brief, intense moments of intimacy during phone calls
- ▶ the erotic thrill of knowing you only have a few days together
- ▶ the emotional good-byes

It's easy to get caught up in the ongoing drama of your love affair rather than looking at the relationship as it really is.

THE GOAL OF TWO LOVERS IN A "NORMAL" RELATIONSHIP SHOULD BE *TO BECOME MORE LOVING AND INTIMATE WITH ONE ANOTHER.*

THE GOAL OF TWO LONG-DISTANCE LOVERS BECOMES *TO SEE ONE ANOTHER AGAIN.*

Here are some of the ways in which this Compatibility Time Bomb can affect you:

1. You don't get to see what your partner is really like.
If you know you have three days to spend with your long-distance lover, you put your best self forward—you make sure you look great, and you try to be as loving and affable as you can. *It's easy to hide the difficult parts of your personality for seventy-two hours so that your partner only gets to see the wonderful parts of you, just as you see only the terrific parts of him.* The problem is that you never really get to know one another. You don't get to see your mate under pressure, in a crisis, when he is tired and cranky, when he is faced with fear, when he is ill. All of these situations reveal a lot about someone's *character*. **There are dimensions of people you experience only when you're with them on a consistent basis.**

2. You avoid dealing with problem areas.
Let's imagine that you haven't seen your long-distance lover in two months, and he's flown in to spend the weekend with you. Over dinner that night, he says something that annoys you. Now you have to make a decision: Do you confront him with what's upsetting you, and risk ruining your weekend, or do you forget about it? Most people choose to avoid the confrontation, fearful that by the time they get through the argument and hurt feelings, half of the weekend will already be over. **The problem with this habit is that you and**

your partner never learn to problem-solve together, or advance the relationship to deeper levels of communication and harmony. The unresolved issues and the unexpressed resentments just sit there like emotional time bombs, waiting to explode. It may look like you have a great relationship on the surface, but you haven't allowed it to move through the transition stage every healthy love affair must experience.

3. <u>You have an unrealistic view of your compatibility.</u>

Long-distance lovers often don't even know how little they have in common because they are too busy entertaining themselves. *If you only have three days with your partner, you will treat it like a minivacation*—you'll spend all your time together; you'll go out to restaurants, movies, shows, etc., you'll have lots of sex; and you'll avoid friends and family. This gives you a very unrealistic picture of your relationship. You may actually enjoy the excitement of the fun weekend more than you enjoy your partner and not even know it. Many couples find themselves extremely disappointed when they finally move to the same city or decide to live together. *"It doesn't feel like it used to,"* they often complain. Of course it doesn't. **It's not a twenty-four-hour-a-day party anymore. It's a full-time relationship, and if you and your partner aren't truly compatible, you'll find out really fast.**

If you and your partner do move to the same town, you are likely to experience:

▶ an increase in arguments and disagreements
▶ a decrease in your sexual activity
▶ a discovery of things about your partner that annoy you

None of these time bombs will necessarily destroy your relationship unless you are unprepared for them or unwilling to deal with them.

When It Can Work

For a long-distance romance to evolve into a healthy, lasting relationship, *both partners will eventually have to live in the same place.* That's the only way you can truly know if you're compatible, and develop the level of intimacy you need to sustain your love. **But while you're still apart, the most successful long-distance affairs are those in which the couple treats the relationship like it is a full-time romance:**

▶ They don't try to make every moment together special, but do normal things together.

▶ They don't try to hide difficult parts of their personality, but are themselves.

▶ They don't edit how they feel, but allow themselves to communicate honestly and deal with conflicts as they come up.

If you follow these guidelines you'll have a much better chance of avoiding this Compatibility Time Bomb.

When It Can't Work

If your partner wants to keep things "light," avoid intimacy and commitment, and isn't interested in working with you to create deeper levels of communication and love, save your airfare and long-distance-phone bills and find a new relationship!

AVOIDING WHO'S WRONG

I have a single friend who recently ended a very frustrating and painful six-year relationship. When I told her the topic of this book, she begged me to let her read each chapter as soon as I'd finished it. "I'm desperate," she explained tearfully. "I can't go on making the same mistakes. I need to understand what I'm doing wrong." I agreed to have her be my first reader.

Late last night the phone rang, and when I answered, it was my friend. "Barbara," she exclaimed in a trembling voice, "I just finished reading the section on avoiding who's wrong. I can't believe how accurate it was. You've described every mistake I've ever made in my relationships. But I feel so angry at you."

"Angry at me?" I answered in shock. "What for?"

"For not writing this book ten years ago, so I could have avoided all this pain," she responded with a chuckle.

She wasn't alone in her desire. I, too, wish I would have understood about Fatal Flaws, Compatibility Time Bombs, and the Ten Types of Relationships That Won't Work. I could have saved myself a lot of heartache. But making many of my own poor love choices, along with helping thousands of people recover from theirs, have helped me to get to the place where I knew enough to write this section.

I hope that this section, on avoiding who's wrong, has helped you understand more about why some of your past relationships didn't work, and has given you a lot to think about in evaluating your present or future relationships. The most uncomfortable part is over. Now that we've looked at everything that can cause a relationship to fail, we'll spend the rest of the book learning about what makes a relationship work!

KNOWING

▼

WHO'S

▼

RIGHT

▼▼▼

The last three chapters were designed to help you avoid partners who are wrong for you, and understand more about obstacles that can prevent your relationships from working. Now it's time to learn about what you should look for when choosing a partner, and how to tell if your mate is right for you.

▼

8

▼▼▼

SIX QUALITIES TO
LOOK FOR IN A MATE

▼▼▼

I frequently travel around the country giving lectures and seminars, and whenever I make a presentation, I always leave room at the end to take questions from the audience. Since many of these people have read my books or seen me on television, they feel they know me, so I'm not surprised when someone asks me something personal. No matter what city I'm in, sometime during my "Ask Barbara Anything" segment, a man or a woman will step up to the microphone and say: *"Barbara, I'm single now, but I've had terrible relationships in the last few years. Can you tell me what kinds of qualities I should look for in my next partner so I don't get hurt again?"*

At this point I usually turn the tables and ask the questioner what kinds of chacteristics have attracted her to mates in the past. I'll hear answers such as *"someone with a good sense of humor," "a person who loves the outdoors," "men who enjoy traveling and eating good food."*

"That's your problem," I respond. **"You're looking for *personality traits* when instead you should be looking for *character*."**

It's taken me years to understand how to answer the question **"What should I look for in a partner?"** because I, like many of you, made most of the mistakes we've talked about in the earlier chapters of this book: falling in love for all the wrong reasons, choosing partners based on one or two appealing things rather than looking at the whole person, ignoring Fatal Flaws. But the most important lesson I've learned about compatibility is one that has changed my life:

▼

THE KEY TO CHOOSING THE RIGHT PARTNER IS TO LOOK FOR A PERSON WITH GOOD CHARACTER, NOT SIMPLY A GOOD PERSONALITY.

▲

Most of us become initially attracted to a mate because of something about their personality—his ability to make you laugh; her softness; his interest in cycling, etc. While these traits might be enjoyable, they aren't what's going to determine whether this relationship truly makes you happy. For that, you have to look for character. **Character determines how a person will treat himself; you; and, one day, your children. It's the foundation of any healthy partnership.** If you think of a relationship as a cake, personality is like the icing, but character is the substance.

This chapter presents six qualities to look for in a partner. Remember, these are different from a list of specific qualities you want in a mate. **Rather, these are the building blocks of good character in a person.** Whether you're single, married, or in between, *learning about these characteristics will help you determine how successful your relationship can be by determining how ready your partner is to be in a loving relationship.* Instead of only asking yourself the question

"Does my partner love me?"

you need to ask

"How capable is my partner of loving, period?"

At the end of each section I've included some questions you can ask your partner that will reveal a lot about his character. If you've been involved with your mate for some time, you may already know the answers to some of the questions, but don't skip them. It's important to think about these in your own mind.

IMPORTANT: **Don't forget to apply everything you read to evaluating yourself and your own qualities as well!**

SIX QUALITIES TO LOOK FOR IN A PARTNER:

1. **Commitment to personal growth**
2. **Emotional openness**
3. **Integrity**
4. **Maturity and responsibility**
5. **High self-esteem**
6. **Positive attitude toward life**

QUALITY

1

▾   ▾   ▾   ▾   ▾   ▾   ▾   ▾

Commitment to Personal Growth

I've listed this quality first because I feel it's one of the most important traits to seek in a partner. If you find someone who's committed to his or her personal growth, you'll have already avoided many of the problems couples face: One person wants to work on the relationship and the other doesn't; one partner tries to talk about the issues and the other refuses; one person sees areas that need improvement and the other is in denial.

Commitment to personal growth means:

▶ **Your partner is *committed to learning* everything he can about how to be a better person and a better spouse.** When you love someone who places a high value on personal transformation, your relationship is guaranteed to be much easier. Whether it's a small fight or a big crisis, your partner should be willing to use everything in your relationship to learn more about becoming more loving and compassionate. *Only when he's committed to learning (along with you, of course!) will your relationship truly become an adventure in personal growth, rather than a power struggle between two people, each trying to be right and make the other wrong.*

▶ He is *willing to receive help and guidance* in the form of **books, tapes, lectures, seminars, and counseling if necessary.** So many relationships experience crisis when one partner recognizes the need for improvement and the other refuses to participate.

There is no way a relationship can work if one partner refuses to seek help when necessary.

This is something to find out in the beginning of a relationship. Don't avoid this issue only to discover when you're in a family crisis that your mate "doesn't believe in counseling" or is too stubborn to pick up a book and learn how to make a relationship work.

▶ He is *conscious of his blind spots and childhood programming,* and is aware of what emotional baggage he has brought into your relationship. We've already seen that *it's not our childhood programming or emotional baggage that destroy our relationships, but our denial of them.* **It's dangerous to become involved with someone who's oblivious to his weaknesses and problem areas.** I'm not saying he has to be an expert on them, but he must at least be open to understanding more about why he's the way he is, and acknowledge that he, like you, is coming into the relationship with some emotional handicaps. You will find that this quality of *humility and lack of pride* really helps to keep your partnership from turning into a battleground.

▶ He has *personal goals for his own self-improvement,* and you can see specific, positive changes in him over time. It's important to find someone who is not only interested in growing but also is doing something about it! Lots of people give lip service to the concept of improving themselves, but when it comes to taking action, they wimp out. *When you see your partner motivating himself by setting goals and achieving them, whether it's to stop smoking, to become more patient with you, or to be more assertive, you'll respect him and have confidence that he won't depend on you to constantly push him or nag him into growing.*

QUESTIONS TO ASK YOUR PARTNER ABOUT COMMITMENT TO PERSONAL GROWTH:

1. What have you learned about yourself emotionally in the past ten years, and how has it changed you?

2. What have you learned from your past relationships, and what do you do differently now?

3. What are your greatest weaknesses, and where do you think they come from?

4. If I asked your past partners to list their biggest complaints about you, what would they be? Do you agree or disagree?

5. What sources of help have you used in the past when you or your relationships were in crisis (books, counseling, etc.)? Did these help?

6. How would you like to change in the next five years? What parts of yourself would you like to get rid of? What qualities would you like to acquire more of?

QUALITY

▼　　▼　　▼　　▼　　2　　▼　　▼　　▼　　▼

Emotional Openness

An intimate relationship is not based on sharing a home, a bed, or a bathroom. It's based on sharing *feelings*. That's why the second quality you should look for in a partner is emotional openness. This means your mate:

▶ has feelings
▶ knows *what* he is feeling
▶ chooses to *share* those feelings with you
▶ knows *how* to express those feelings to you

I can't tell you how many excuses I've heard from men and women in unhappy relationships about why their partner can't express feelings:

► *"His father never told him he loved him, so he can't tell me."*

► *"She was really hurt by her ex-husband, so she has a hard time showing me that she cares."*

► *"He never shows me what's going on inside him. I think growing up in an alcoholic family made it scary for him to have feelings."*

All these evaluations are very accurate, but they miss the point.

IF YOUR PARTNER CAN'T IDENTIFY AND SHARE HIS FEELINGS WITH YOU, HE'S NOT READY TO BE IN AN INTIMATE RELATIONSHIP

What's the purpose of being with someone who is emotionally shut down? **Staying in a relationship with a person who cannot share feelings is a form of self-punishment.**

Another way to describe emotional openness is "emotional generosity." We think of people as being generous with their money, or their time, but it's so important to find a mate who is generous with his love. Generosity means to give freely, abundantly, and without restriction. This means a partner who tells you how much he loves you and shows you how much he appreciates you. I don't mean once a year, on your anniversary, or when he's had a few drinks, or only when you threaten to leave. **You deserve to have someone in your life who shows you his love and appreciation on a consistent basis.**

The opposite of emotional generosity is emotional stinginess—hoarding love and emotions as if they were in limited quantity and offering you tiny pieces of one's heart. Emotionally stingy people will make you practically beg for love; they'll make you pull their feelings out of them, and then they'll expect you to make a big deal about the tiny scrap you received. These people probably never learned how to love, but that's not your problem. *Unless you want a full-time job as a teacher, avoid relationships with emotionally stingy partners!*

Emotional openness in a partner gives you access to his inner world. It is his way of offering you the key to his heart. It's the true fulfillment of the promise you make when you decide to be together. Don't put up with anything less.

QUESTIONS TO ASK YOUR PARTNER ABOUT EMOTIONAL OPENNESS:

1. **Do you feel comfortable expressing your feelings to the people you love? To whom in your life right now do you often say "I love you?"**

2. **What feelings are difficult for you to talk about? What feelings are easy? Has this changed over time?**

3. **Are there parts of yourself you don't feel comfortable sharing? Why do you think that is?**

4. **When you do open up and share your emotions, how do you feel afterward?**

5. **Do you think your inability to express yourself has ever caused problems in your relationships?**

6. **If I asked your past partners whether you were emotionally open, what would they say?**

QUALITY

▼　　▼　　▼　　▼　　**3**　　▼　　▼　　▼　　▼

Integrity

I'll never forget the time I was counseling a couple with marital problems, and the wife complained that she couldn't trust her husband. When I asked him if her accusation was correct, he defended himself by answering, "I only lie when I'm not comfortable telling the truth." What a bargain! The scary part was that he seriously believed there was nothing wrong with his dishonesty.

I couldn't disagree more. **Honesty, integrity, and trustworthiness are essential ingredients for a healthy relationship.** Knowing that you can count on your partner to be truthful with you at all times will give you a tremendous sense of security. On the other hand, if you live in constant fear that your partner is somehow lying to you, it'll be next to impossible to relax in the relationship. You'll be tense, doubting, and resentful. The long-term effects of loving someone you don't trust are devastating both to your self-esteem and to your love affair. As I emphasized in my book *How to Make Love All the Time,* **not telling the truth is the most significant way couples kill passion and destroy their intimacy.**

People who frequently bend the truth may have a "life isn't fair" attitude, and they consider dishonesty a strategy for getting an advantage. In other words, something is inherently wrong with their value system. And I can tell you from painful experience that *when you live with a liar, you end up covering up for him and eventually becoming a liar yourself.*

Finding a partner who has integrity means seeking:

▶ **Someone who is honest with himself:** There are many people who don't lie to you but lie to themselves. Honesty begins at home, so to speak. *That means you should avoid mates who are masters of self-deception.* You may tell yourself your boyfriend is an honest person, but then you remember that he avoids facing his dependence on alcohol, or that he claims it's over between him and his ex-girlfriend even though they talk almost every day. It's not that he's a liar—he's just not very good at being honest with himself.

▶ **Someone who is honest with others.** Does your partner lie to his clients or associates, all in the name of "business"? Does your girlfriend hide the truth about her life from her family? Does your mate often justify doing things at work you feel are dishonest? *If you doubt your partner's integrity, you'll lose respect for him,* and it'll be difficult for you to trust his behavior toward you.

▶ **Someone who is honest with you.** Whenever I meet friends I haven't seen in several years, they always remark how calm and serene I appear. I know that this can be attributed in part to how secure I feel in my relationship and how deeply I trust Jeffrey. What a fabulous feeling to love someone who, time and time again, proves to me that I can count on him always to be truthful. I contrast this with my last very painful relationship, in which I didn't ever completely trust my partner. I never quite knew where he was when he went out, or how he handled his finances, or whether he actually did what he had promised to do.

A partner who is honest:

1. will not hide parts of his life or personality from you
2. will not tell you only what you want to hear in order to protect himself
3. will share the truth with you without your having to trick him into admitting it, or pry it out of him

▶ **Someone who doesn't play games.** Games belong on the playground, not in relationships. Yet many adults can't have relationships without playing emotional games: "I won't tell you how I feel and you have to guess," or "I'll tell you things I know will make you jealous, and then I'll feel in control." All of these games involve dishonesty. **Look for a partner who is up front about how he feels and what he wants, and someone whose actions match his or her words.**

When your partner is consistently honest with you, you will naturally trust him.

QUESTIONS TO ASK YOUR PARTNER ABOUT INTEGRITY:

(Obviously, if your partner is an incurable liar, he'll answer these questions dishonestly, but trust your gut instincts and watch his actions to see if they reflect trustworthiness.)

1. **Do you think partners should be honest about everything in a relationship, or do you think some things should be kept private? For instance . . . ?**

2. **Have you ever been lied to or betrayed in a relationship? What happened? How did it make you feel?**

3. **Have you ever lied to or betrayed someone in a relationship? What happened? Would you do it again?**

4. **What things, if any, would you lie about in a relationship? An affair? Unhappiness with your partner's appearance? Etc.**

5. **If I asked your past partners if you were honest and trustworthy, how would they answer? Why?**

6. **What kinds of things do you feel are inherently wrong, and what wouldn't bother you (cheating on income tax, taking office supplies home from work, littering, not returning money you found, etc.)?**

7. **Are you telling me the truth right now?** (Watch eyes closely for reaction!)

QUALITY

4

Maturity and Responsibility

There are people who just aren't ready to be in a committed relationship. They may be very lovable; they may even love you very much. *But if they haven't reached a certain level of maturity, you'll feel like you've adopted a child rather than found a lover.*

For those of us who enjoy rescuing others, this is a quality to be especially adamant about finding in a partner. Otherwise you'll probably end up feeling, **"I LOVE MY MATE SO MUCH—I JUST WISH HE'D GROW UP!"**

Here are some signs that your partner is mature enough to have a relationship:

He (or she) can take care of himself. If your partner has grown up sufficiently, he'll be able to:

► earn enough money to support himself
► know how to keep his living space relatively clean
► know how to feed himself

You may think I'm joking, but I'm very serious! I've heard countless stories from women and men who've fallen in love with someone who couldn't take care of themselves. These weren't twenty-one-year-olds, either! These people were always out of work, borrowing money from family and friends, or living in chaos.

I remember a woman who called my radio show to ask my advice about her boyfriend. She was forty-four and he was forty-seven. They'd dated for six months and she really liked him, but was suspicious because he never invited her back to his apartment. In fact, in the time they'd been together, she'd never even seen where he lived. One night she insisted that he show her his place.

"Barbara," she told me conspiratorially, *"I've never seen a dwelling this filthy in all my life. There were dusty piles of magazines three and four feet high on the floor. There were clothes strewn everywhere; not just a few items, but hundreds of things! I don't think this man ever put his clothes away! And the kitchen! It looked like it hadn't been cleaned in decades! There was old food crusted over everything, and of course pots and dishes in more piles. I was sick to my stomach. Now, what I want to know is this: Do you think I should keep dating him?"*

I had to control myself to keep from laughing. Since I'm a firm believer in the principle *that our outer world is a reflection of our inner world,* I was sure that, from her description, this guy she was dating was a real mess! It was obvious that part of him had never grown up enough to take care of himself, so I doubted that he could emotionally take care of her.

I've worked with a lot of young people (late teens, early twenties) through my seminars, and I always feel concerned when I see a couple this age planning to get married, or deciding to have a child. Many of them can hardly take care of themselves, or are just learning how, and aren't really ready for the responsibility of a partnership, let alone a family.

He's responsible. Responsibility means doing what you say you're going to do. It means remembering to pay the bills, keeping your promises, showing up on time, and not letting people down. Responsibility isn't saying you're responsible but acting irresponsible. **It isn't a concept—it's an action.**

Part of maturity is being responsible and being accountable. We don't give children a lot of responsibility because we know they're not mature enough to handle it. *When you find a partner who's irresponsible, you have, in a sense, stumbled upon a child in an adult's body. Lovable, perhaps even sympathetic, but certainly not ready for an adult relationship*—that is, unless you don't mind being disappointed all the time.

Everyone deserves to be loved, but not everyone's ready for the responsibility that goes along with an adult relationship. Trust me—it's easier to make your love affair work when your partner is a grown-up!

He's respectful. One of the ways in which we note the maturation of children is by their increased respect for the world around them and the people in it. A child who didn't respect any boundaries and took his brother's toys learns not to touch what is not his. Instead of leaving out the milk and cookies after having a snack, he learns to respect his mother's time by putting them back in the refrigerator. Rather than shouting and banging on the table when he's in a restaurant, he learns to respect the environment he's in and moderate his behavior.

In this same way, look for maturation in a partner by noticing how respectful he is of:

► your feelings
► your boundaries
► your time
► your possessions
► his possessions
► our environment
► his employees, employer, or coworkers
► other people's feelings

QUESTIONS TO ASK YOUR PARTNER ABOUT MATURITY AND RESPONSIBILITY:

1. Are you usually on time or late for appointments, etc., in your life?

2. In what area of your life would you say you are the most irresponsible (finances, health, returning phone calls, etc.)?

3. Have you been fired from your jobs, or have you quit? If you were fired, what were the reasons?

4. Do you feel you act more as the caretaker in your relationships, or as the one who's taken care of?

5. If I asked your past partners, would they say you were very responsible, very irresponsible, or somewhere in between? On what would they base these conclusions?

6. Do you consider yourself sensitive to other people's feelings?

7. **Do you usually return things when you borrow them from people?**

8. **How do you feel about littering?**

Note: Aside from just asking questions, pay attention to how your partner lives his life. That will tell you everything you need to know about this quality.

QUALITY

▼   ▼   ▼   ▼   **5**   ▼   ▼   ▼   ▼

High Self-Esteem

You've probably heard it said before, but it's true:
YOUR PARTNER CAN ONLY LOVE YOU AS MUCH AS HE LOVES HIMSELF.
   One of the biggest mistakes we make in choosing partners is focusing on how much our mate loves and treats us, not how he treats himself. I know a man who was sure he'd met the woman of his dreams. "She'll do anything for me," he boasted. "She's so giving and so loving. She makes me feel like the greatest guy in the world." He neglected to notice that this woman had no self-esteem. She was afraid to make a move without him; she constantly criticized her appearance and insisted she was fat, even though she was bulimic; she interpreted any suggestions he gave her as condemnations. **She loved him, but not herself, and soon he realized that the love she lavished on him was really** *hungry love,* **not full love.**

A PERSON WITH LOW SELF-ESTEEM LOVES *IN ORDER* TO FEEL GOOD ABOUT HERSELF. A PERSON WITH HIGH SELF-ESTEEM LOVES *BECAUSE* SHE FEELS GOOD ABOUT HERSELF.

The healthier your partner's sense of self-esteem, the stronger your relationship will be. That's why it's important to look for these signs of self-esteem:

► **Your partner takes pride in himself.** If your mate walks around apologizing for his life and seems embarrassed by who he is, or is constantly putting himself down, then he has no pride in himself. You need a partner who has some satisfaction with who he is now and who he's becoming. I'm not talking about arrogance, or false bravado masquerading as self-confidence. True pride gives someone a sense of solidity and inner strength. *Another good way to tell is to ask yourself if you're proud of who he is.*

► **Your partner doesn't abuse himself, but takes good care of himself.** I know a man who grew up with a tremendous amount of shame. He drank, he smoked, he abused drugs and sex. Then somehow he found his way to my seminars in Los Angeles. Two weeks later he stopped drinking. He came back for another seminar, and a week later he stopped smoking. He did four more seminars in a row and gave up every vice he had. When a friend asked him why, after years of attempting to get clean, he finally did it, he answered: **"I loved myself too much to do that stuff anymore."**

▼

THE MORE YOU LOVE YOURSELF, THE HARDER IT WILL BE FOR YOU TO ABUSE YOURSELF PHYSICALLY OR EMOTIONALLY.

▲

You can tell how someone feels about himself by observing how he treats himself: the food he eats, the environment he lives in, the way he takes care of his body, his car, his possessions. All of these are reflections of self-esteem. Someone who mistreats himself and doesn't mind it won't mind mistreating you, either.

► **He doesn't allow others to abuse him.** "I'm married to a wimp," a middle-aged woman complained to me once while I was signing autographs. "He lets everyone push him around. His boss doesn't respect him. His own brother takes advantage of him all the time, and my husband won't stand up to him. The worst part is, he says he doesn't love me anymore!"

"How could he?" I answered. "He doesn't love himself."

One very clear symptom of low self-esteem is the way you let other people treat you.

THE MORE YOU LOVE YOURSELF, THE LESS YOU'LL ALLOW OTHERS TO MISTREAT YOU.

This is why victims are poor choices for partners, even though loving them might make you feel needed. **All the terrible things they complain that others have done to them are merely reflections of their own low self-esteem.**

▶ **He expresses his self-confidence by taking action in his life.** *True self-esteem manifests itself in action.* It inspires us to take chances, go after our dreams, and reach out beyond our comfort zone. You can always spot someone with self-esteem because he's *doing* something. In contrast to this is **the procrastinator, a person with low self-esteem, who avoids action because he's scared to death of failing and feeling even worse about himself.** Look for partners who do something about their goals instead of just talking about them.

QUESTIONS TO ASK YOUR PARTNER ABOUT SELF-ESTEEM:

1. **What are you the most proud of about yourself and your life?** (Notice whether he has a very difficult time finding anything to say.)

2. **What kind of emotional abuse or mistreatment have you tolerated in the past? Why did you put up with it? Would you tolerate it now?**

3. **What do you do to show your love for** *yourself* **(bubble baths, massages, special vacations, etc.)?**

4. **What are your worst health or living habits?**

5. **Do you procrastinate a lot of the time, much of the time, or not much at all?**

6. **What risks have you taken in your life? What was the most recent risk? Are there any risks you've been avoiding taking?**

QUALITY

▼ ▼ ▼ ▼ **6** ▼ ▼ ▼ ▼

Positive Attitude Toward Life

There's an old saying, *"There are two kinds of people in the world: positive people and negative people."* If you had to spend the rest of your life with one of these two, which would you choose? Tough decision, right?! Unfortunately, we often fall in love with someone without discovering whether he has an essentially positive view of the world, or an essentially negative one, and it really makes a difference.

Negative people:

► always focus on the problems, and resist solutions
► always find something or someone to complain about
► allow fear and worry to rule them
► are cynical and pessimistic about the future
► don't trust easily

Positive people:

► always focus on finding the solution
► turn obstacles into opportunities and adversity into lessons
► trust in their ability to make a difference
► believe that things can always get better
► use their vision to change their reality

Naturally, it follows that negative people create similarly negative relationships, and positive people create equally positive relationships. No surprise, then, that having a love affair with a negative person is about as much fun as listening to someone slowly drag chalk across an old blackboard.

Love is a positive force: It thrives in an atmosphere of positivity and starves in an atmosphere of negativity. That's why it's so important to find a partner who has a positive attitude. You'll be able to tell by spending a little time with someone whether he's positive or negative. Look for the symptoms I just listed.

Relationships are much easier when you're with a positive person. You work through conflict faster; there's less blame and more cooperation. Most of all, there's more love.

▼

QUESTIONS TO ASK YOUR PARTNER ABOUT A POSITIVE ATTITUDE TOWARD LIFE:

1. **Do you feel people are essentially good or essentially bad?**

2. **When lots of things go wrong at once, how do you react? What goes on in your mind? Give an example from your recent past.**

3. **What are some of the most important lessons you've learned about pain in your life?**

4. **If you could sum up your philosophy of life in a few sentences, what would it be? Has it changed since you were younger?**

5. **If you had to explain why the world is the way it is to your children, what would you say?**

6. **Do you believe things always turn out for the best? Whether your answer is yes or no, explain why.**

▲

Taking the time to discuss these six categories of questions with a new partner will reveal much about his character and will help you determine whether he can be the kind of person you want to spend your life with. And talking about these with your longtime mate may surprise you! You might learn things about your partner you didn't know, and the quizzes will help you focus more clearly on problem areas in your relationship.

If you've finished this chapter but didn't answer all the questions about YOURSELF, you avoided a wonderful opportunity for your own personal growth! **Go back and read the chapter again, this time concentrating on evaluating your character.**

9

▾▾▾

SEXUAL CHEMISTRY: WHAT TURNS YOU ON AND WHAT DOESN'T

▾▾▾

▶ Are you in a relationship but sometimes wonder if you'd be sexually happier with another partner?

▶ Are you single and find the partners you're sexually attracted to are the ones who aren't good for you?

▶ Do you know someone who would make a great spouse except for the fact that you feel no chemistry between the two of you?

▶ Do you ever worry that your partner's not attracted enough to you, or that you're not attracted enough to him?

Life was so much simpler before we discovered sex. Remember when you were seven or eight and had buddies of the opposite sex? It was so easy to hang out together riding bikes or playing games. You knew that grown-ups did things like holding hands and getting married, but it didn't interest you one bit, and besides, it seemed really gross. "I'm never kissing a boy!" you vowed to your friends. "I'm never going to act goofy around girls!" you promised your pals.

And then, sometime between ages ten and thirteen, you were struck by a plague that ravages all adolescents: *hormones!* And all of a sudden, the other sex looked very different to you, especially certain people. Now, if you were a girl, all boys weren't the same anymore—a few of them looked *really good.* When you saw them in the hallway at school, you got a funny feeling in your stomach. When you stood near them, your heart started beating rapidly. Just the thought of that one special guy gave you goose bumps! **You didn't know it then, but you were having your first experience of SEXUAL CHEMISTRY.**

Sexual chemistry turned a boy you thought of as a friend into someone who made you melt. It took a girl you wouldn't have been caught dead with a year before and transformed her into the star of a fantasy that kept you up each night. *It divided everyone you knew into two very distinct categories: the ones you were "attracted to" and the ones you weren't.*

WHAT IS SEXUAL CHEMISTRY?

Many years have passed for all of us since our first crush, and yet sexual attraction is as mysterious a process now as it was then. For one thing, it's hard to define. **You either feel it, or you don't.** Have you ever had a friend describe a fabulous man to you, assuring you that this guy had everything a woman could want, and you became very excited to meet him, only to find when you're finally face to face that there's "no chemistry"? Or have you ever found yourself powerfully attracted to someone you had nothing in common with, didn't respect or approve of, and with whom you would never want to spend your life? This is what's so exasperating about understanding sexual attraction. **It seems we often feel it too much under the wrong circumstances and not enough under the right ones.**

Over the course of a relationship, sexual chemistry will naturally fluctuate: It can grow as you become closer; it can diminish as you build emotional walls between you; it can even be lost and reignited. But one thing is for sure:

▼

SEXUAL CHEMISTRY NEEDS TO EXIST BETWEEN YOU AND YOUR PARTNER *IN SOME FORM* IN ORDER TO DISTINGUISH YOUR RELATIONSHIP FROM A FRIEND-SHIP.

▲

After all, what's the difference between how you feel toward your friends and how you feel toward your partner? *What makes your partner more than just a best friend?* The answer is: the sexual, erotic connection between you. **It binds you together in a very primal, very physical way that's difficult to experience with someone unless you have sex with that person.**

One way to define "sexual chemistry" is as a kind of **resonance.** You and your partner resonate together. The dictionary defines resonance as:

> *"energetic vibrations of a body produced by application of a periodic force of nearly the same frequency as that of the free vibration of the affected body."*

Even though this term is used most frequently to describe a certain quality of sound, the principle of how sound waves resonate can be applied to people as well. In simple terms, **when something of one frequency comes into contact with a "body" (or in this case, a person) with a similar frequency, the energetic vibration between the two is called resonance.** We experience this resonance in different ways, one of which is sexual attraction. It certainly feels like an energetic vibration! And that's really what sexual energy is.

Why You're Turned On by Some People and Not by Others

If sexual chemistry occurs when there's resonance between two people, then what causes that resonance in the first place? Scientists and sociologists have only just begun to study this psychic, invisible dimension of our lives. Whether you're a skeptic or a believer, you've probably experienced picking up "vibrations" without realizing it. I'm sure you've met people and either really liked or disliked them before they even opened their mouth to say anything. You're picking up their energy. If they're full of love, compassion, and forgiveness, and you are, too, you'll probably feel "good vibes." If they're they holding a lot of negativity inside them, such as anger and bitterness, and you aren't, you'll probably feel "bad vibes." **But if you have the same kinds of emotions inside you, you will resonate.**

To understand why some people's "vibrations" turn you on, let's go back to our analogy of sound. Sound is also a vibration, but a very manifest one that we can actually hear. Every piece of music vibrates at a different frequency. A piece of classical music, for instance, produces a different vibrational quality than a piece of heavy metal rock music. Or there might be a very explosive symphony by Beethoven that has an even more intense vibrational effect on you than a rock love song. Your body feels different when you listen to each of these types of music, and each produces a very different effect on your nervous system. *You enjoy listening to sounds (or music) with which your nervous system resonates.* Just as sounds give off certain energies, so do people. We each have several different "categories" of energy or vibrations in our lives:

▶ Your *physical vibration* is the sum of everything you do to your body with food, cigarettes, drugs or alcohol, exercise, or sex, and can also be affected by strong mental or emotional vibrations.

▶ Your *mental vibration* is the sum of all your thoughts, judgments, and beliefs.

▶ Your *emotional vibration* is the sum of all your feelings, past and present, including all your emotional programming.

▶ Your *spiritual vibration* is the sum of your sense of peace with yourself and your world, your spiritual philosophy, as well as a reflection of all your other vibrations combined.

YOU RESONATE WITH (OR ARE TURNED ON BY) PEOPLE WHOSE VIBRATIONAL ENERGY IS SIMILAR TO YOURS.

So when you find yourself sexually attracted to someone, it probably means the two of you have very similar vibrations in one of more area—physical, mental, emotional, or spiritual. This doesn't necessarily mean you will be compatible partners, however:

PHYSICAL ATTRACTION AND COMPATIBILITY ARE NOT THE SAME THING.

Physical attraction is one element of a compatible relationship, but it alone will not be enough to make you and your partner compatible. For total compatibility you'll also need mental

attraction, emotional attraction, and spiritual attraction (see Chapter Ten). Otherwise your relationship will be a case of Lust Blindness, based purely on your sexual resonance.

INSTANT ATTRACTION VS. GRADUAL ATTRACTION

One of the biggest mistakes many of us make in looking for the right partner is judging that person too hastily. *If you meet someone and aren't instantly attracted to them, it doesn't necessarily mean that you won't* **become** *attracted to them as you get to know them better.* Sharing your thoughts and feelings with one another may create strong mental and emotional resonance that will spark sexual resonance. *The attraction should not just be based on how your partner looks, but also who he is and how you feel about yourself when you're with him.* For this reason, gradual attraction may actually be more genuine than "lust at first sight." **You're attracted to the whole person.**

In Chapter One I told you the story of how I almost missed the chance to have the most wonderful relationship of my life with my partner Jeffrey because of my habit of looking for instant attraction. I knew Jeffrey for two years and never would have considered myself attracted to him. It had nothing to do with his looks—he's incredibly handsome. He was just so different from the types of men I'd chosen in the past (he was healthy!) that I didn't even consider the possibility that I could fall in love with him. It was only after getting to know what he was like on the inside and developing a powerful emotional, mental, and spiritual resonance that the feelings of sexual attraction began to emerge.

Looking back, it's hard to believe I ever wasn't wildly attracted to Jeffrey, because that's the way I feel now. But we needed time to create enough resonance between us before we could recognize and appreciate the wonderful symphony our separate energies create when they come together. How grateful I am that I gave the relationship time to develop instead of judging it before it even had a chance to blossom!

Falling in love with your best friend can be the most fulfilling emotional experience of your life. **Studies report that couples who were friends before they became romantically involved have more successful and satisfying marriages.** From my own experience, I believe this is because they build a solid foundation of communication and compatibility upon which the relationship can truly grow. *If you become involved with someone based only on chemistry and attraction, you may wake up one morning and find out that you don't even like the person!!*

If you're trying to break the habit of "Lust-At-First-Sight," you'll need to be more patient in your new relationships and give the true attraction a chance to reveal itself. **It's important to remember, however, that giving sexual chemistry some time to develop does not mean staying in a passionless relationship for months and years with the hope that you'll wake up one day and suddenly and miraculously find yourself attracted to your partner.** Although there are instances when two people have known one another for five or ten years as friends and all at once they realize they've been in love all along, it's more common for us to linger in unsatisfying partnerships because we're afraid to face the truth.

WHEN YOU LOVE SOMEONE YOU'RE NOT ATTRACTED TO

One of the most painful questions I'm frequently asked is about the importance of chemistry in love relationships:

"Is it possible to have a lasting relationship with someone I'm not really attracted to?"

People who ask me this question are usually involved in a relationship they wish were different. They feel love for their partner but don't feel sexually attracted to them. *They don't want to leave, so they try to rationalize their lack of sexual chemistry and make it "okay."*

My honest response to this question is: **"No, I don't believe it's possible to have a healthy, lasting, romantic relationship with someone whom you aren't attracted to,** *at least for anyone who wants to include sexuality as part of their life."*

Perhaps if a couple met when they were both quite elderly and no longer had an interest in sex, they wouldn't need more than a strong friendship as a foundation to live together happily. But there's no reason why people in their seventies and even older can't enjoy active and fulfilling sex lives, so I don't like to use this example. Besides, it's not sixty- or seventy-year olds who usually ask me about love without attraction—it's men and women in their twenties, thirties, and forties.

Here are some of the reasons why you might attract or stay with partners to whom you're not sexually attracted:

280 ▶ KNOWING WHO'S RIGHT

1. You are avoiding true intimacy. A sexual connection binds a couple together in a very special way. *There's nothing more intimate than taking someone inside your own body, if you're a woman, or putting a part of yourself into someone else, if you're a man.* When you're making love, you create tremendous intimacy between yourself and your partner. **Although it may look like you're avoiding sex, becoming involved with someone to whom you aren't attracted may actually be a way you're unconsciously avoiding intimacy in your life.** Since you know you aren't going to have a strong sexual relationship, you're naturally protected from feeling too vulnerable. This will be especially true if you have a pattern of choosing partners with whom you have no chemistry.

2. You are avoiding sex. Some people aren't just avoiding intimacy by selecting mates they aren't attracted to, they are also avoiding sex. If . . .

▶ you've experienced any form of sexual molestation or abuse
▶ you've been raped
▶ you've felt sexually controlled by previous partners
▶ you were brought up with negative sexual programming

. . . then you may consciously fall in love with people who don't turn you on sexually. In this way you get to avoid sex. You may not be aware that you have these sexual issues. You may even bemoan the fact that you keep attracting partners in whom you're not sexually interested. *But if a lack of chemistry is a recurring theme in your relationships, you may need to do some work on healing your sexuality.*

3. You are trying to maintain a position of control. When you feel sexually attracted to someone, you are, in a sense, giving that person some control over you. It's as if your mind is saying, "You affect me so strongly that you make me want to lose control around you." *If you have issues with needing to be in control, or being afraid of being controlled by others, you may choose partners toward whom you feel no or little sexual attraction in order to keep yourself "safe."* Because you don't feel a strong sexual pull toward them, you get to maintain a certain emotional distance, creating the illusion that you hold more of the power in the relationship.

HOW WE COVER UP OUR LACK OF SEXUAL FULFILLMENT

I'll never forget the woman who came up to me at a seminar and, with a pained expression on her face, asked me if I thought it was important for her to be sexually attracted to her husband. When I answered that yes, I felt it was very important, an amazing thing happened. Her facial expression changed before my eyes, and she looked at me with a stiff smile. "Well, I think sex is overrated," she responded loudly. "There are many more profound ways to love someone other than just sexually." I felt sad as I watched her walk away, and even sadder when I found out from her best friend that she hadn't had sex with her husband in six years! *Like many of us, she was sexually unhappy, but was an expert at covering it up with rationalizations and excuses.*

▼

SEXUAL EXCUSE CHECKLIST

Here are some common excuses I hear from people who don't feel sexually attracted to their partners and don't want to deal with the situation. See how many of these you relate to.

1. We're not much different from other couples.

▶ *"Most couples end up not having much sex as they get older anyway, so I don't think it's such a big deal if we aren't that sexual now. I mean, the honeymoon can't last forever, right?"*

One of the ways in which we justify our lack of fulfillment is by finding other people who are unfulfilled and using them as evidence that we're not unusual. This excuse is just as ludicrous as if you told yourself, "Lots of people get cancer, so it's no big deal if I get it."

2. He's such a nice person, who cares about sex?

▶ *"I was wildly attracted to my last boyfriend, but the relationship was a nightmare. He always lied to me, and made me feel really insecure. My new partner is the opposite—so sweet and polite, and really considerate of my feelings. I feel like I've finally found a nice guy, and even though I'm not really attracted to him, the good things in the relationship make up for it."*

282 ▶ KNOWING WHO'S RIGHT

This person is swinging from one extreme to another. She used to choose relationships based on "lust blindness," but since that didn't work, she's taking the opposite tack by choosing a man she's not attracted to, and assuming that will make her happy. What she's failing to see is that **it wasn't the sexual attraction that caused her pain in her past relationship, but the lack of compatibility with her partner in other areas.**

3. **It's not that I don't want sex, we just never seem to find the time.**

   ▶ *"When Kevin and I first met, we were both really busy with school, so we never really had much time for sex. After the wedding, I was responsible for packing up our apartment and moving us to a new town, so that took a lot of energy. Then I got pregnant, and was sick a lot, and since our son was born, I haven't really been in the mood for sex. I love Kevin, but something always seems to get in the way of our being sexual together."*

   This woman has convinced herself that it's not her lack of attraction to her partner that's the problem, but her lack of time. If she's asked whether she enjoys sex when they rarely engage in it, she'll be forced to admit that she doesn't, and that **she uses work and children as excuses to cover up the real problem: She's not attracted to her husband. COUPLES WHO NEVER SEEM TO "FIND THE TIME" FOR SEX ARE AVOIDING THE SEXUAL PROBLEMS IN THEIR RELATIONSHIP.**

4. **I'm not that interested in sex anyway.**

   ▶ *"Lately I just haven't been feeling very sexual, period. I gained about twenty pounds and have been really stressed out about work, so sex is the last thing on my mind. That's why it doesn't bother me that my husband and I aren't having sex right now. In fact, I prefer it that way."*

   This is denial in its purest form—convincing yourself that sex isn't important to you, and therefore, feeling attracted to your partner is unnecessary. The truth is that **this woman has some deep sexual issues that she gets to avoid by having an asexual relationship with her husband.**

5. **She's such a good wife and mother/he's such a good provider.**

   ▶ *"Maureen is such a loving mother to the kids, and a great support to me. I couldn't ask for a better wife. I've accepted the fact that I'm not attracted to her in a sexual way, and I think we both can live with that."*

   ▶ *"Paul and I are like best friends. He's a fabulous provider and gives me a wonderful life-style. Our sex life is pretty nonexistent, from my side mostly, but I'd be crazy to give all of this up just to have good sex with someone else."*

   These two people are not only being unfair to themselves but are ripping off their partners as well. They've both settled for a marital arrangement that "looks good" to the world and fits their picture, even though each is unsatisfied. Instead of dealing with their issues, they talk themselves out of them. **This man and woman are in just the type of situation that makes them ripe to have an extramarital affair.**

▲

If one or more of these sexual excuses sound familiar, it's time to stop lying to yourself and give your relationship the attention it deserves.

HOW IGNORING YOUR LACK OF SEXUAL ATTRACTION FOR A PARTNER CAN DESTROY YOUR RELATIONSHIP

Ignoring the lack of chemistry between you and your partner is really another of our compatibility time bombs. It will eventually cause both you and your partner tremendous pain:

▶ *You'll miss the opportunity to bond with your partner in a way in which you do not bond with anyone else.*

▶ *You'll hurt your partner by constantly rejecting him (unless, of course, he isn't attracted to you either!).*

▶ *You'll make yourself prone to sexual infidelity.*

This third risk is by far the most destructive. I've seen so many cases where people ignored their lack of attraction to a partner, telling themselves it wasn't that important, only to wake up six months or five years or twenty years later and find themselves intensely sexually attracted to someone else, or worse, involved in a complicated affair.

▼

WHEN YOU STAY IN A RELATIONSHIP WITH SOMEONE YOU AREN'T ATTRACTED TO, YOU'RE SETTING YOUR-SELF UP FOR EVENTUALLY CHEATING ON THAT PERSON.

▲

Here is a story of a couple with this problem:

HOW CARLOS ENDED UP SLEEPING WITH HIS WIFE'S SISTER

Carlos and his wife, Wendy, attended one of my seminars in hopes of saving their ravaged marriage. Wendy stood up on Friday night and announced she wanted to forgive Carlos for cheating on her but didn't know if she could because of the circumstances. When I asked her what they were, she answered: *"My husband not only cheated on me, he cheated on me with my sister."*

The next morning Carlos pulled me aside to explain. "I'm ashamed to admit it, but what Wendy said was true. I had a six-week affair with her sister, Stacie. I just don't understand it, Barbara. How could I do anything so awful?"

I suggested he do some deep soul-searching over the weekend to figure it out, and the next morning Carlos approached me again, and I could tell by the tears in his eyes that he'd had a breakthrough.

"I think I figured it out," he explained. "I haven't wanted to admit it, but **the truth is, I've never been sexually attracted to Wendy. She's more like a best buddy.** She was the first girl who ever loved me just for me, not how much money I had or what I could offer her. She didn't care that I was a plumber and didn't have a fancy job, like other girls I'd dated. I was so happy to feel so totally accepted by a woman that I guess I didn't pay much attention to our sex life. *I knew I loved Wendy very much, but now that I look back, I see that I avoided having sex with her from the beginning.* I thought my lack of desire was a sign of maturity, but it never went away, and a physical attraction toward her never developed."

"Wasn't she suspicious?" I asked Carlos.

"Frankly, I think she was relieved at first. Wendy hadn't had a lot of sexual experience, so my lack of interest took the pressure off her. A few years into our marriage, she started asking me questions about it, and I'd blame it on work or whatever. The truth was, I felt very sexual, but not toward Wendy.

"When her sister, Stacie, moved to California, she stayed with us for a month, and the energy between us was intense. Barbara, I wanted to run away, because **I felt all the attraction for Stacie I would have given anything to feel for Wendy.** Things got better once Stacie moved out, but last year, when Wendy went to a business conference out of town, she had Stacie promise to come over and cook me dinner. I tried to tell her I'd be fine, because I didn't trust myself alone with Stacie, but Wendy insisted. I was like dry wood being lit by a match—we just ignited together. We both felt awful afterward and vowed we would never do it again, but the passion was too intense. *I know I was terribly wrong to cheat on my wife, but am I wrong to want to have a good sex life?* I've tried, but I can't live without that kind of passion anymore."

Carlos was right—although his affair had devastating effects on the whole family, it did have one positive result: **Carlos was no longer in denial. The affair forced him to face the sexual frustration he'd kept secret from himself for so long.** He and Wendy did a lot of healing together that weekend, but agreed to separate. *They were in a relationship that couldn't work because there was no sexual compatibility.*

You Can't Create Sexual Chemistry

IF YOU HAVEN'T FELT SEXUALLY ATTRACTED TO YOUR PARTNER FROM THE BEGINNING OF YOUR RELATIONSHIP, YOU'LL BE UNLIKELY TO DEVELOP THOSE FEELINGS OVER TIME.

One of the hardest things I ever have to tell a couple is that I don't think their relationship has enough compatibility to work. They often come to me hoping that a miracle will allow them to avoid facing the fact that it's over. (We'll talk later about how to tell if your relationship can survive or not.)

If you and your partner used to, at one time, feel very attracted to one another but have lost that sexual spark

through the years, *you may be able to reignite it by doing some serious emotional healing*. I know because this is what I help people do in my seminars. **BUT IF YOU'VE NEVER FELT THAT CHEMISTRY, AND GOT TOGETHER ANYWAY, AND STILL DON'T FEEL IT, YOU PROBABLY NEVER WILL.** (An exception: If you've never felt sexually attracted to anyone, and suspect you have a problem with your own sexuality, it's possible that with some professional help you can slowly discover sexual feelings toward your partner as you heal yourself.)

If I had the formula to make people attracted to one another, I'd probably be a billionaire! People would pay anything for an elixir that created sexual chemistry. Through all of my books, seminars, and tapes, I feel confident that I can help a couple who has lost the sexual magic, but I can't help a couple who never had it. **That's why it's so important that you make sure *before* you become seriously involved with someone that the right kind of chemistry exists between the two of you.**

How to Tell If You Have Enough Sexual Chemistry with Your Partner

Here's a quiz to help you determine how sexuality attracted you are to your partner. This is different from a quiz that would determine how happy you are with your sex life, since **it measures *how you feel about your partner's sexual attractiveness not his ability as a lover or the frequency of your lovemaking*.**

► You can take this quiz about your present partner.
► You can take the quiz about previous partners (how you *used to feel* about them.)
► Ask your partner to take the quiz with you.

I know it's scary to be honest about this topic, but don't avoid it—*the more you understand about your relationship, the better your chances of not getting hurt. So answer honestly.*

▼

YOUR SEXUAL CHEMISTRY QUOTIENT

Read each statement and ask yourself how accurately it describes your feelings:

If you feel this way ALMOST ALWAYS   Give yourself 4 points

If you feel this way FREQUENTLY   Give yourself 3 points
If you feel this way SOMETIMES   Give yourself 2 points
If you feel this way ONCE IN A WHILE   Give yourself 1 point
If you feel this way RARELY OR NEVER   Give yourself 0 point

1. I like the way my partner looks in clothing.
2. I like the way my partner looks naked.
3. I like the way my partner's skin feels.
4. I like the way my partner smells.
5. I like the way my partner tastes.
6. I like the way my partner holds me.
7. I like the way my partner kisses me.
8. I like the way my partner touches me when we aren't having sex.
9. I like the way my partner touches me when we are having sex.
10. I look forward to having sex with my partner.
11. When I think about having sex with my partner, I feel physically aroused.
12. I feel sexually excited when my partner's body is pressed against mine.
13. When I don't have sex with my partner for a while, I miss it.
14. I like the way my partner moves his or her body.
15. I think my partner is sexy.

Now total your points:

► **50–60 points: YOUR PARTNER REALLY MAKES YOU SIZZLE SEXUALLY!** You are highly attracted to him or her, and it doesn't take much for him to turn you on. *Make sure you're compatible in other areas of your relationship—the chemistry is so strong that you could be a victim of lust blindness if your relationship isn't well balanced.* Pay attention to those questions that produced lower scores and discuss the results with your partner.

► **36–49 points: YOU FEEL NATURALLY ATTRACTED TO YOUR PARTNER, BUT THERE ARE OTHER PROBLEMS THAT ARE INTERFERING WITH YOUR ABILITY TO ENJOY HIM OR HER SEXUALLY.** Chemistry isn't the issue—there's lots of it—but *you may have emotional resentments that are affecting your sexual closeness.* It's also possible that you aren't totally happy with your partner's sexual technique, or that *you have some blocks in your* *own sexuality that are preventing you from fully enjoying your relationship.* Think about these issues and communicate honestly with your partner about problem areas.

▶ **21–35 points: YOU MAY NOT WANT TO ADMIT IT, BUT YOU ARE NOT REALLY ATTRACTED TO YOUR PARTNER.** It's possible that you never were, or perhaps the problems in your relationship have turned you off completely. *Ask yourself why you are staying in this relationship.* Is it convenient? Are you afraid you can't do better? Are you protecting your partner, or your children? *You are not sexually happy with this person. Get some professional help and either work on trying to find the passion again, or get out.*

▶ **0–20 points: YOUR PARTNER IS A TOTAL TURNOFF!** What are you doing with him or her? You must spend your time either physically disgusted, numb, or avoiding your mate as much as possible. *You may have such low self-esteem that this is what you think you deserve, or you could have some serious sexual blocks due to past trauma. You deserve to feel happier than this. Stop lying to yourself and end this relationship.*

Remember, this quiz doesn't test your overall compatibility, **it only tests how attracted you are to your partner.** So:

▶ You could score very high on this test (50–60 points) but still have a bad relationship overall.

▶ You could score in the middle of this test (36–49 points) but still have a strong relationship that happens to have some sexual and emotional problems.

If you score very low on the test (0–35 points), please think carefully about the information in this chapter. You probably don't have enough natural attraction to your partner ever to have a fulfilling sexual and romantic relationship. Stop waiting for it to happen, and focus on getting back in touch with your needs. This is *not* the way love is supposed to feel!

WHEN YOU AND YOUR PARTNER AREN'T SEXUALLY COMPATIBLE

Remember that earlier I explained sexual chemistry is *not* the same as sexual compatibility? **You may feel a lot of sexual chemistry with your partner but be sexually imcompatible** with him or her. Here are some situations that can create sexual incompatibility:

REASONS FOR SEXUAL INCOMPATIBILITY

1. **You and your partner don't physically fit together.**
2. **You and your partner have different sexual frequency requirements.**
3. **You and your partner have different Sexual Styles.**
4. **You or your partner is sexually addicted or dysfunctional.**

---

1. YOU AND YOUR PARTNER DON'T PHYSICALLY FIT TOGETHER.

This will only sound amusing if it's never happened to you, but if it has, you won't laugh reading this. Some people's bodies just fit together better than others, and some people's bodies don't fit together at all. I frequently receive heartbreaking letters from men and women complaining that their relationship isn't working because the two partners aren't physically compatible. Women write about men whose penises are too large to fit comfortably inside, or so small that they can't feel anything during intercourse. Men write about women with vaginas so tight that intercourse becomes extremely painful for the male partner, or vaginas so large that the man feels lost when he enters. **These mismatched lovers end up dreading sex because it's so physically uncomfortable, and the problem creates tremendous tension in their relationship.**

If the physical differences aren't extreme, a couple can work together to adapt their sexual behavior to alleviate the problem. **However, if the physical differences are extreme, a couple will have a difficult time finding sexual happiness together.**

This situation becomes more complicated when a couple decides to wait until after they're married to have sexual intercourse. I recently met a woman who shared a sad story with me. She and her husband had been married for thirty-two years but almost never had sex! *It seems she'd decided to stay a virgin until she got married, and on her wedding night discovered that her husband's penis was so large that it virtually couldn't fit inside her without causing horrific pain and bruising.* This woman went from doctor to doctor, but none could offer any remedy for the couple's embarrassing predicament. Since she refused to have sex with her mate, he began having affairs about five years into the marriage, affairs she knew about but tolerated because of the circumstances. They finally decided to get divorced after over three decades of sexual incompatibility.

"I'm a Catholic, and I was taught to wait," she told an audience of women with tears in her eyes, **"but please don't make the same mistake I did. Find out if you and your partner will be physically good together before you get married."**

I can't tell you how to make your sexual decisions when you're single, but like this unfortunate woman, I, too, am concerned about couples who have no sexual knowledge of one another before they make a permanent commitment. *If you're planning to remain celibate until you're married, at least take the time to have a very frank discussion with your partner about physical compatibility in order to avoid any sexual blocks on your wedding night!*

2. YOU AND YOUR PARTNER HAVE DIFFERENT SEXUAL FREQUENCY REQUIREMENTS.

▶ "I like to make love several times a week. My wife only wants sex a few times a month. We fight about it all the time, and it's poisoning our relationship. What can we do?"

▶ "My boyfriend wants sex at least once a day, and sometimes twice a day on weekends. When we first met I felt flattered that he was so turned on by me, but now I almost dread sex. It feels like a chore. Can you help us?"

▶ "My husband can go without sex for months at a time, and I walk around constantly horny. I don't want it all the time, but sometimes would be nice. When I talk to him about it, he says sex isn't important to him, but it is to me. Do you think we're just incompatible?"

All of these couples have one thing in common: Their sexual compatibility is threatened by the differences in their sexual frequency requirements. This is not about whose sexual rhythms are right and whose are wrong, but about the fact that they're *different enough to produce conflict.*

No two people are exactly alike, so naturally one partner's desire for sexual contact won't always coincide with his or her mate's. On the night you're in the mood, he's exhausted from work. The morning he's suddenly aroused, you wake up with cramps. These moments when you and your partner are sexually out of sync are normal parts of any long-term relationship. *The problem arises, however, when you're almost always out of sync because your sexual rhythms are so different from those of your lover.*

The good news is, in many cases, you and your partner can work through this crisis with professional guidance and honest communication. Perhaps the man who wants sex every day is using it as a tension reliever, not a way to make love to his wife. By developing other means of reducing stress in his life, such as exercise or meditation, and by dealing with conflicts rather than avoiding them, he may find his need for constant sex balances out. And perhaps the woman who only wants sex twice a month is avoiding intimacy with her partner. Maybe she doesn't like the way he makes love to her; maybe she has some sexual issues in her past that have turned her off to sex. Or perhaps she doesn't feel good about her body and sexuality and has numbed herself to that part of her relationship.

There are reasons why you either want or don't want sex. *Exploring these and discussing your feelings with an understanding mate can help you and your partner find a common ground of sexual frequency that makes both of you happy.* **However, if your partner insists that "This is just the way I am" and shows no interest in either compromise or communication, you must face the fact that your sexual frequency conflicts make you incompatible.**

3. YOU AND YOUR PARTNER HAVE DIFFERENT SEXUAL STYLES. Each of us has a Sexual Style that reflects the many aspects of our personality. You might be Miss Romantic or Mr. Speedy, Miss Control Freak or Mr. Sensitive, to name just a few.

Your Sexual Style will reflect:

▶ your past sexual experiences
▶ any emotional programming you have about sex from childhood
▶ your level of comfort or discomfort with your body
▶ your level of self-confidence
▶ your level of emotional openness or fear
▶ your attitude toward intimacy
▶ how much you feel you deserve love and pleasure
▶ how much you know or don't know about sex

In addition, a person's Sexual Style can and will change over time as he or she changes physically, emotionally, mentally, and spiritually.

▼

THE CLOSER YOUR SEXUAL STYLE IS TO THAT OF YOUR PARTNER, THE MORE SEXUALLY COMPATIBLE YOU'LL BE; CONVERSELY, THE FARTHER APART YOUR SEXUAL STYLES, THE LESS SEXUALLY COMPATIBLE YOU'LL BE.

▲

How can you figure out someone's Sexual Style? The only way I know of is to have sex with him or her. Soon you will know all there is to know! You will either love it, hate it, or like some parts but not others. And your partner will have his or her own opinions about your Sexual Style.

▶ **In a good relationship, you and your partner will create a Sexual Style that's a synthesis of the best parts of each of you.** For instance, when Alan met Victoria, his Sexual Style was very different from hers. She was a very emotional lover, and Alan was a much more physical lover. By learning more about themselves and from one another, Alan began opening up more in bed and allowing himself to feel more emotion, and Victoria started giving herself permission to be more sensual and lusty. Their Sexual Styles became increasingly compatible as their relationship blossomed.

▶ **In a bad relationship, one partner will sacrifice or modify his Sexual Style to please the other or to avoid conflict.** Susanna was attracted to Charlie when she first met him but very uncomfortable with his Sexual Style. Charlie was into a lot of sexual fantasy, X-rated movies, and role-playing in bed, whereas Susanna's Sexual Style was more grounded in intimacy and love. Because she didn't want to lose Charlie, Susanna did whatever he wanted in the bedroom, but as the weeks went by, Susanna became more and more resentful, until she stopped wanting to have sex at all. Charlie became frustrated and eventually left her. He actually did her a favor, because the relationship wasn't healthy.

If your Sexual Style and your partner's clash, examine the rest of your relationship and you'll probably find similar conflicts. After all, sex is just an expression of who you are emotionally and intellectually. So if your emotional style and mental style aren't compatible with your partner's, your Sexual Style most likely won't be, either. (See Chapter Ten for more about overall compatibility.)

What if your Sexual Style is very different from your partner's and it's causing problems between you? Some couples who start out with different Sexual Styles work together to learn more about themselves and all those elements that contribute to Sexual Style I mentioned earlier. Through constant communication, a willingness to make their relationship work, and professional guidance, if necessary, they actually improve their sex life. Other couples with very different Sexual Styles try to work on solving their problem, but fail. They are simply such different people that they're incompatible in many areas. It all depends on you and your partner, and how willing you are to use your sex life as an opportunity to learn many things about yourselves.

The truth is: **Different Sexual Styles can sometimes create sexual incompatibility, but just as often they serve as an impetus for a couple to work together as a team to grow in love, sensitivity, and maturity.**

4. YOUR PARTNER IS SEXUALLY DYSFUNCTIONAL. In Chapter Six, *Fatal Flaws*, we discussed sexual dysfunction at length and explained why it's so destructive to relationships. Just to remind you, I included three categories of behavior under sexual dysfunction:

1. **Sexual addiction and obsession**
2. **Lack of sexual integrity**
3. **Sexual performance problems**

If your partner has a problem in any of these areas, you may not be sexually compatible with one another. *It all depends on how severe the problem is and how willing your partner is to change or get help* (or if you're the one with the problem, how willing you are to change or get help).

NO MATTER HOW MUCH YOU LOVE SOMEONE, YOU'LL HAVE A DIFFICULT TIME TRANSCENDING THE PAIN THAT PERSON'S SEXUAL DYSFUNCTION CAUSES YOU.

If it hurts to read this, and you know this is a problem in your relationship, make sure you've read about sexual dysfunction in Chapter Six very carefully.

When the Sexual Chemistry Disappears

One of the most frightening feelings in the world is waking up next to your partner in the morning and, as you watch him sleep, realizing that you aren't sexually attracted to him anymore. I wrote my first book, *How to Make Love All the Time,* in hopes of helping couples avoid making the common relationship mistakes that eventually destroy the passion they used to feel. **Often the chemistry isn't gone—it's just buried underneath piles of unexpressed feelings and bad habits. With hard work and emotional retraining, it's possible not only to rediscover the passion but also to experience more love and intimacy than you did before.**

Sometimes, however, the chemistry disappears because you and your partner have grown in separate directions. Remember, we defined sexual chemistry as resonance:

IF YOU AND YOUR PARTNER BEGIN TO RESONATE ON VERY DIFFERENT VIBRATIONAL LEVELS, YOU WILL NOT FEEL ATTRACTED TO ONE ANOTHER ANYMORE.

This is an important point to understand. *It's not that you stop feeling attracted to your partner, and therefore the relationship stops working.* **It's that you stopped feeling attracted to your partner because the relationship stopped working.** When you and your partner stop resonating physically, emotionally, intellectually, or spiritually, you will stop resonating sexually.

Yesterday I took a break from writing this chapter and had lunch with a friend I'll call Dianne. I like Dianne because she's a woman completely devoted to her personal growth. She's spent the past five years facing her addictions, her codependency, and her denial. As part of that process, she recently ended a ten-year relationship. When Dianne asked me which chapter I was working on, I told her it was this one.

"That's appropriate," she said with a laugh. "One of the reasons I finally left Spencer was because I had turned off to him sexually. It's strange, because in the beginning of our relationship I was crazy about him."

I explained my concept of sexual resonance to Dianne, and all of a sudden her eyes lit up. "I get it!" she exclaimed. "For the past five years, I was growing in so many areas of my life. I changed my diet, I changed the way I communicated, I changed from victim consciousness to empowerment consciousness. Even though Spencer was trying, he didn't change that much. **According to what you're saying, we began vibrating at very different frequencies. You know, it really felt as if suddenly we were in two different worlds. I still loved him, but I couldn't feel connected to him as I did before.**"

"That's why you stopped feeling attracted to him," I continued. "There wasn't enough resonance left between you to create sexual chemistry."

I was glad to have helped Dianne understand more about sexual chemistry and her relationship. I hope, through this chapter, that I've helped you understand more, too.

Sex is really just a mirror for us—a mirror that reflects the state of our mind, our heart, and our soul. Knowing this, your sex life can transform from something mysterious and confusing to something enlightening and magical.

10

▼▼▼

COMPATIBILITY: FINDING OUT WHO'S RIGHT FOR YOU

▼▼▼

We've finally arrived at the most exciting part of the book, the chapter where you get to put everything we've talked about together and use it to discover exactly what kind of partner is right for you! Whether you're looking for a relationship, recovering from one, or committed to one, I know the exercises that follow will help you focus on what you want and need from a mate.

This chapter includes sections on:

1. **HOW TO TELL IF YOU'RE READY TO HAVE A RELATIONSHIP**
2. **HOW TO MAKE A COMPATIBILITY LIST**
3. **HOW TO TELL IF YOU AND YOUR PARTNER ARE COMPATIBLE USING THE COMPATIBILITY FORMULA**

Throughout this chapter I'll be asking you to do some writing and make some lists, so have a notebook and a pen handy. I'll also be reminding you of some important points from earlier chapters so you can apply them directly to your own love life.

IMPORTANT: It's normal to feel a little nervous starting out on this chapter. If you're in a relationship, you might be thinking, *"Uh-oh, what if I find out my partner and I aren't*

compatible? Maybe I'll just skip this chapter." If you're single, you might worry that you'll do the exercises and find out you aren't ready to be in a relationship! NO MATTER HOW YOU FEEL, DON'T AVOID THIS CHAPTER. Trust me—it'll help you create the loving relationship you deserve.

<u>STEP ONE</u>

HOW TO TELL IF YOU'RE READY TO HAVE A RELATIONSHIP

If you aren't emotionally ready to be in an intimate relationship, you'll have a difficult time determining whether you're with the right person. *The relationship won't feel right because of your own problems, not because you aren't compatible with your mate.*

▼

ARE YOU READY FOR LOVE?

Here are some questions to ask yourself to help determine whether you're ready to have an intimate relationship.

1. Am I still in love with an ex-partner?
2. Am I still carrying tremendous resentment and rage toward an ex-partner?
3. Do I often feel spiritually or emotionally empty within myself?
4. Do I dislike the person I am?
5. Do I feel I have very little that's valuable to offer a mate?
6. Do I have any addictions I'm not dealing with?
7. Do I feel so lonely and desperate that I'm totally miserable without a relationship?
8. Do I feel no one would want to be in a relationship with me?
9. Do I find it almost impossible to feel any emotion?
10. Am I unwilling to talk about my feelings with others?

▲

If you answered YES to even one of these questions, you may not be emotionally ready to have an intimate relationship with anyone. Either you haven't recovered sufficiently from a pervious relationship to give your heart to a new person, or your self-esteem is so low that you can't possibly love another person, or you feel so empty inside that you have nothing to offer except your extreme neediness. If you answered YES to questions nine or ten, you need to find your own emotions before you can expect someone else to be with you.

If you answered YES to some of these questions and you're already in a relationship, you are, no doubt, aware of the problems your lack of readiness is causing. *You may need some time away from your partner to find yourself, or heal whatever is preventing you from being totally available. You aren't being fair to your mate by expecting him or her to deal with what are your blocks to intimacy.*

There are times in our lives when we're ready to become involved with another person, and times when we need to be alone. **If you suspect you aren't ready for love, go on a "Relationship Fast" and work on improving your relationship with yourself.** When you can take this quiz and answer NO to the questions, you're ready to fall in love.

STEP TWO

HOW TO MAKE A COMPATIBILITY LIST

When I wrote my first book, *How to Make Love All the Time,* I talked a little about the importance of making a Compatibility List for both singles and couples. Over the past five years I've received countless letters from readers about their experiences making a list, and I'm excited to be able to update the process for you in this chapter.

If you are in a relationship that's working well, your Compatibility List can help you locate problem areas as well as remind you of how much you have to appreciate about your partner. If your relationship is troubled, your Compatibility List can help you understand what is and what isn't working between you and your mate, and make it easier to decide whether it's time to separate. If you're looking for a new relationship, your Compatibility List acts like a shopping list, directing you toward partners who are right for you and helping you avoid partners you don't need and who will be a waste of time.

In Chapter Nine we talked about the resonance between two people as what attracts them to one another. **Your Compatibility List will clarify and define how you "resonate" in ten different areas of your life, and therefore reveal what kind of resonance, or compatibility, you're looking for in a partner.**

The first step is making your Compatibility List. Later in this chapter I'll explain how you can use your list and my Compatibility Formula to determine how compatible you and your partner are.

Here's how to make a Compatibility List:

▶ **Find a quiet place where you won't be disturbed.**

▶ **Write down the qualities you seek in a mate in the following ten categories** (I've included a brief list of examples from each category):

---

1. Physical Style

Appearance
Eating habits
Personal fitness habits
Personal hygiene

EXAMPLES

Well built, dark hair
Eats healthfully/no meat
Exercises regularly
No drugs or alcohol
Cares about appearence
Likes clothes/dresses well
Keeps body clean

---

2. Emotional Style

Attitude toward romance and
    affection
How he treats you
How he expresses feelings
How he treats the relationship

EXAMPLES

Always very affectionate
Supportive of me and my
    dreams
Cries easily
Expresses feelings easily
Makes romantic gestures
Committed
Sentimental about special
    occasions
Proud of me and shows it
Faithful and devoted

---

3. Social Style

Personality traits
How he interacts with others

EXAMPLES

Warm and friendly
Very outgoing, aggressive
Likes socializing
Good sense of humor
Down to earth/practical

Sophisticated
Kind and sensitive
Likes to play and be light
Stands out in a crowd

---

4. Intellectual Style

EXAMPLES

Educational background
Attitude toward learning
Attitude toward culture
Attitude toward world affairs
Creative expressions

Well educated/college +
Creative mind
Interested in culture
Interested in world events
Likes learning new things
Enjoys philosophical
    discussions

---

5. Sexual Style

EXAMPLES

Attitude
Skill
Ability to enjoy

Enjoys frequent sex
Very sensual
Sensitive, skilled lover
Seductive
Likes to cuddle
Easily aroused—no hangups

---

6. Communication Style

EXAMPLES

How he communicates
Attitude toward
    communication
Other forms of expression

Loves talking
Verbally articulate
Good writer/sends cards
Takes feedback well
Willing to discuss problems
Tells me what's going on inside
    him

---

7. Professional/Financial Style

EXAMPLES

Relationship with money
Attitude toward success
Work and organizational habits

Financially responsible
Hard worker
Ambitious in career
In a field that helps others
Well organized
Generous with himself and
    others
Enjoys good things in life
Honest and ethical

8. Personal Growth Style

Attitude toward self-
improvement
Ability to look at self and
change
Willingness to work on
relationship

EXAMPLES

Committed to learning about
self
Reads books on growth
Attends seminars
Sees own shortcomings
Enjoys discussing growth
Makes concrete changes

9. Spiritual Style

Attitude toward Higher Power
Spiritual practices
Philosophy of life
Moral views

EXAMPLES

Believes in God
Enjoys meditation and prayer
Open to the mystical
Optimistic outlook on life
Compassionate toward less
fortunate
Respectful of all living things

10. Interests and Hobbies

EXAMPLES

Loves to travel
Enjoys music
Loves to dance
Loves dogs
Loves entertainment (movies,
theater)

You can make your Compatibility List as long as you like. I've found that *the more specific you are on your list, the more helpful it'll be to you in determining whether you're in the right relationship.* I suggest you work on your list during one session, then put it down for a day or two. During that time you'll probably remember other qualities you want to include. Then look at the list again and add your new items to it. *One way to be thorough is to remember qualities that were missing from past relationships that caused conflict or problems, and to include them.*

Making a Compatibility List will teach you a lot about yourself. When you're done with it, read it over and ask yourself:

▶ **Which of these qualities do I feel I possess?**
▶ **Which of these qualities do I wish I possessed?**

You may be surprised to find that your Compatibility List not only describes your ideal partner *but also your ideal picture of you!*

I suggested in my book *How to Make Love All the Time* that if you're single, you should carry a copy of your Compatibility List in your wallet or purse at all times. Read it often. Share it with your friends. *I believe the list can actually act like a magnet, attracting that special person into your life.* I've heard some incredible stories from people who have followed this advice and reported that soon after they wrote their list, they met their ideal partner.

Later in this chapter I'll explain how to use this list with a **Compatibility Formula** that will determine how compatible you are with a particular partner. That's when the fun begins!!

STEP THREE

HOW TO TELL IF YOU'RE COMPATIBLE WITH YOUR PARTNER

Now it's time for you to apply everything you've been reading about to your relationship. I've divided this section into several parts based on how long you've known your partner:

▶ **0 to three months**

▶ **three to six months**

▶ **six months or longer**

I've done this because there are certain things you can find out about your partner within a few weeks of knowing him, but others may take several months to discover. **Therefore, deciding whether or not you're compatible with someone should happen in stages. At each stage of involvement you should decide whether you're compatible enough to go on to the next stage of involvement.**

Stage One: 0 to Three Months—the New Relationship

Let's say you've determined that you're ready for a relationship; you've made your Compatibility List, and you've met someone you're very interested in. **How can you tell if the relationship is worth pursuing, or if it's going to be a waste of your time?**

Here is a **new relationship checklist** which will help you figure out whether to continue with someone or to stop seeing him.

You'll recognize some of the questions from earlier chapters in the book. Within the first few months of a new relationship, you should be working on this checklist.

NEW RELATIONSHIP CHECKLIST

1. I've asked my partner a lot of questions about himself in the following areas, and received answers I feel good about.

Family background and quality of relationships, past and
    present ☐
Past love relationships/reasons for breakups/lessons learned ☐
Attitudes about love, commitment, children ☐
Sexual attitudes and preferences (including contraception) ☐
Sexual history (including discussion of AIDS) ☐
Spiritual or religious philosophy and practices ☐
Personal and professional goals ☐
Financial habits, background, and goals ☐
Attitude about *personal growth,* counseling, books, etc. ☐
Attitudes and behaviors about *food, exercise, and health* ☐
Attitudes or history with *addictions* ☐
Ethics, morals, and values ☐

Obviously I'm not suggesting that you meet your partner for your first date, and after the waiter takes your order, you pull out a questionnaire with four hundred questions you want answers to! But over several months of dating someone **you need to have conversations about these topics to really get to know him or her.** There's nothing wrong with bringing up the topic by simply saying, *"I'd like to know more about you. Tell me about all your ex-girlfriends and why the relationships didn't work, and then I'll tell you about my love history,"* or *"How do you feel about God and religion? Are they important to you? Have your views changed over the years?"* **Remember: If you and a partner can't even talk about these things, you aren't ready to be in an intimate relationship with one another.**

2. I'm not making the Six Big Mistakes We Make in the Beginning of Relationships (see Chapter Four).

I'm asking enough questions (see above). ☐
I'm not making premature compromises. ☐
I'm not giving in to Lust Blindness. ☐
I'm not giving in to material seduction. ☐

I'm not putting commitment before compatibility. ☐

I'm not ignoring warning signs of potential problems (see rest of checklist). ☐

Before you become too involved, make sure you aren't making these common mistakes. Remember: It's easy to be so excited to have finally found someone you like that you fall into these six traps. Stop, take a deep breath, and check before you go forward. *If you feel confident that your relationship is on the right track, continue with it. If you aren't sure, take some space from it for a week or two, then see how you feel about your partner.* **Slowing down can't hurt, and it may help you avoid becoming more involved in a potentially painful relationship.**

Stage Two: Three to Six Months— The Developing Relationship

When you first meet someone you spend most of your time trying to figure out if you like him enough to keep seeing him. **If you make it to three or four months, your relationship will probably become "serious." You consider yourself "in love"; you're officially a couple. At this point you should consciously stop and decide whether it's in your best interests to continue deepening this relationship.**

THE THREE- TO SIX-MONTH PERIOD IS A CRUCIAL STAGE OF A RELATIONSHIP, DURING WHICH YOU ARE GOING TO BECOME MORE EMOTIONALLY INVOLVED. THEREFORE YOU WANT TO BE SURE YOU'RE MAKING THE RIGHT DECISION BEFORE MAKING YOURSELF EVEN MORE VULNERABLE.

This is the time to ask yourself some more serious questions about your partner's character, since you're starting to see beyond his outer shell and getting to know the real person inside. *You also need to be honest with yourself about how this relationship is making you feel.* The following checklists will help you evaluate the situation.

DEVELOPING RELATIONSHIP CHECKLIST

1. I've checked my partner for Fatal Flaws (using the criteria in Chapter Six) and found him to be clear of them:

CLEAR

Addictions ☐

Anger ☐

Emotional damage from childhood ☐

Victim consciousness ☐

Control freak ☐

Sexual dysfunction (as far as you know at this point) ☐

Hasn't grown up ☐

Emotionally unavailable ☐

Hasn't Recovered from past relationships ☐

2. I'm not in one of the Ten Types of Relationships that Won't Work (see Chapter Five).

I do not care more about my partner than he does about me. ☐

My partner does not care more about me than I do about him. ☐

I am not in love with my partner's potential. ☐

I am not on a Rescue Mission. ☐

I do not have my partner on a pedestal as a role model. ☐

I am not infatuated with my partner for external reasons. ☐

I have more than just partial compatibility with my partner. ☐

I did not choose my partner in order to be rebellious. ☐

I did not choose my partner only as a reaction to a previous partner. ☐

My partner is available. ☐

3. I've tested my sexual chemistry with my mate (see Chapter Nine) and scored at least 36 of 60 points, indicating that there is basic sexual attraction between us. ☐

If you determine that your partner is healthy, your relationship is healthy, and the attraction is there, you'll feel a lot more confident going ahead to the next level of intimacy.

Stage Three: Six Months or Longer—a Serious Relationship

Once you've been with a partner for six months or longer, you're probably asking yourself, "Is he the one for me?" You know you love one another; you think you get along well. Now you begin to wonder if there's anything that could interfere with the happiness of this relationship. This is the time to go through the following checklist, since it will help you become clear about potential problems that could sabotage this relationship.

SERIOUS RELATIONSHIP CHECKLIST

1. I have checked my relationship for Compatibility Time Bombs (see Chapter Seven), discussed any potential problems with my partner, and, if necessary, made agreements with him about how to handle these issues.

Significant age difference ☐
Different religious background ☐
Different social, ethnic, or educational background ☐
Toxic in-laws ☐
Toxic ex-spouse ☐
Toxic stepchildren ☐
Long-distance relationship ☐

2. I've found the Six Qualities to Look For in a Mate (see Chapter Eight) in my partner.

Commitment to personal growth ☐
Emotional openness ☐
Integrity ☐
Maturity and responsibility ☐
High self-esteem ☐
Positive attitude toward life ☐

THE COMPATIBILITY FORMULA

Now you're ready to look at all the aspects of your relationship and determine how compatible you and your partner are together. I've created a Compatibility Formula that will give you an accurate analysis of how much you're getting what you need from your mate. Here's how it works:

Get out your Compatibility List. Make sure you've written down at least four or five items you want under each category. *The more complete your list is, the more accurate the Compatibility Formula will be.*

You're going to assign a point value to each item on the list based on how much of that desired quality or behavior your partner possesses. For instance, let's say that under "emotional style" you listed the following qualities you want in a partner:

> **Always very affectionate**
> **Supportive of me and my dreams**
> **Cries easily**
> **Expresses feelings easily**
> **Makes romantic gestures**
> **Committed**
> **Sentimental about special occasions**
> **Proud of me and shows it**
> **Faithful and devoted**

You will "grade" your partner as to how much he demonstrates these qualities using this scale:

Almost always	5 points
Frequently	4 points
Sometimes	3 points
Occasionally	2 points
Rarely or never	1 point

So if your partner is **frequently** affectionate, but not always, you'd give him **4 points** next to that item.

Always very affectionate   **4 points**

Next you'd ask yourself how supportive your partner is of your dreams. Maybe he supports you in some areas but not in others, and that's been a problem. So you would give him **3 points** for **sometimes.**

Supportive of me and my dreams   **3 points**

Then you check the next item: cries easily. "My partner cries once in a while, but it's hard for him," you think. "I wish he did cry more and show more vulnerability." So you give him **2 points for occasionally.**

Cries easily   **2 points**

Step-by-step Instructions for Using the Compatibility Formula

1. **Go through your entire Compatability List and grade your partner based on how much he fulfills the items you've listed. Use the system we just described.**

2. **At the end of each section, total the possible score, then total your partner's actual score.**

To determine the *possible score,* multiply the number of items in that category by 5 points. So if you listed nine items under "emotional style," you multiply that by 5 points and come up with a possible perfect score of 45 points. To determine your partner's *actual score,* simply add up the number of points you wrote next to each item.

Sample:

Always very affectionate	4
Supportive of me and my dreams	3
Cries easily	2
Expresses feelings easily	3
Makes romantic gestures	3
Committed	5
Sentimental about special occasions	5
Proud of me and shows it	5
Faithful and devoted	5

Total: 35

You should have two numbers, or totals, at the end of each section.

Sample:

POSSIBLE SCORE	PARTNER'S ACTUAL SCORE
45	35

Now divide the first number (the possible score) into the second number (your partner's actual score).

WHEN YOU DIVIDE YOUR PARTNER'S ACTUAL SCORE BY THE POSSIBLE SCORE, YOU'LL GET A NUMBER THAT REPRESENTS THE PERCENTAGE OF COMPATIBILITY YOUR PARTNER IS GIVING YOU IN THAT CATEGORY.

So if under "emotional style" your partner's possible score was 45 and his actual score was 35, you divide 45 into 35:

$$35 \div 45 = .777 \text{ or } \textbf{77 percent compatible}$$

If in another category, your partner's possible score was 25 and his actual score was 23, you divide 25 into 23:

$$23 \div 25 = .92 \text{ or } \textbf{92 percent compatible}$$

At the end of your list, total all ten categories to arrive at a *total possible score*. Then total all the actual scores to arrive at your partner's *total actual score*.

Next, divide your partner's total actual score by the total possible score to get a total compatibility percentage:
Sample #1:

TOTAL POSSIBLE SCORE	TOTAL ACTUAL SCORE
230	197

$$197 \div 230 = .856 \text{ or about } \textbf{86 percent compatible}$$

Sample #2:

TOTAL POSSIBLE SCORE	TOTAL ACTUAL SCORE
220	134

$$134 \div 220 = .609 \text{ or about } \textbf{61 percent compatible}$$

IMPORTANT NOTE: Make sure each of your ten compatibility categories has roughly the same number of items listed, give or take a few. For instance, maybe "physical" has seven, "emotional" has eight, and "social" has six. DO NOT make a list that is much shorter or much longer than the other nine, or it can throw off the Compatibility Formula. For example; if most of your lists have six to nine items, that's fine. But if one list has only two items, or twelve, it may affect your final score. (If you're mathematically proficient you can adjust the scoring accordingly, but it could get complicated!)

A SAMPLE COMPATIBILITY EVALUATION

Roxanne and John

Roxanne, twenty-eight, has been dating John, thirty-one, for about nine months. Here's her compatibility evaluation of John:

1. Physical Style

	JOHN'S SCORE
Cares about eating well	3
Good build/works out	4
No addictions (smoking, etc.)	5
Takes care of himself	4
Dresses nicely	2
Not a lot of body hair	5
Good-looking	4

Possible score: 35   Actual score: 27
Percentage of physical compatibility: 77

2. Emotional Style

	JOHN'S SCORE
Likes touching and holding me	3
Makes the relationship important	3
Expresses feelings easily	2
Romantic	2
Not afraid of commitment	2
Sentimental about special occasions	3
Likes being a couple and tells his friends about us	2
Doesn't make me jealous	4
Sensitive to how I feel	3

Possible score: 40   Actual score: 24
Percentage of emotional compatibility: 60

3. Social Style

	JOHN'S SCORE
Likes having fun	3
Has an easy time being with people	2
Enjoys parties, groups	1
Funny	3
Reliable	3
Commands respect from others	2
Warm and friendly	3
Considerate	3
Polite and respectful	5

Possible score: 45   Actual score: 25
Percentage of social compatibility: 55

4. Intellectual Style

	JOHN'S SCORE
Good education	5
Well read	5
Knows about lots of things	5
Interested in world events	5
Smart	5
Likes teaching me what he knows	5

Possible score: 30   Actual score: 30
Percentage of intellectual compatibility: 100

5. Sexual Style

	JOHN'S SCORE
Good lover	3
Comfortable with his body	2
Likes to kiss and touch a lot	3
Appreciates me sexually	2
Makes love, not just sex	1
Wants sex a few times a week but not more	1

Possible score: 30   Actual score: 12
Percentage of sexual compatibility: 40

6. Communication Style

	JOHN'S SCORE
Talks about his feelings and thoughts	3
Enjoys discussing ideas with me	2
Tells me when he's upset instead of clamming up	1
Open to my opinions and feelings	3
Expresses himself clearly so I understand	3
Doesn't lose his temper a lot—calm	1

Possible score: 30   Actual score: 13
Percentage of communication compatibility: 43

7. Professional/Financial Style

	JOHN'S SCORE
Responsible financially	5
Cares about getting ahead	5
Organized and efficient	5
Frugal and conservative with money	5
Has good taste	3
Honest in his work	5
Plans for the future	5
Reasonably successful/owns own home or condo	5

Possible score: 40   Actual score: 38
Percentage of professional compatibility: 95

8. Personal Growth Style

	JOHN'S SCORE
Interested in growing	2
Has worked on himself through counseling or books	1
Would discuss our problems and work with me on solving them	1
Is honest with himself about his problems	1
Flexible and willing to change	2

Possible score: 30   Actual score: 7
Percentage of personal growth compatibility: 23

9. Spiritual Style

	JOHN'S SCORE
Believes in God	3
Christian	5
Goes to church sometimes	1
Positive view of the world	2
Appreciates creation and God's gifts	1
Accepts my spirituality and involvement with church	2

Possible score: 30   Actual score: 14
Percentage of spiritual compatibility: 46

10. Interests and Hobbies

	JOHN'S SCORE
Enjoys cycling	5
Likes museums and art	5
Cares about the environment	4
Likes food and dining out	5
Likes camping	4

Possible score: 25   Actual score: 23
Percentage of interest compatibility: 92

Roxanne's overall compatibility summary for John:

TOTAL POSSIBLE SCORE	TOTAL ACTUAL SCORE
335	213

Percentage of total compatibility with John: 63

What Your Total Compatibility Percentage Means

Once you have scores in each category, and a final score, you can assess your overall compatibility with your partner. When I did the research for this book, I asked dozens of people to use this Compatibility Formula to evaluate their partner. I also used the formula myself, and I not only evaluated my present partner but also scored several former partners to see what percentage of compatibility we had. After comparing the scores of the relationships, I came up with a scale that I feel is highly accurate in interpreting your compatibility percentage.

80–100 PERCENT COMPATIBILITY: You and your partner are highly compatible. There is enough overall resonance in values, habits, behavior, and goals to create consistent harmony and enjoyment between you. Naturally, there will be areas of less compatibility. *Notice in which categories your partner scored a lower percentage. These will probably be the areas of greatest conflict in your relationship, and the topics you fight about the most!*

No relationship will be 100 percent compatible, since no two people are completely alike. The closer your score is to 100 percent, however, the better you'll get along and the more fulfilled you will feel. This doesn't mean you should feel bad about your lowest area of compatibility:

THE AREAS IN WHICH YOU AND YOUR PARTNER EXPERIENCE THE GREATEST CONFLICT IN YOUR RELATIONSHIP WILL BE YOUR GREATEST TEACHERS.

Perhaps you and your mate have 86 percent overall compatibility, but you notice that in the social category he scored only 65 percent. You can be sure there are important lessons for both of you around the topic of personality style. Maybe your list asks for someone dynamic, outgoing, and aggressive like yourself, but your partner is quiet, introspective, and cautious. It's possible that you're together so you can learn to be more like him and balance your need to always be active, while he may need to learn to take more risks and become a little more like you. This becomes your LEARNING AREA in the relationship.

Partners with compatibility of more than 80 percent usually have one or two major LEARNING AREAS. **The rest of their strong compatibility gives the relationship a firm foundation upon which to work through the weaker areas.** *If you have three or four areas with tremendous conflict, however, you won't just be* *learning from one another—you'll be clashing constantly.* (When this is the case, your overall score would probably be much lower than 80 percent.)

It *is* possible to have an incompatible relationship even if you score 80 percent or higher. Perhaps the area of lowest compatibility is so important to you that it outweighs the good compatibility in the others. For instance, your partner scores an overall 81 percent, but in the personal growth style category he scores only 53 percent. If your growth is highly important to you and you're experiencing constant conflict every time you try to talk about problems or explore new ways of loving, you may find it impossible to stay in the relationship in spite of all the good that exists. I'll talk more about this in the next few pages.

It's also possible to score a high percentage and be incompatible because of the other factors we've examined in the book: You and your partner might be compatible in many ways but have a Toxic in-law problem that he's unwilling to deal with. Or perhaps your mate is ideal for you in all ten areas—except that she's an alcoholic and in major denial. **Remember: Even one Fatal Flaw or Compatibility Time Bomb can be powerful enough to sabotage an otherwise well-matched partnership.**

If you and your partner are committed to growing together, *you can use the results from this formula to strengthen your compatibility with one another.* Naturally, you both need to make your list and do your evaluation. Share them together, talk about what you need more from each other, and make new commitments to give your partner more of what each other needs. When I used this formula, **I scored my partner twice—once for how he was when we first met, and once for how he is now.** The results were exciting: Jeffrey scored many points higher when I graded him now versus the way he was when we first began our relationship. He had the same experience in making his list about me. We talked about this afterward and agreed that all the hard work we've done to communicate our own needs and learn to fulfill each other's needs has really paid off. **We've actually become more compatible over time, and used our LEARNING AREAS to stretch ourselves into more loving, caring partners.**

70–80 PERCENT COMPATIBILITY: This relationship is *partially compatible,* with some significant areas of incompatibility that are producing conflict and discomfort for both partners. If you score your mate at this percentage level,

you're probably feeling confused and torn about whether your relationship is right for you. Your dilemma is understandable, and I hope by using this formula you can see why: You're very compatible in some areas and very incompatible in others. **This does not necessarily mean that you need to end the relationship.** *It does mean that you need to communicate honestly with your partner about those areas in which you aren't happy, and hopefully agree on a plan of action you can both take to remedy the situation.*

Stop making excuses such as "We're a lot better off than most couples," or "Look at all the good things we share together." This may be true, but you aren't feeling fulfilled, and *time will only make the situation worse, not better.* You might consider working with a professional counselor or therapist who can help you focus on the problem areas and transform them into powerful learning experiences. **If your partner refuses to participate in improving the relationship, you may need to face the fact that you're not with the right person for you. You aren't miserable, but you aren't as happy and loved as you could be, and you're cheating yourself.**

What I said earlier about Fatal Flaws and Compatibility Time Bombs is true for the 70–80 percent group as well—especially with less than 80 percent compatibility, you may not have enough of a foundation to fight off the destructive effects of these other problems.

0–69 PERCENT COMPATIBILITY: You are most likely *not* in a relationship with the right person for you. You may feel you love your partner. You may have years of history together, but you aren't resonating in enough areas to create a consistently loving, enjoyable partnership. *You've probably developed a high tolerance for tension, conflict, struggle, loneliness, and pain because you haven't been getting what you want, and yet you're still with this person.* I know it's painful to read these words, but if you're honest with yourself, you'll realize you've been secretly feeling this way for a while. Perhaps you've dreaded facing it, and have avoided looking at your relationship until now. Perhaps you stayed for other reasons, such as children, finances, or illness. **But the fact is that this relationship is causing you more unhappiness than it is happiness.**

The lower your percentage is, the worse your relationship is. If your partner scored in the fifties or sixties, your relationship is extremely incompatible. If he scored less than 50 percent, it's a nightmare! *Even with professional help, there are probably too many areas of inherent incompatibility for the two of you ever to be right for one another. It's not that you or he is bad or wrong—you just don't belong together.*

Evaluating Your Ten Compatibility Categories

The easiest way to get an overall picture of the **balance of compatibility** in your relationship is to list the percentages of compatibility in all ten areas. Each area reflects many aspects of your being, but some categories reveal more about certain parts of you than others:

▶ Your **value system** is reflected in your personal growth, spiritual, physical, and professional categories.

▶ Your **emotional programming** is reflected in your emotional, sexual, communication, social, and professional/financial categories.

▶ Your **background** is reflected in your professional, intellectual, and interest categories.

IMPORTANT: Each of us has certain compatibility categories that are more important to us than others are. For instance, if you're a professional athlete you might care more about finding a high percentage of compatibility in your physical category than you would in your spiritual or personal growth categories. In that way, the physical category would really be worth more than one tenth of the Compatibility Formula. On the other hand, if you're a minister, the spiritual category would be more important to you than the physical, and even if you had a low percentage of physical compatibility, it might be outweighed by a high percentage of spiritual compatibility. Take this into account when evaluating your ten categories.

Let's look at some examples:

ROXANNE AND JOHN

Roxanne and John have been dating for nine months, and Roxanne has been confused about whether or not to continue the relationship. When we look at her compatibility evaluation of John, we can see why she's been having so many problems. John's overall compatibility with Roxanne is 63 percent, much lower than what would be needed to create a harmonious relationship. However, when we examine the percentage of compatibility in each category separately, we understand more about Roxanne's dilemma.

CATEGORY	COMPATIBILITY PERCENT
Physical style	77
Emotional style	60
Social style	55
Intellectual style	100
Sexual style	40
Communication style	43
Professional/financial style	95
Personal growth style	23
Spiritual style	46
Interests and hobbies	92

Roxanne and John have what in Chapter Five I called "partial compatibility." Their intellectual and professional styles are highly similar, and their interests are perfectly matched. This explains why Roxanne was attracted to John in the first place. He's intelligent, successful, and worldly. He also happens to share Roxanne's passions for cycling, camping, and dining. Naturally, Roxanne thought she'd met the man of her dreams. **The strong partial compatibility Roxanne and John share created the illusion that they were right for one another.** *It wasn't until several months into the relationship, when Roxanne started wanting more emotional connection and intimacy from John, that their inherent incompatibility began to surface, and the relationship quickly deteriorated.*

Here's a diagram of what "partial compatibility" looks like:

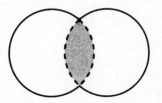

The shaded area is the area of shared compatibility. As long as Roxanne only focuses on that part of her relationship, it will appear that John is perfect for her. But as soon as she focuses on her emotional/social needs, the trouble begins. In every area that affects the dynamics of a relationship, (emotional, sexual, social, and spiritual) John is completely different from Roxanne. And look at that 23 percent compatibility in personal growth style. To John, growth means that his stock portfolio increases in value!

Using this Compatibility Formula not only helped Roxanne realize that John was not the right one for her, but also gave her a clear understanding of *why* the match was so wrong. This made it a lot easier for her to end the relationship without worrying that she was making a horrible mistake, and helped her focus on what she needed to look for in her next partner.

REMINDER: Use the Compatibility Formula to evaluate your former partners. You will have some interesting revelations about your past choices, and some fun, too. If you're presently single, you can use your Compatibility Formula right now, before you even meet a new partner.

MONICA AND CHARLES

Monica's Compatibility List for Charles was used as our prototype earlier. When Monica tallied his scores and applied the formula, she and her husband, Charles, came out 91 percent compatible, which is very high. But Monica says she's been feeling some unhappiness with the relationship, **so when she individually lists the results from all ten categories, she'll get a clear picture of the trouble spots in the relationship.**

CATEGORY	COMPATIBILITY PERCENT
Physical style	100
Emotional style	86
Social style	93
Intellectual style	83
Sexual style	73
Communication style	83
Professional/financial style	95
Personal growth style	100
Spiritual style	100
Interests and hobbies	96

What can you see about Monica and Charles's marriage from looking at this list? First of all, it's obvious why they're together:

Their value systems are almost identical, as reflected in the personal growth, physical, and spiritual categories. This means they operate on a very solid foundation of shared vision. Their personalities are also very similar, as reflected in their professional/financial, social, and interest categories. In most of these areas they experience little or no conflict.

The problem area in their relationship is the one with the lowest percentage: their sex life.

Enjoys frequent sex	2
Very sensual	3
Sensitive, skilled lover	5
Seductive	2
Likes to cuddle	5
Easily aroused—no hangups	5

Looking at that category again, Monica sees that although she's very satisfied with Charles's ability as a lover, and his affectionate nature, she's not happy with the infrequency with which they have sex and the minimal effort Charles makes to be romantic and seductive. This is an area Monica and Charles need to work on together. Fortunately, they have so much compatibility in the personal growth area that they shouldn't have a problem improving their sex life. Monica also notices that Charles's emotional and communication styles are not quite as compatible with hers as she'd like (not uncommon between men and women, by the way). This is also something they continually need to discuss and uplevel.

A Picture of a Compatible Relationship

A truly compatible relationship will resonate in the majority of areas while still maintaining the individuality of each partner. It might look something like this:

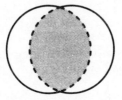

The differences add spice, challenge, and opportunities for growth, but the majority of the relationship is a strong, central core of resonance and harmony. I believe that for a relationship between two people to last a lifetime, their two spheres of individuality will, over the years, merge more and more into one. If the opposite happens, and their two spheres move apart, they'll have a difficult time living together happily and harmoniously, and they may need to separate.

Only You Know Who's Right for You

When I first began writing *Are You the One for Me?* I was very concerned about the chapter on compatibility. I knew I needed to give my readers some guidelines and formulas with which to assess their relationships, but I was adamantly opposed to presenting some brief compatibility quiz where I would profess to tell you how happy you were in your relationship based on my questions. I spent a lot of time thinking about how I could support you in evaluating your relationship *based on your own standards and needs, not mine.* Out of this concern came my idea for the Compatibility List and formula. I'm happy with the results, and I hope these tools have helped you become clearer about your love choices.

Ultimately, all that matters is your own happiness and what *you* think of your relationship, not what I think. So if your partner came out 63 percent compatible with you, and I said that's probably not good enough, but you still think your relationship can work, go with your feeling. I hope it will work, and I'll be happy to have been wrong. My categories are simply general comments on what I've found to be true much of the time. They aren't set in stone; they're not scientifically accurate. So use them if they serve you, and if they don't, go on to the next section!

For those of you who like simplicity and hate percentages, division, and math of any kind, here's a Sixty-second Compatibility Test you can use to see how well matched you are with someone. I sometimes suggest this to people who want to get an instant sense of how they feel about a particular partner. It's also fun to talk about at parties and on dates. Let me warn you, however, that these four little questions are deceptive—answering them can be a more intense experience than you expect it to be. Ready? Here goes:

THE SIXTY-SECOND COMPATIBILITY TEST

Ask yourself the following four questions about your prospective or present partner:

1. Would I want to *have a child* with this person?
2. Would I want to have a child *just like* this person?
3. Do I want to *become more like* this person?
4. Would I be willing to spend my life with this person *if he never changed from the way he is now?*

If you answered yes to all four questions, you're probably compatible with one another. If you answered no, ask yourself why not.

Have you figured out that answering these four questions could take you as long as reading this whole chapter again? I didn't promise you that they'd be easy—just that there would be no math!

The quest for understanding compatibility may not seem as compelling as the search for passionate, romantic love that, in spite of all odds, binds two people together. But as the philosopher Friedrich Nietzsche said:

> "It is not lack of love but lack of friendship
> that makes unhappy marriages."

With love *and* compatibility, I know it'll be much easier for you and your partner to live happily ever after.

11

▼▼▼

COMMITMENT:
MAKING AND KEEPING ONE
WHEN IT'S RIGHT
AND LETTING GO
WHEN IT'S WRONG

▼▼▼

If you never want to see a man again, say,
"I love you. I want to marry you.
I want to have your children . . ."
They leave skid marks.
COMEDIENNE RITA RUDNER

▼▼▼

Here's an idea for an interesting evening: Get a bunch of single people together, bring up the topic of "commitment," and watch the intense reactions. You'll notice most of the women get a kind of hungry look of longing on their faces, while the men will act as if you're torturing them by making them even talk about it. "The C Word" as I call it, seems to have that effect on people, evoking powerful emotions of hope and happiness, resistance and fear.

During the two years when I did my radio show in Los Angeles, I must have received thousands of phone calls about commitment:

▶ **"How do I know when I've been with my boyfriend long enough to expect a commitment?"**

▶ **"My girlfriend is pushing me to ask her to marry me, but I don't feel ready. How long should I wait?"**

▶ **"I've been married for two months, but I only knew my husband for six months before the wedding. We're having problems, and I wonder if we made a commitment too soon."**

So far, this section of the book has looked at the importance of chemistry and compatibility in choosing the right partner. Now it's time to add the third component, commitment.

YOU AND YOUR PARTNER NEED THREE INGREDIENTS TO MAKE YOUR RELATIONSHIP WORK:

1. **CHEMISTRY**
2. **COMPATIBILITY**
3. **COMMITMENT**

Without commitment, your relationship will be superficial and directionless. You and your partner won't be able to experience the depth of love and intimacy that can come only when you've truly committed yourselves to one another.

Here are some of the values of making a commitment in your relationship:

▶ **Commitment gives your relationship purpose.** A relationship without commitment is like a boat without a rudder in the ocean—it has no power of its own to seek a particular direction. It's at the whim of every current and every breeze. Commitment gives your relationship purpose and direction and thus allows it to move forward, rather than round and round in circles.

▶ **Commitment invests you in your relationship.** *The difference between being with someone without a commitment and with a commitment is the same as the difference between renting*

324 ► KNOWING WHO'S RIGHT

or buying a house. Most people are much less careful and conscious about their treatment of an apartment or home when it is not theirs. All of that changes when you purchase your first house. Suddenly you notice every scratch and every stain. You watch your children, friends, or pets like a hawk to make sure they aren't spilling on, chipping, or damaging your precious property.

Once you fully commit to a partner, you treat your relationship differently because more of you is invested in it. This allows your relationship to grow and thrive in ways it cannot without that commitment.

▼

WHEN YOU MAKE A COMMITMENT TO A RELATIONSHIP, YOU INVEST YOUR ATTENTION AND ENERGY IN IT MORE PROFOUNDLY BECAUSE YOU NOW EXPERIENCE *OWNERSHIP* OF THAT RELATIONSHIP.

▲

► **Commitment creates emotional safety.** Can you imagine renting an apartment or office space without a lease? At any moment, your landlord would have the right to throw you out on the street. Imagine the kind of tension you would live with knowing his commitment to you was so tenuous. This is the same underlying tension that exists in relationships that have no commitment as their foundation. **You experience a lack of safety that produces a constant state of unconscious anxiety.** I'm not talking about dating someone for three months without a serious commitment. *I'm talking about being sexually and emotionally involved with someone over a significant period of time without receiving a commitment from that person as to his or her hopes or plans for the relationship.*

Naturally, commitment doesn't totally protect you from pain or loss, just as a lease doesn't protect you from being evicted, or from your landlord selling the building. But it does reflect your partner's **intentions,** and that gives you a level of emotional safety that allows you to relax in the relationship.

► **Commitment creates freedom.** Many people have negative associations with the word "commitment." Often, men, in particular, resist commitment because they identify it with *limitation and loss of freedom.* **I believe that commitment has the opposite effect:**

It frees you from expending your emotional energy in many different directions and allows you to focus it on one person. You're free to immerse yourself in the relationship, to love and give fully with no restraints. This creates an experience of letting go, of surrendering, not to your partner, but to love itself. This only becomes true, of course, when you are with the *right person.*

▼

MAKING A COMMITMENT TO THE *RIGHT PERSON* WILL EMOTIONALLY LIBERATE YOU. MAKING A COMMIT-MENT TO THE *WRONG PERSON* WILL EMOTIONALLY IMPRISON YOU.

▲

Why We Fear Making Commitments

Whenever people tell me their partner is afraid of making a commitment, I remind them that it's not the fear of commitment that's the problem, *but rather an unconscious, underlying fear.* I've found four basic fears that keep us from feeling comfortable making commitments:

COMMITMENT FEAR

▼　　▼　　▼　　▼　　**1**　　▼　　▼　　▼　　▼

Fear of the Future

I've often heard men and women who are reluctant to commit to their partner claim that making a commitment would be a dishonest act. "How can I promise my girlfriend I will always love her?" a man will ask. "What if in ten years we grow apart, or what if she cheats on me and I leave her? Then I've broken my commit-ment."

With one of every two marriages ending in divorce, it's natural to experience a lack of confidence and certainty when commiting to a partner. We live in an unpredictiable and sometimes frightening world. None of us knows what the future holds. The more aware you become of this fact, the less comfortable you might feel making commitments *if you think that commitment means promising someone how you'll feel and behave at a future date.*

My response is this:

I believe when we make a genuine commitment, it can only be *a commitment to fully loving our partner in each moment, and for so long as the relationship allows us to also love and respect ourselves,* rather than a commitment to the amount of time our love will last.

For instance, you can commit to a marriage and later discover that your partner isn't willing to work on the relationship, or to stop drinking or abusing you or your children. If you feel strongly about keeping your commitment, you'll find yourself in a terribly painful dilemma. "I promised to stay in this marriage," you tell yourself, "but I'm miserable." On the other hand, if you're committed to the act of loving as long as it's healthy for you, you'll be able to end that relationship *once you've done all you could to save it,* because *you're keeping a commitment you made to yourself.*

I'm *not* suggesting that the moment you experience a little discomfort, you should break your commitment. I'm saying that if you or your partner have been resisting making a more serious commitment to one another because of your fear of the future, you may want to redefine the meaning of commitment so it feels honest.

COMMITMENT FEAR

▼   ▼   ▼   ▼   **2**   ▼   ▼   ▼   ▼

Fear of Being Hurt

Most people who have ever been divorced or gone through a major breakup tend to become somewhat "commitment phobic." After all, you have evidence that giving your heart totally to someone causes you pain and sorrow. As a recently wounded friend of mine put it, "Why would I want to volunteer for combat again after what I just went through?"

I can totally sympathize with this point of view, having been married and divorced not just once, but several times. (Premature commitment was one of my favorite pastimes!) However, one of the important lessons I learned along the way was:

▼

IT'S NOT FALLING IN LOVE OR MAKING A COMMITMENT THAT EVENTUALLY CAUSES US SO MUCH PAIN—IT'S MAKING A COMMITMENT TO THE *WRONG* PERSON.

▲

I hope you can understand the distinction here, because it's one of the most important points in this book. Avoiding commitment because you've been hurt emotionally is as unnecessary as if you decided you're never going to eat out again because you got food poisoning in one bad restaurant! Just choose your restaurants more carefully. And that's been my message throughout these chapters. When you make more intelligent love choices, relationships become a source of joy, not heartache.

In many ways, those of us who have made the biggest mistakes in love are in a much better position to make better choices the next time, *if we learn from our past and choose partners with whom we're truly compatible.* We know the cost of not paying attention to the problems in our relationship, or of not asking for what we want from our mate. So if you've been feeling handicapped by your past, why not change your attitude and consider yourself *extra qualified* to create successful relationships!

COMMITMENT FEAR

▼ ▼ ▼ ▼ **3** ▼ ▼ ▼ ▼

Fear of Choosing the Wrong Person

If you've ever been frightened of making commitments, you've probably had this awful fantasy:

You've been in a relationship for a while with someone you love very much, but have been afraid to make a commitment, worried that one day you'll meet someone "better" or with whom you're more compatible. You've put off making any decisions for a long time, and finally you decide that your paranoia is foolish, and you agree to marry your partner. You have a perfect wedding and a glorious honeymoon. Several weeks after you return, you're standing in a store, or at a meeting, and as you look across the room, your heart stops. Your eyes stare into those of someone you instantly know is your true soulmate. You fall in love on the spot. You always knew he was out there, just as you imagined him. You've never felt like this before. And then, all of a sudden, you gasp: **"Oh, my God," you think, "I'm married!"**

Am I the only one who has ever had this nightmare? From the research I've done, I don't think I'm alone. It's natural to worry when you're committing yourself to someone, hopefully for a lifetime. You wonder, if I just waited a little bit longer, would someone even more right come along? How can I be 100 percent sure that I'm not making a mistake? It's as if we all would like God to come down and say, in my case, **"Hi, Barbara. Listen, I know you've been wondering whether you should marry Jeffrey. Let me reassure you that he is indeed the one I had in mind for you, so trust me, you're not making a mistake. Feel better now? Good. Gotta run. Lots to do in heaven. Bye, bye."** Whew! Now that God told me I'm making the right choice, I can relax.

Unfortunately, we don't get that kind of supreme reassurance about our love choices. I believe that some degree of doubt is normal when you contemplate making a permanent commitment to a mate. *However, more than a little doubt may be a warning sign from your heart that you're not making the right choice.* Ultimately, only time will tell if your choice was correct. After all, it's not as if it's totally up to fate. **It's up to you to choose a compatible partner and commit to making the relationship work.**

If you're contemplating commitment but have serious concerns about your partner, make sure you read every chapter in this book *twice* **and carefully do all the exercises.** I've designed all the quizzes and checklists to alleviate as many of your doubts as possible and to give you hard evidence that'll determine whether you and your partner will be compatible.

COMMITMENT FEAR

▼ ▼ ▼ ▼ 4 ▼ ▼ ▼ ▼

Fear of Turning Out Like Your Parents

"I don't want to get married to my girlfriend," a man told me once. "Right now, our relationship is great. We have a wonderful time; we have great sex; we appreciate one another. If we get married, we'll end up just like my parents and every other married couple I see. We'll start picking on each other all the time; my girlfriend will get fat and I'll get out of shape; we'll take each other for granted. **I'm sorry, but I refuse to let marriage ruin my relationship!**"

Whenever I ask audiences how many of them would like to have a relationship just like their parents had, almost no one raises their hands, and most people burst into uncomfortable laughter. It's sad but true that few of us witnessed healthy and happy marriages while we were growing up. So it's natural for us to feel reticent about "settling down" with one person, even more so for children from divorced families. That phrase "settling down" itself sums up the less than positive view of marriage—it will bring us *down* rather than raising us up! Many people I've worked with feel:

COMMITMENT = BOREDOM, LOSS OF FREEDOM,
DRUDGERY, NO FUN, NO SEX

Part of the problem is that we've inherited *our parents' definition and picture of commitment* but haven't taken the time to redefine for ourselves what we want commitment to look like. Commitment, with or without marriage, doesn't automatically produce a set of predetermined experiences. *You* have the freedom to create the experiences and give the meanings you want to your relationship. *I feel it's important for any couple, whether they're considering commitment or are already committed, to take time to discuss what they want their commitment to mean and how they want their relationship to look.* Sometimes just doing this eradicates your concerns about making a long-term commitment and turns your fear into excitement!!

Are You Commitment-Hungry?

▶ Do you gaze with longing at bridal magazines, dreaming of the day when you'll be qualified to buy stacks of them?

▶ Do you mentally marry and have kids with each new man you meet, all within the first few minutes of meeting him?

▶ Do you dread checking the box marked "single" on applications and other forms?

▶ Do you secretly hate your friends who keep meeting nice, eligible men and getting married?

▶ Does the term "mother-in-law" actually turn you on?

If you answered yes to any of these questions, or remember when you would have, then you understand the term "commitment-hungry" firsthand. I hate to sound sexist, but I've found that women are "commitment-hungry" to a much larger extent than men, for obvious sociological reasons. (Read my book *Secrets About Men* for more clarification.) **When you're commitment-hungry, you're looking for a commitment rather than looking for a good relationship.**

Commitment-hungry people often end up making premature commitments, one of the big mistakes we make in the beginning of relationships. *They're so anxious to get a commitment from their partner that they pay little or no attention to the quality of the relationship itself.* All too often they wake up after they've moved in together or gotten married, and find themselves in a totally incompatible relationship.

I used to receive calls on the radio from commitment-hungry women all the time. I could tell within the first few minutes of the call that they were in this category:

"Dr. De Angelis, I need your help. I've been going with my boyfriend for seven months, and I really want to get married, but he says he's not ready. I'm twenty-one and he's twenty-two, and I really love him. I want to be engaged by next Christmas. Should I give him an ultimatum?"

My answer to people like this was always the same: **"What's the rush?** Why are you in such a hurry to become engaged or get married?" The question was really rhetorical, since I already knew the answer. **Commitment-hungry people (and I used to be one, so I know) have a deep need to belong to someone.** The key is that they are more concerned with the "belonging" part than with who the "someone" is. From the moment they get into a relationship, they push for commitment, often alienating their partners and actually prolonging the process. Sadly, many women in this category are trained to be commitment-hungry by their mothers, who were probably commitment-hungry themselves. You'd be suprised at how many young women in their late teens and early twenties feel pressured to find a man and get married.

Getting married before you have created a strong, mature, loving relationship is simply irresponsible, even more so if you decide to have children right away. All the excitement of being engaged will end. All the planning and preparation for the wedding and honeymoon will be over. And you will be left with what was underneath all that glamor and activity all along: an underdeveloped, immature relationship. This is why folk wisdom says, *"The first year of marriage is hell."* **The truth is that the first year and many more years of marriage are hell if you aren't ready to be married in the first place.** When you have built a solid foundation of communication, trust, and respect, the first year of marriage is *heaven.*

If you are commitment-hungry, work with the exercises in this book to understand more about yourself and your needs. *Take the time to fill yourself up from within.* Discover who you are and what your special contribution is as a human being. Stop pushing so hard, and instead focus on building the strongest, most loving relationship you can.

The Four Levels of Commitment

I was discussing the topic of commitment in one of my women's seminars last year when one of the course participants stood up and shared this story: It seems she met a very nice man and had been dating him for about two months. Things were heating up between them, and she decided that before she went any farther, she needed to know how he felt about the future of the relationship. One night, toward the end of their date, she told him that to continue seeing him and deepening their intimacy, she needed some kind of commitment.

"My partner got very quiet," she recalled, "and made some excuse about being too tired to get into a serious conversation. I figured that I caught him off guard and that we'd discuss it the next day. But the next day he didn't call, or the day after that, or even a week later. I called him and left messages, but he seemed to be ignoring me. At first I was hurt. Then I got really angry because I couldn't understand what had happened.

"I decided I couldn't stand not knowing anymore, so one day I waited for him outside his office. When he saw me, his face turned bright red. I told him I hadn't come to try to get him back but to find out why he ran away so fast.

" 'I really liked you,' he answered, 'but I just wasn't ready for marriage, not now, anyway. I need more time to get to know you. I guess I didn't know how to tell you that. I'm really sorry.'

"Marriage?" I exclaimed in shock. "Who said anything about marriage?

" 'Well, you did,' he responded with a puzzled look on his face. 'You told me you didn't want to go any farther without a commitment.'

"I couldn't believe my ears," she told all of us in the seminar. "All I wanted from him was an agreement that we stop seeing other people and be sexually monogamus. The poor guy thought I wanted a proposal!"

Many of us make the same mistake the woman's unfortunate date did: *We equate the word "commitment" with the word "marriage."* You meet someone and like them, and at a certain point feel you need to make some kind of commitment to solidify the relationship, so you ask yourself, "Would I ever want to marry this person?" If it's too soon to be able to answer that question, which it probably is, you become confused and wonder, "What do I do now?"

I've found there are **four basic levels of commitment a relationship passes through as it grows.** Here is a description of each one. I think you'll find them helpful in understanding your own relationships and knowing when it's time to move on to the next level:

COMMITMENT LEVEL

▼　　▼　　▼　　▼　　**1**　　▼　　▼　　▼　　▼

Commitment to Be Sexually and Emotionally Monogamous

If you're single and dating, you'll probably spend some time getting to know a new partner. This period corresponds to the "new relationship" category in Chapter Ten. At some point, *within weeks and certainly by a few months,* you'll need some kind of commitment in order to go forward. This should be a commitment to be sexually and emotionally monogamous.

▼

COMMITMENT LEVEL 1 AGREEMENTS:

▶ You and your partner agree that this is your **one and only intimate relationship,** and commit to putting your time and energy into sharing with one another and no one else.

▶ You and your partner agree that you are each other's **only sexual partners** ("sex" meaning everything from kissing to intercourse—whatever level you are participating in), and you agree to the sexual guidelines I discussed on page 116.

▲

If your partner refuses to make a Level 1 Commitment, I strongly urge you to say good-bye right then and there. **Your relationship will not be able to grow without monogamy, and if your partner doesn't respect and value you enough to offer you that commitment, he's not worth waiting for.**

COMMITMENT LEVEL

▼   ▼   ▼   ▼   **2**   ▼   ▼   ▼   ▼

Commitment to Work Towards a Partnership

Once you and your partner are monogamously dating, you'll probably spend several more months deepening your knowledge of one another and testing your compatibility. This correlates with what we called a developing relationship in Chapter Ten. When you feel . . .

► your relationship is getting better and better
► you're sharing most aspects of your time and life together
► you're starting to think as "we"

. . . then you're ready for a Level 2 Commitment: working towards a partnership. **This means you acknowledge that you've become a couple, an entity within yourselves.** (When I was young, we used to call this "going steady.")

▼

COMMITMENT LEVEL 2 AGREEMENTS:

► You and your partner agree that **your relationship is special and worth nurturing.**

► You and your partner agree that your relationship has **the potential to be a lasting partnership.**

► You and your partner agree to work together, honestly communicating feelings, looking at your own blocks to intimacy, and learning to understand one another **in order to create that potential lasting partnership.**

▲

It's during this developing stage of relationships that a lot of us make the mistake of **not** getting a Level 2 Commitment. You assume you partner seeks a possible future with you—otherwise why would he be saying he loves you and spending all that time with you? You don't actually talk about your assumptions, and one day, months later, your heart gets broken when you bring up marriage or something comparable and he responds by saying, *"I never said we would have a future together. I don't love you that way."*

DON'T STAY IN A DEVELOPING RELATIONSHIP FOR MORE THAN FOUR TO SIX MONTHS WITHOUT GETTING A LEVEL TWO COMMITMENT.

COMMITMENT LEVEL

▼   ▼   ▼   ▼   3   ▼   ▼   ▼   ▼

Commitment to Spend Your Future Together

Once you've agreed to work on creating a partnership together, you could spend six months to several years building that partnership, depending on how old you both are and the circumstances surrounding your relationship. **My advice is: The younger you are, the more time you should spend before agreeing to a Level 3 Commitment.** If you're in your early twenties, you probably need several years of learning relationship skills and emotional maturity to give your love a strong foundation. If you're in your thirties, have had serious relationships, and are very clear about who you are and what you want, you may not need (or want to spend) this much time developing a partnership, and may be ready to commit to a future together within the first year. Each case will be different.

You're ready to make a Level 3 Commitment when:

▶ You've created a strong and healthy partnership that's functioning well almost all the time.

▶ You feel sure that you want to spend your future together, if not the rest of your life.

▶ You have no desire to investigate anyone else as a possible partner.

▶ You feel totally loved and appreciated by your partner almost all the time.

COMMITMENT LEVEL 3 AGREEMENTS:

▶ You and your partner agree that **you want to spend your future together.**

▶ You and your partner agree to **formalize your commitment** by either
  1. becoming engaged to be married
  2. planning on becoming engaged as soon as you can
  3. deciding to live together

▶ You and your partner agree to continue working on your-selves and the relationship **to eliminate any remaining doubts or obstacles to a successful lifetime commitment.**

You've probably noticed that a Level 3 Commitment is an agreement to spend the foreseeable future together, but not the indefinite future, as in forever. *You know you want to spend your life together, but for various reasons you aren't totally ready to formalize that desire (that would be a Level 4 Commitment).*

Making a Level 3 Commitment will look different from couple to couple, depending on how traditional or nontraditional your values are and on the circumstances surrounding your relationship. Here are some examples of couples and their Level 3 Commitments.

ANNIE AND CHRIS—BECOMING ENGAGED

Annie, twenty-nine, and Chris, thirty-one, have known each other for eighteen months. Neither of them has ever been married before, and both work at careers they enjoy. They've spent the past year sharing each other's lives, getting to know each other's families, and talking about the future they each want for themselves. From all this work they've created a strong, loving partnership that both want to maintain for the rest of their lives. Even though they've discussed marriage, they've never made any concrete decisions. So Chris decided to formally propose to Annie and they became officially engaged. They planned their wedding for a year later, giving them time to strengthen their bond further before they make that Level 4 Commitment.

Chris and Annie are both fairly traditional in their values. They decided not to live together until after the wedding, although they spend many nights at each other's apartment. **An engagement was the perfect Level 3 Commitment for them.**

JOAN AND KEITH—DECIDING TO LIVE TOGETHER

Joan, thirty-six, and Keith, thirty-eight, have been together for two and a half years. Joan has been married once before (no children), and both Joan and Keith's parents were divorced, so from the beginning they've worked very hard to communicate honestly and create the kind of relationship they both hope is possible. Their union is strong and healthy, and they know it's time to take it to a new level. Neither of them, however, is ready to get married. Joan has no plans to have children in the near future, possibly never, and *questions whether becoming legally married is the form she'd like her relationship to take. Keith agrees, and although he can't imagine his future without Joan, he knows he's still working through his negative views about marriage.* **After discussing their feelings, they decide to move in together.** This represents a powerful new commitment for them both, and a preparation for the next level of love.

Joan and Keith are not a traditional couple; therefore, becoming engaged doesn't contribute as much to their relationship as living together will. They're both comfortable with this option, since it serves two purposes:

▶ **It gives them a higher level of commitment.**

▶ **It gives them time to live together domestically and heal their fears and concerns about marriage or a similar arrangement.**

The Pros and Cons of Living Together Outside of Marriage

It would be remiss of me to talk about commitment levels without discussing living together. In the past few decades, millions of couples of all ages have chosen to live together, either as a prelude to marriage or in place of marriage. **Note:** *If you have strong judgments about living together due to your religious or moral beliefs, please understand that I'm looking at this issue purely from a psychological point of view.* For the rest of you, I feel it's

important to understand both the positive and the negative consequences of living with someone you love.

THE CASE FOR LIVING TOGETHER

*There is a part of me that feels, after having seen so
many dysfunctional and incompatible relationships over
the years, that all couples should live together before deciding to get married.* I wonder how many unhealthy relationships
would have ended if the two partners had tried being together
twenty-four hours a day and come face to face with the issues they
were avoiding by seeing each other only on weekends or a few
nights a week.

Here are some of the benefits of living together:

► **You discover sides of your partner's personality you
cannot know about unless you live together.** There is no way
you can get to know a person whom you see intermittently as well
as if you lived together. It's a lot easier for someone to be on his best
behavior for three hours during a date than it is for him to maintain
that behavior day after day when you live under the same roof.
When you live with someone you uncover habits, attitudes, and
behaviors you never see otherwise. You see him in his natural habitat,
his home, and thus become exposed to sides of his personality that
may be hidden from you if you're just dating. You see him when he's
tired, sick, angry, frustrated, and grumpy. *Living together requires a
sharing of power and control; it demands compromise and flexibility from both partners.* **You get exposure to the full range of
his emotional reactions.**
I've heard so many nightmare stories about people marrying,
and once they've moved in together, discovering things about their
mate that are unacceptable. Marriage is tough enough without any
unpleasant surprises.

► **You discover more about whether your life-styles are
truly compatible.** Some men make great lovers in a romantic affair,
but lousy husbands. Some women are fantastic part-time companions
but terrible full-time wives. *You may enjoy loving someone but
hate living with him.* The qualities that encourage you to fall in
love with someone and have a great time seeing him may not be

enough to create day-to-day harmony once you move in together. You may find out your partner's life-style doesn't fit with yours, something you'd never know unless you shared the same living space over a long period of time.

▶ **You discover how capable your partner is of true partnership.** Living together requires a sharing of power and control; it demands compromise and flexibility from both partners, since you're merging the habits and desires of two unique individuals. You may not find out how willing or capable your mate is of true partnership until you commit to living together. **Only when you have to make decisions together about finances, food, household responsibilities, acquisitions, etc., do you truly discover what kind of team player your partner is.**

THE CASE AGAINST LIVING TOGETHER

Here are some possible negative consequences of living together:

▶ **You can destroy the relationship by expecting too much from it when it's still developing.** Although I personally feel living together with a mate can be a valuable experience at a certain stage of the relationship, I also feel that *living together prematurely is a big mistake.* I've counseled too many couples who moved in together for the wrong reasons:

▶ to save money
▶ because one had a nicer place
▶ so they could spend more time together
▶ because one partner was afraid of losing the other

▼

LIVING TOGETHER BEFORE YOUR RELATIONSHIP HAS REACHED A SIGNIFICANT LEVEL OF COMMITMENT, MATURITY, AND EMOTIONAL STABILITY CAN ACTUALLY SPEED UP THE DISINTEGRATION OF THE RELATIONSHIP.

▲

If your relationship isn't ready to handle the pressures of living together, it might fall apart under the strain brought about by living together prematurely.

▶ **You can become emotionally lazy.** If moving in with someone feels like a goal to you, and you live together before you're ready, you risk becoming emotionally lazy in the relationship. You may avoid conflict in order to keep the peace, especially if you haven't learned to work through conflict together. You may give your partner less attention and appreciation since he or she is there all the time, or neglect the relationship in other ways.

YOUR LIVING ARRANGEMENT IS NOT YOUR RELATION-SHIP—IT'S ONLY ONE EXPRESSION OF YOUR RELATIONSHIP.

One of the most common mistakes couples make is becoming emotionally lazy, but this is even more of a risk for couples who live together before they've established a strong emotional bond.

▶ **You can avoid furthering your commitment to one another.** You may have heard the saying, *"Why buy the cow when you can get the milk free?"* I think it was used by many of our mothers in their attempt to convince us that boys wouldn't marry us if we had sex with them, since they were already getting what they wanted. I've heard this same argument about living together—**that if a man is living with you and enjoying the benefits of domestic life, he has no reason to ask you to marry him.** I have to agree that in some cases this may be true, especially if you haven't received a Level 3 Commitment before you move in together, and if you haven't known one another for a good length of time. *Some commitment-phobic men (or women) might hide behind living together to experience the intimacy they crave but also to avoid making the final commitment of marriage.*

I don't believe the solution is to refuse to move in with someone before you're engaged or married, unless that feels right to you. *If you're considering living with someone but want the formal structure of marriage somewhere down the road, you need to discuss all this before you actually move in together in order to avoid any misunderstandings. You may want to come up with a time projection—nine months or a year, for instance—at which point you'll reevaluate your relationship and decide whether you feel ready to marry.*

COMMITMENT LEVEL

▼　　▼　　▼　　▼　　**4**　　▼　　▼　　▼　　▼

Commitment to Spend the Rest of Your Lives Together

You are ready for a Level 4 Commitment when:

▶ You've had a Level 3 Commitment for some time (engaged, living together, etc.) and *have worked through whatever obstacles or emotional issues were in your way.*

▶ You have total trust and faith in your relationship and its ability to continue to grow and survive whatever adversity it faces.

▶ You feel excited about exploring deeper levels of love, intimacy, and surrender with your partner.

▼

COMMITMENT LEVEL 4 AGREEMENTS:

▶ You and your partner agree that you want to spend the rest of your lives together.

▶ You and your partner agree that as lifelong mates, your relationship becomes your creation, your "child," **and you will cherish, protect, and nurture that child called your partnership.**

▶ You and your partner agree to any other commitments you both feel are important to inaugurate your new level of oneness.

▲

For most people, a Level 4 Commitment is expressed by becoming legally married. For others who are less traditional, it may be expressed in a nonlegal ceremony, or in another private way in which they consecrate their relationship. Whatever form it takes, a Level 4 Commitment is the highest form of commitment you can make to another person.

The Real Meaning of Marriage

I believe strongly that it's not a wedding ceremony or a license that creates true commitment. **Marriage is not a piece of paper.** It's not wearing a ring or collecting photo albums of your vacations. It's not saying, "We've been married for twenty-five years."

▼

MARRIAGE IS A WAY OF LOVING, HONORING, AND CEL-EBRATING YOUR PARTNER DAY BY DAY AS AN EXPRES-SION OF YOUR COMMITMENT TO ONE ANOTHER.

▲

In this way, marriage is an active, participatory process, not a static state. You aren't married because you had a big party, or because you sent in twenty-five dollars to the county, or because everyone thinks you are. *You are truly married when you and your partner resonate together mentally, emotionally, physically, and spiritually.* **I believe that the real act of marriage takes place in the heart, not in a church or synagogue or hotel ballroom. It is a choice you make, not just on one special day but over and over again, and that choice is reflected in the way you treat your partner.**

When a woman calls me on the radio, or writes me a letter and tells me she's been married for twenty years and is miserable because her husband is abusive, won't talk to her about their problems, cheats on her, or drinks and treats her like dirt, but she doesn't want to leave and "break up the marriage," I always respond in the same way: *"You don't have a marriage—you have a living arrangement."*

A marriage is a partnership, a union, not a battleground. **The moment you stop treating one another with love and respect, your marriage ceases to exist. Once you start living with anger and distrust of your partner, he is no longer your husband.** You may be living together, but you are not married. You may wait years to finally end the relationship, but *you were emotionally divorced when you closed your hearts to each other.*

I find that so many young people live with the dangerous misconception that when they get married, something wonderful will happen to the relationship. "When we finally get married, I know things will get better," they tell themselves. **I feel that deciding to marry invites a certain kind of spiritual accelera-tion or intensity into your life. Marriage becomes like a big**

magnifying glass—it will amplify or exaggerate whatever conditions existed before the marriage took place. If you have a fabulous relationship, marriage will make it better. If you have a rocky relationship, marriage will make it even more turbulent. Whatever problems you had before will seem more disturbing afterward. Whatever strengths you had will appear more substantial.

How do you know when you are ready to get married? Aside from encouraging you to work with all the checklists I've given you, I suggest you ask yourself:

"Do I feel married to my partner right now?"

If you already feel that oneness and resonance in your hearts, *then marriage becomes a celebration and consecration of the connection you have already worked hard to create.* Your wedding formalizes that celebration, but the state of marriage already exists between the two of you.

I don't believe anyone has the power to marry you any more than you already are. I *do* believe that offering your marriage to God or a Higher Intelligence for blessing is tremendously empowering. It's a way of honoring your Source for the gift of love you've found in one another, and asking for continued clarity and vision so you can expand that gift.

Naturally, your own beliefs are what's important. I wanted to share my thoughts with you since, over the years, people have told me my ideas have helped them clarify their views on marriage.

ANSWERS TO YOUR QUESTIONS ABOUT COMMITMENT

Here are some of the most common questions I'm asked about commitment, and my answers:

▶ **"How can I tell if someone has a problem with commitment?"**

You know by now that I strongly believe most relationship problems are surprises only because we didn't pay attention to warning signs along the way. Therefore, the best way to spot a commitment-phobic person is to follow the commitment-level guidelines in this chapter. *That means you should ask your partner how he feels about commitment during the new relationship stage, and pay attention to his answers!* Then make sure to get the appropriate commitments for each level as time passes. ***Don't avoid discussing it. Don't put it off.***

If your partner resists making the commitment you need and refuses to work toward it, it's up to you to end the relationship. **If he's really frightened of commitment and thinks he can get away with staying with you without making one, he will.** You need to honor your own needs and standards and stick to what you know is right.

▶ **"My partner says he wants to make a serious commitment to our relationship and our future but that he's 'not ready.' What does that mean? Is he just making excuses?"**

Your partner is telling the truth when he says he's not ready to make a commitment. The question you need to ask him is, *"Why aren't you ready?"* **If he doesn't know the reasons he's resisting becoming more involved, he can't do anything to improve or heal the situation.** His saying, "I don't know what it is" shouldn't be an acceptable answer to you. Your response should be, "Well, if you want to keep seeing me, find out!" Otherwise you can go for months and years living in emotional limbo while you wait for him suddenly to wake up one morning and discover that his fear of commitment is gone.

It's scary for someone to look at his or her emotional programming and old hurts. Let your mate know you understand his discomfort but that you also value yourself and your emotions too much to stay in a relationship indefinitely without knowing the direction it's taking.

Take some time to think about the circumstances in your partner's life. Are there genuine problems that prevent him from being ready to commit, such as a messy divorce he's just recovering from, or financial pressure he's under? Discuss these with him.

Another important step you need to take is asking your partner *when* he thinks he might be ready, and what it will take to get him ready. You have a right to know what kind of time period he's talking about. Ask him to do this revealing exercise—it might help him get in touch with his own feelings about commitment:

I'll be ready to make a serious commitment/get married when _____ .

This is a fill-in-the-blank exercise. The person taking it should repeat the sentence at least ten times. Example:

I'll be ready to make a serious commitment/get married when:

▶ I own my own home
▶ I have $50,000 in the bank
▶ I'm thirty years old
▶ I never feel turned off by my partner
▶ I see an example of a happy marriage

▶ **"I've told my partner I need a commitment from him and he told me he's 'working on it.' How long should I wait?"**

That depends on what "working on it" means. For some people it means, "I'll tell you I'm working on it to get you off my back and buy some time." For others it might mean he is seriously examining his emotional programming in order to understand his fear of commitment. **You need to ask your partner what he means by "working on it."** Ask him HOW he is working on it. Is he going to therapy, reading books, attending a men's group, talking to other married men? **WHAT SPECIFIC, CONCRETE ACTION IS HE TAKING TO WORK ON IT?**

Don't just accept "I'm working on it" as an answer. You'll feel a lot better staying in the relationship while he's working on it if you know what that means. There's nothing wrong with a person confronting his fears of intimacy. In fact, it's healthier and more honest than someone who blindly throws himself into a relationship and then later puts up emotional walls. So support your partner in his self-analysis, *but make sure you're somehow included in the process and that you're kept informed of his progress.*

Make sure, however, that you're not looking for a premature commitment. For instance, *if you've only known one another a short while and are anxious to get engaged or married, you, not he, may be the one with the problem.* Reread the sections on premature commitment.

▶ **"My partner keeps promising me he'll buy me an engagement ring soon, but it never happens. Should I give him an ultimatum?"**

I don't know about you, but I wouldn't feel too thrilled accepting an engagement ring from a man I pressured to propose to me. What's the point? The real issues are: Why is he resisting, and what are his concerns? *Forcing him to buy you a ring is manipulative and childish.* You should be more concerned with solving the problems in the relationship. **On the other hand, if he cannot get clear on these issues and will not talk about why, you need to accept the fact that this relationship is not what you hoped it would be, and move on.**

I do believe in giving ultimatums when necessary, but only after you've exhausted all other possibilities. For instance, if you've known someone a few months and he's been frequently late in picking you up, you wouldn't say, *"If you're ever late again, don't bother coming over."* That's a very controlling form of behavior. On the other hand, if after a year of dating, your partner is still chronically irresponsible, you can say, *"If you don't agree to get some professional counseling starting within the next few weeks, I don't want to continue this relationship."*

Notice how specific that ultimatum was. The more specific you are when giving an ultimatum, the better your results will be. The other person knows what you expect of him, and will have an easier time complying with your demand. For example:

"If we don't get married soon, I'm leaving" (WRONG WAY).

"I need you to agree to go with me to a counselor to talk about why you won't set a wedding date, and I need you to do this within the next two weeks; if you won't, then I have to leave" (RIGHT WAY).

Ultimatums can be useful in waking us up to areas we've been in denial about, or forcing us to stop procrastinating about something we've been avoiding. But like any powerful tool, they need to be used sparingly and with sensitivity.

▶ **"How do I handle my relationships if I know I'm not ready for any kind of serious commitment? I'm only twenty-two and don't want to get married for a long time."**

If you are just interested in dating and learning more about yourself and people, you can be a lot more flexible with regard to how compatible you are with partners. Whereas a 70 percent compatible relationship might be unhealthy for someone who was ready for a long-term commitment, it would be perfectly acceptable for a young person enjoying himself or herself. It's still important, however, to pay attention to all the things we've talked about in the book so you don't get hurt and build emotional walls. **You don't need to be in ideal relationships, but you shouldn't stay in bad ones either.**

▶ **"I'm in love with two people at the same time. Is it possible to be committed to them both?"**

I could spend hours answering this question, but here's the short version:

AFFAIRS DON'T WORK. THEY END UP HURTING EVERYONE.

You may feel you're getting different needs met from each partner, but you aren't being fair to either one, even if they claim your other relationship doesn't bother them. *Don't use an affair to fill the holes in your primary relationship.*

If you're in love with two people, you need to take a serious look at what you want and need from a partner. **Use the tools I've given you in this book to make a choice.** Until you commit to one person, you won't be able to truly experience healthy love with either of them.

▶ **"It seems like my partner and I have been stuck between Commitment Levels 3 and 4 for a long time. We love one another and know we want to be together, but we're both scared of getting married. Will we be stuck here forever?"**

Some people have no problem making the transition from knowing they want a future together to actually doing something about it, while others struggle with their fears and doubts. *This might be especially true if you or your parents were divorced, or if you've been hurt very badly in the past.* **Rather than just waiting for the fears to clear, confront them head on.** Make a list of your fears and share them with your partner. Talk honestly about each one, together or with the help of a counselor. Work on understanding the real source of those fears. If they are largely due to your old emotional programming, they may not disappear until you actually take the plunge and make the commitment. If they are due to other factors, making concrete changes in your relationship will help. **You need to find a balance between a) ignoring your fears and blindly plunging ahead, and b) giving your fears so much power that they immobilize you.**

How to Know When to Break Your Commitment and End a Relationship

One of the most painful things in life is admitting to yourself that the relationship you're in isn't working and that it's time to leave. You wish you could go to sleep, wake up the next morning, and have everything be different, but you can't. You wish your partner would magically become the person you want him to be, but he won't. You know you've put off making the decision long enough and that it's time to say good-bye.

I believe that you should do everything in your power to salvage a troubled relationship. That includes using all possible sources of outside help, including *professional counseling, seminars, books, support groups, recovery programs, etc.* However, you may reach a point at which you feel you cannot or do not want to continue with your partner, and at that point you need to decide to stay or to go.

It's time to end your relationship when:

▶ **You realize you are incompatible.** If there's one thing you should understand after reading this book, it's that you and your partner must be compatible for your relationship to work. *If you aren't, your love alone will not be enough to overcome the inevitable problems. Only when you have found a new, compatible relationship will you realize how right you were to leave the incompatible one behind.*

▶ **You realize you have no sexual chemistry between you.** If, after reading this book, you recognize that you and your partner don't have enough chemistry to make your love more than a good friendship, you need to set both yourself and your partner free to find a complete union with a more suitable mate.

▶ **You and your partner have grown in two different directions.** I strongly believe that we often come together with a mate for a certain length of time in order to be each other's teachers, and when we have learned the necessary lessons, we need to go on. You and your partner may have grown tremendously in your years together, and given each other great emotional gifts. *However, you may have arrived at what I call the Divided Path, a point at which you are destined to travel in different directions.*

When your goals and styles of growing are too different, it will no longer be healthy or emotionally fulfilling for you to stay together.

The hardest part about reaching the Divided Path is that your love for your partner may not have changed, and that makes it even more difficult to say good-bye. I know, because I've arrived at the divided path several times in my life. All I can say to reassure you is that each time, my new path brought me greater happiness, wisdom, and love than I had ever known before.

▶ **Your partner has a Fatal Flaw he will not deal with.** There are millions of men and women who have had the heartbreaking experience of having to leave someone they loved because that person refused to face his or her own Fatal Flaws. We've seen how toxic Fatal Flaws are, whether it's alcoholism, drug abuse, addiction to pornography, or rage. **As I mentioned in Chapter Six, if your partner will not seek help in battling his problem, or is in total denial that he even has a problem, you have no healthy choice but to end the relationship.**

▶ **Your partner refuses to work on your relationship.** This is perhaps the saddest reason of all you may have to end a partnership, and the biggest waste. **If your partner refuses to face or discuss your problems and will not agree to any outside help in solving your conflicts, he has broken his commitment to your relationship as much as if he had an affair.** He may be scared; he may have had an abusive childhood; he may have a wonderful, loving heart somewhere inside him. *The fact remains that unless he's willing to be an active participant in your partnership, there is no partnership, and you must leave.*

If you're presently struggling with making the painful decision of whether to stay or leave, I hope the information in this book has helped you feel more certain about your choice, and given you confidence that, although it's not easy, you're doing the right thing.

PRACTICING RECOMMITMENT IN YOUR RELATIONSHIP

Some of the nicest requests I ever get are from couples who have been through my *Making Love Work seminars* and ask me to perform a remarriage or recommitment ceremony for them. Often I'll hear statements such as:

▶ "We've been married for fifteen years, but until we worked with you, we never really understood what commitment meant. Now we realize we've never really been married the way we want to be, so we need to have a new ceremony."

▶ "My husband and I were so emotionally shut down to one another and to ourselves that marriage was something we were doing because it was expected of us. We feel so much in love now, and really want to get married again because now we *feel* married."

I feel that practicing regular recommitment is an important part of any growing relationship. It reminds you of your agreements with one another and offers you an opportunity to make new ones. It helps you remember the true meaning of marriage as a continually renewing experience. *Yearly anniversaries are a perfect time to recommit to your partner.* Instead of just buying cards or going out to dinner, why not really honor your relationship by committing to him or her for another year? Remarriage or recommitment ceremonies are also wonderful events to share with your friends, family, and children. By demonstrating your love to one another, you are setting a wonderful example for others to aspire toward.

Whether you've just transformed your relationship into one that's more loving and want to celebrate it, or have survived hard times together and want a fresh start, or simply like the idea of regular renewal, recommitment as a ritual will add a new dimension of joy and intimacy to your partnership.

LIVING YOUR COMMITMENT

The other day I asked a group of people I was working with to share their definitions of commitment. The first few answers were what I expected: "giving 100 percent"; "surrendering"; "being there completely." Then a man stood up and told me if I really wanted to understand commitment, I should think about ham and eggs.

"Ham and eggs?" I asked.

"Yep, ham and eggs," he replied with a sly smile. **"Here's the difference between involvement and commitment: The chicken is involved, but the pig is committed!"**

After I finished laughing, I had to admit that he had a point. Many of us think we're committed to our partners, but we only give them pieces of ourself and our love periodically, like a chicken offering its most recent egg. True commitment isn't expressed in an occasional "I love you" or anniversary card. *Rather, it's a constant awareness of a sacred process you and your partner have entered into together to experience the highest joys and lessons that love has to offer.* This high commitment is reflected in every moment of your relationship, in the way you listen to one another, the way you touch, the way you give, and the way you receive. It transforms mere partnership into union and fills your every action with meaning. When you have the privilege of making this kind of complete commitment, you have truly given yourself a wondrous gift.

12

▼▼▼

THE ADVENTURE
OF LOVE

▼▼▼

I've always believed that reading a book on personal growth is like taking an exciting adventure with the author as your guide. The moment you open the book and read the first page, it's as if the writer reaches out her hand and says, "Come, let me share my vision with you and show you new ways of seeing life and seeing yourself. If you allow me to be your guide, I'll open doors to feelings and understandings you've never experienced before. I know the journey might be a little frightening at times, because I've taken it, too, but I promise to make it as safe as possible. I'll be right beside you the whole way." And as you turn each page, your fear of what you might discover about yourself becomes relief as you realize that you don't have to make the same mistakes you've made before. And suddenly you become excited about how many more choices you have than you ever thought you did.

Are You the One for Me? is meant to be just this kind of journey, and I hope it's been a rewarding one for you. I know that learning about your Love Myths, emotional programming, and all the wrong reasons to choose partners doesn't always feel good in the moment, but it empowers you by giving you the freedom to do things differently. So be proud of yourself for your willingness to grow, and find your highest dreams of love again. Trust your new ability, with the Compatibility Formula and the other tools you've received, to know when it's right, and create the partnership you've always dreamed of.

The adventure of this book is almost finished, but now, with all you've learned, an even more important journey awaits you, my favorite adventure—The Adventure of Love; for of all the exciting places we could visit, and exotic paths we could travel, love is the greatest adventure of all. The majestic sights it will reveal to us are not without, but within. It shows us the wonders of the heart and the magnificence of our ability to feel. It opens our eyes to the truth about who we are and who we are meant to be. As we allow love to touch us, it touches our very spirit, and we are blessed. It is a journey that, when taken, totally transforms us so that we will never be the same again.

Like all great expeditions, The Adventure of Love requires great emotional courage. It demands that you risk and change and grow, and just when you think you can rest, it demands that you grow some more. But through that growth you are rewarded with the experience of being fully and magnificently alive. *You feel more than you ever have before, and thus you become more than you have ever been before.*

The farther and deeper you go into your love adventure, the clearer it becomes that your true destination is not at some point in the future but is here and now, and that the goal is not to arrive somewhere but to be fully present where you already are. *You come to understand that loving isn't something you do to get a result— it's an action that, in itself, fills you with joy and therefore fulfills its own purpose at each moment.*

When you are traveling with someone who isn't right for you, the journey of love may take you down many difficult paths and offer you many painful lessons. **Only when you've found the right partner for your traveling companion will your journey, though always challenging, become one that truly brings you happiness. And only with the right partner can you use your relationship not to "fall in love" but to "ascend in love."** I believe, after all, that The Adventure of Love, in its highest form, helps us pierce the illusion of our aloneness in the world by offering us an opportunity to transcend the limits of our single self and experience a merging of selves, or oneness, with our beloved. *In this way, love is a doorway into the divine.* So choose your traveling companion with great care, since it is into his or her eyes that you will be gazing to catch a glimpse of God.

Thank you for allowing me to travel with you for a while. I wish you love and peace on your journey.